Also by Pete Davies

FICTION

The Last Election

Dollarville

NONFICTION

All Played Out

Storm Country

Twenty-Two Foreigners in Funny Shorts

I Lost My Heart to the Belles

This England

Mad Dogs and Englishwomen

The Devil's Flu

INSIDE THE HURRICANE

FACE TO FACE WITH NATURE'S DEADLIEST STORMS

Pete Davies

AN OWL BOOK
Henry Holt and Company
New York

For my parents

Henry Holt and Company, LLC
Publishers since 1866
115 West 18th Street
New York, New York 10011

Henry Holt® is a registered trademark of
Henry Holt and Company, LLC.

Library of Congress Cataloging-in-Publication Data
Davies, Pete, date.
Inside the hurricane: face to face with nature's
deadliest storms / Pete Davies.—1st ed.
p. cm.
Includes bibliographical references.
ISBN 0-8050-6611-X
1. Hurricanes.   I. Title

QC944 .D39   2000
551.55'2—dc21   00-029562

Henry Holt books are available for special promotions and
premiums. For details contact: Director, Special Markets.

First published in hardcover in 2000 by
Henry Holt and Company

First Owl Books Edition 2001

Designed by Jennifer Daddio

Printed in the United States of America

1   3   5   7   9   10   8   6   4   2

CONTENTS

INSIDE THE HURRICANE

1

AT THE
BAYMAN BAY

Shaped like a rough stone dagger pointing downward, the island of Guanaja lies thirty miles north of the Caribbean coast of Honduras. It's the most easterly of the three main Bay Islands—a chain of rock and coral whose shrimp boats and dive resorts produce a small but growing source of revenue for that impoverished Central American republic.

In 1998, one of the best of those resorts celebrated twenty-five years in business. Founded by a U.S. military diver named Tom Fouke after he'd retired from service in Panama, the Bayman Bay Club is a discreet cluster of luxury cabins hidden amid dense tropical forest on the steep slopes of Guanaja's western shore. Connected by walkways snaking through mango trees and coconut palms, high above a pristine white beach with a wooden dock and dive shop, the cabins are barely visible from the azure sea; only the pointed roof of the four-story clubhouse juts out through the thick canopy.

In August of that hallmark year for the Bayman, Chris and Alice Norris spent a week at the resort on their honeymoon. A lively, attractive young couple, they got on well with Fouke and his wife, Linda—so much so that, with a TV crew coming to film a travel piece, they offered these good-looking newlyweds free board for a few extra days to hang around the place while the cameras rolled.

The Norrises were sorely tempted, but they had jobs to get back to in Rochester, New York. Chris was a computer programmer with Xerox, Alice was a pediatric nurse, they'd just bought a new car—so they did the responsible thing and went home, and pretty soon they were regretting it. They weren't a couple to knuckle down for forty years and cash in pension plans; Chris especially was a free spirit, plainly not a man who'd be happy too long doing the nine-to-five.

Originally from Montreal, now twenty-eight years old, Chris was a muscular, genial figure with black curly hair and a raffish goatee. He was a surfer; he'd spent time in California and Jamaica, and at college in South Carolina he'd been a lifeguard on Myrtle Beach. So when Tom Fouke phoned Rochester a few weeks later to offer the couple work as his operations and administration managers, Chris Norris was ready to jump at that chance.

Alice was ready to jump alongside him. Four years younger than her husband, a tall, willowy woman with long hair falling halfway down her back, she was feeling pretty burned out with her job. They'd both loved it at the Bayman and, she thought, Chris had maintenance and construction experience, she knew food service—they could do this. They went to Vermont to talk it over with her parents, and it was settled that they were moving to Honduras. They sold the car and all their furniture; the lease on their flat conveniently ran out, and on Saturday, October 24, they landed on Guanaja to start a new life.

It was a happy day. What, after all, could there possibly be to worry about? True, a few people at work had asked Alice, "Don't they have hurricanes down there?" She shrugged and told them there hadn't been a hurricane on Guanaja in twenty years, not since Greta in '78. She said later, "It didn't even cross our minds. It was the last thing you'd think about."

Settling in that first Sunday, she did notice that the water inside the reef was different. On her honeymoon two months earlier, it had been like clear blue glass all week; now it was choppy, rough, and tinged gray. Still, the sea couldn't be honeymoon-perfect all year round, could it? The guests were out diving, everything was normal; she thought no more about it.

At 7:15 the next morning, Monday, October 26, Chris Norris woke his wife. He told her, "There's a hurricane coming. In six hours."

Alice's first thought was that she hadn't even unpacked yet. It's a thought she now acknowledges to have been somewhat irrelevant. The storm bearing down on Guanaja was called Mitch, and it would give Alice Norris the worst three days of her life.

L
ike most Atlantic hurricanes, Mitch was born in West Africa as a seedling disturbance called a tropical wave. As air flows westward toward the ocean, the atmospheric imbalance between the burnished, arid Sahara and the cooler, moister tropic shores to the south of it plants a series of kinks in the wind. Sparked by the friction of contending air masses, thunderstorms start igniting from each of these chafing glitches in the sky.

About every three days through the summer and beyond, one wave after another heads out to sea in a turbulent procession of rain and lightning. Each wave is a snag of disorder tucked into the atmosphere; each one of them is heading toward America, and each one of them has the potential to become a hurricane.

On 8 October 1998, one such bundle of disarranged weather passed through the Ivory Coast; it moved out into the Atlantic two days later. It took a week to traverse the ocean; it didn't start getting organized until October 20, by which time it was in the south-central Caribbean. Then satellite pictures started showing telltale cloud patterns banding together; thunderstorms were beginning to circle around the heart of the wave.

Late the following day, after a plane from the United States Air Force Reserve had investigated this disturbance, the National Hurricane Center in Miami formally classified it as a tropical depression. The wave was now a system with a closed circulation; the wind was rotating around a core of low pressure.

On the afternoon of October 22, these spinning winds rose in speed above thirty-nine miles an hour. This is the marker point where tropical depression becomes tropical storm; it's the moment when a system gets christened, as a simple means of alerting the public that this item needs watching. After Alex and Bonnie, after Danielle and Georges, Mitch was the thirteenth named system of 1998—and by any measure, it would turn out unluckier than any storm that year, or virtually any other year on record.

Over the broiling, humid waters above the junction of the Panamanian isthmus with Colombia, Mitch became a hurricane in the small hours of

Saturday, October 24—the same day that Chris and Alice Norris would land on Guanaja. At that moment, it was a shade under 400 miles south of Jamaica, traveling due north, and it had winds topping seventy-four miles an hour. On the Saffir-Simpson scale, it was now a Category 1 hurricane.

The Saffir-Simpson scale was devised in 1971 to grade the damage that wind and storm surge can do in different orders of hurricane. Herb Saffir is a structural engineer; Bob Simpson was director of the National Hurricane Center at that time. To a certain extent, the classification prescribed in the scale that bears their names is arbitrary—but if you're in the path of the storm, it helps a lot to know what's coming.

A Category 1 hurricane is "minimal." Trees and mobile homes will be damaged, but not much else; low-lying coastline might get some flooding, with small boats parted from their moorings. It's disruptive, it can certainly kill people, and you'd probably prefer not to be there, but—unless the rain in the system brings severe flooding inland—only rarely will it be an epic disaster.

By ten o'clock on Saturday morning, as Mitch was crossing deep water on its way toward Jamaica, its winds had climbed above ninety-seven miles an hour. It was now a Category 2, a "moderate" hurricane—in which trees start falling, billboards and road signs start flying, and mobile homes take major damage. More solid buildings might start losing roof tiles, and the coast where the hurricane makes landfall will take a pounding; small piers and marinas will be battered if not wrecked, and shoreline evacuation becomes strongly advisable.

That Saturday morning, Tom and Linda Fouke were at their home base in Fort Lauderdale. Like their manager Don Pearly at the Bayman Bay, they were watching the weather reports, and they knew Mitch looked likely to get considerably worse yet. At that point, they were praying for the people of Jamaica, of Cuba and the Caymans.

Then Mitch started veering northwest. On Saturday evening, as the Norrises settled in at the Bayman, the hurricane started lumbering toward Central America. The winds rose above 112 miles an hour, and Mitch was now a Category 3. This is the point where a hurricane becomes formally defined as "major," or "intense"; by now, this was the kind of storm that you definitely don't want to experience.

By Saffir-Simpson's definitions, damage in a landfalling Category 3 will be "extensive." It'll bring down large trees, and lots of them; any tree still standing will be stripped of branches and foliage. Mobile homes will be destroyed, and even sturdier structures will lose at least part of their roofs. Along the coast, a storm surge nine to twelve feet above normal high tide will cause serious flooding; if your escape route is over low land, you'll need to be gone at least three hours before the eye of the storm arrives.

On a small island like Guanaja, of course, there's no place to escape to.

Early on Sunday morning, Mitch passed over the Serranilla Bank, crossing latitude 16 North, the line of latitude that runs roughly parallel with the coast of northern Honduras. The forecast at this point was that the Bay Islands would be spared; the hurricane would pass north of them and crash into the coast of Belize, or into the Yucatan Peninsula. The media duly poured into Cancún and Belize City, passing a flood of evacuees heading out in the other direction. Thousands of tourists left Cancún; the people of Belize City and the cays offshore moved fifty miles inland, seeking safety in the artificial capital of Belmopan.

By now, the warnings coming out of Miami were in deadly earnest. About nine o'clock that Sunday morning, with winds rising above 132 miles an hour, Mitch became a Category 4. The damage in such a storm will be "extreme." Smaller buildings lose their roofs altogether; mobile homes become matchwood. If you have anything you want to save in there, take it with you, because you're unlikely otherwise ever to see it again. Given appropriate coastal geography, the storm surge can be a wall of water maybe fifteen or eighteen feet tall. Depending on the terrain, it can reach as much as six miles inland; even substantial structures will take severe impacts from the battering force of the waves and all the debris borne upon them. Anyone within a couple of miles of the beach would be seriously ill-advised to stay there.

Mitch's path was still northwest. By three o'clock on Sunday afternoon it was parallel with Guanaja, but 350 miles to the east of it; still Belize and the

Yucatan seemed most threatened. The slower a hurricane travels, however—and Mitch was grinding across the ocean at a crawl, at barely ten miles an hour—the less predictable its movements. It was going slowly because competing atmospheric systems couldn't decide which way they were going to send it; in this situation all the science, all the computer models, all the instruments and satellites and airplanes, all the human wisdom and experience in the world can too easily get a storm like this one wrong—and they did.

That Sunday afternoon, Mitch stopped edging north. Its path was now due west, and the Bay Islands lay square before it. When Tom and Linda Fouke got home that evening in Fort Lauderdale, the Weather Channel showed a huge, angry red vortex bearing down directly on Guanaja—on the business they'd spent twenty-five years building, certainly, but on 10,000 people as well, virtually all of them living only feet from the sea. "We went to bed that night," says Tom, "in fear and terror."

By six o'clock on Monday morning, with winds topping 155 miles an hour, Mitch was a Category 5 hurricane. Saffir-Simpson now states bluntly that the destruction in such a storm will be "catastrophic." Even ten miles from the beach, on low-lying land in a Category 5 you may well not be safe from a storm surge that can be, to all intents and purposes, a tidal wave—a mass of water rising twenty feet or more above normal high tide. And if you don't drown, what are you going to hide in? Never mind mobile homes, entire buildings are now pulped and blown away. The air fills with a barrage of flying glass, wood, and metal; roofs part from walls as easily as you'd peel the lid off a yogurt carton.

This will be happening all through the heart of the storm—and in a storm as big as Mitch, that central zone of destruction can be fifty miles wide, or wider. Consider that when Andrew passed just south of Miami, it reduced to rubble an area of southern Dade County larger in size than the entire city of Chicago. Now consider that Andrew, compared to Mitch, was a wristwatch set beside a watermelon.

Mitch was the worst kind of storm possible on this earth, and it was still growing, becoming the fourth strongest hurricane in the Atlantic basin this century. It was still toying with its target, too—making feints to the north, pausing and lurching as if undecided where to go. Whichever way it turned, however, for the staff of the Bayman Bay this storm was now too close to hope that it might leave them unscathed. They had a hurricane plan, and that morning they started putting it in place.

After living through Fifi and Greta in '74 and '78, Tom Fouke had built two bunkers at the resort, two concrete boxes cemented into the hillside. One lay beneath the bar and the management's office in the basement of the clubhouse; the other was under Don Pearly's cabin at the far end of the resort, two hundred yards away along the twisting walkways through the trees. In one respect they were lucky; forty guests had left on Saturday and, with Mitch disrupting air services already, only eight had flown in with the Norrises.

The guests would go in the bunker under Pearly's house, with Don, Chris, and Alice to look after them; it was a space about thirty feet by twenty. The local staff would go beneath the clubhouse; it was a smaller room, about fifteen by twenty, but it had an outer sheltered area that would serve as extra space if Mitch didn't turn out too bad. Don told the staff to round up their families from the settlements of Mangrove and Savannah Bight at the north end of the island; the stilt houses on the shore there weren't likely to survive. Parents, wives, and children came into the resort, and the number of islanders to be housed in the second bunker rose to thirty-five.

Meanwhile, Chris Norris and the staff lashed down everything they could—the kayaks, the diesel air compressors that took teams of twenty men to shift—and they boarded up the bunker windows. They used Sheetrock and plywood outside, then nailed mattresses to the walls to cover the windows inside, to stop the glass blowing in on them if the outer boards were torn off. Alice remembers it as a crazy morning; in shock at first after Chris woke her, she hurriedly set about storing food and first-aid kits in the bunkers, and packing everything away in the clubhouse.

They thought they had very little time; there was a fair bit of confusion, and a lot of them were scared. As their preparations started to fall into place the wind was picking up, gusting harder and stronger, and there were ten-foot waves coming in over the reef. But still Mitch was undecided; the hurricane crept toward them, a little north of the islands, leaving them to wait and wonder through the afternoon how bad it might be.

On Monday evening, Chris guessed the wind was topping eighty miles an hour; Alice began to think it was time to get stowed away in the bunkers.

She was sitting at the bar in the clubhouse, and by now the wind was making her deeply uncomfortable—then one of the guests said, "This is OK. I don't think it'll get much worse than this."

Alice felt relieved. You're right, she thought, this isn't too bad. I can handle this. We'll spend the night in the bunker, and it'll be better in the morning.

It wasn't. By the small hours of Tuesday morning, it was worse than anything she could possibly have imagined—and it would stay that way for the next sixty hours.

N ormally the worst of a major hurricane passes over its victims in eight to twelve hours at the most. It's a horrendous experience, but with luck it's a relatively short one. It may not feel too short at the time, of course—but often the aftermath poses many greater and more enduring problems than the event itself.

For Guanaja, Mitch was different. The tempest stalled, and sat over the island for two whole days and three interminable nights. With only one deceptive lull, for two days and three nights the people of the island were subjected to winds roaring more or less continuously out of the northwest at 130, 150, sometimes 180 miles an hour, with gusts inside that blasting substantially stronger yet.

One resident would say later, "I lost my sense of balance for days afterward. If I coughed or laughed, I had to put my hands out to keep from falling over. Because no hurricane lasts the way this one lasted. Normally they hit, the eye passes, then they hit you back from the other way—but this one didn't seem to have no back nor front to it. It just went on and on."

"It went on so long," said Alice Norris, "I thought it would never end. You try not to think about it, but it's so hot and sweaty inside the bunker and the water's seeping in, three or four inches deep, and you can't sleep, and you're waiting for something to crash into the building, and all the time the noise is just totally incredible. I thought I'd be able to hear trees and cabins falling, but I couldn't hear anything but the wind. It's like a freight train circling right around the bunker, it's *so* loud, and then the gusts come in with this deep, deep vibration, and you just *cringe*. I wish I could have seen it—but I wouldn't have gone out there for a million dollars."

The bunker had a steel door; it took three men straining against it with their shoulders to open it even a tiny bit against the wind, and sometimes they couldn't open it at all. The first night, no one ventured out anyway—then, at first light on Tuesday morning, the storm seemed to calm a bit. Chris Norris and Don Pearly stepped out to find twelve-foot seas inside the reef—but the dock was still standing, and the wind had dropped. They took the guests to the clubhouse to get some air and breakfast—then the wind picked up again, and around them the cabins started falling apart.

Two window shutters flew through the dining room, louvered chunks of wood four feet by six and two inches thick. The lull hadn't lasted much over half an hour; hastily they got the guests back in the bunker. For Chris Norris, however, his battles with Mitch were only just beginning.

A tree had fallen on the water main, and the tanks were draining; they had to fix the pipe or run out of water. Through winds now back above 100 miles an hour and rising (so if you jumped in the air, you were carried six to ten feet forward at a time) Chris crawled and scrambled up the hillside with the resort's fishing guide to mend the pipe, trying to listen for falling trees as they worked.

Around them, roofs were coming off buildings; when the gusts came in, they were strong enough to pick up whole cabins and explode them. "We knew we had to get the water repaired," said Chris, "so you just focus on that. The mission is water. I've been through emergencies before, and you try to do what needs to be done, and you try not to get panicked and scared. There's plenty of time to be panicked and scared back in the bunker. Better just to do the task at hand."

It took three-quarters of an hour to fix the pipe. As they were heading back down the hill, the roof came off Cabin 9 and flew thirty-five yards past them into the forest—but they weren't done yet. Now they had to get to the generator room and shut the power down, before they had broken live lines whipping about the place. The morning was gone by the time they'd done that—then Chris got down to the clubhouse and looked out to sea.

The swells were nearing twenty feet now, but far out he could see a series of larger waves coming in. Thirty feet tall, four or five of them one after the other, they stood high out of the ocean, great ridges of water. Well, he thought, the dock's gone when those arrive. They didn't just take the pier, either—they took the dive shop, the compressor room, the boathouse, the equipment rental room, and the dive staff's housing too. It was all shattered in minutes, leaving nothing on the shore but the main entranceway up on the hillside. That was concrete—but with everything else torn away from in front of it, it only lasted a few minutes longer.

After that, Chris didn't go anywhere near the sea. He knew a five-foot wave inside the reef was a rarity, so these waves were unimaginable. He wouldn't even want to venture a guess at what lay beyond them in open water. What he did know was that the wind was getting back to the worst it had been during the small hours that morning; it was time to make sure everyone was safely back in the bunkers, and then hole up for a second night. He thought they were all secure, they could ride it out—then at one in the morning Don Pearly's wife, Eli, sat bolt upright and said, "Ernesto doesn't know where the staff bunker is."

Ernesto was a new chef; he'd only arrived a few days before and when they'd counted the staff into the bunker, they'd forgotten about him. So now Chris Norris had to go out and find him. He cut a six-foot length of climbing rope, looped one end around his right wrist, and tied a knot in the other end. It was maybe a hundred yards up to the staff cabins; the walkways were clogged with debris, with splintered lumber and the trunks and branches of fallen trees. He moved in stages of ten yards or less through the howling, spray-soaked dark, lashing the rope to tree stumps or concrete foundation posts at every halt as he peered into the blackness to see which way to go next.

When he got to what remained of the staff cabins, he found Ernesto hiding under his bed in three inches of water. He was gibbering with terror. The roof was peeling off, and the walls would surely follow. Chris had to yell the man's name for five minutes before it registered that he was there. Half pushing, half carrying, he forced Ernesto down the slope toward the staff bunker. Sixty feet above the sea, the air was full of salt. The wind tore the breath from their mouths. As they fought their way down the hillside, Chris realized with a thrill of horror that he could *see* this wind; that the air had become a solid, visible force all around him.

You know how, when a car's hot after you've driven it, you can see the heat rippling off it? The wind was like that; he could see the gusts coming through the darkness, he could see masses of air physically ripping toward them. It wasn't absolutely pitch-black; they were in a wet gray murk, with these twisting, shimmering bodies of wind tearing through it.

As each one approached, in rapid fire he'd see one tree and another and then the next buckling, snapping, and splintering before the blast, leaves and branches tearing away and vanishing; it looked like a special effect, but it wasn't, it was all too dreadfully real. In these gusts he and Ernesto couldn't stand, they couldn't move—they just lay flat, lashed to the strongest anchor Chris could find, clinging to the rope, waiting for it to pass, then darting, crouching, stumbling to the next point to tie down again, fighting for their lives through a wreckage of downed trees and smashed cabins.

It was an obstacle course in a nightmare; rescuing Ernesto took an hour. When he got him to the staff bunker, Chris didn't go in; he hammered on the door, shoveled the man in there, slammed the door shut, then tried to get back to his own shelter. The path was now totally blocked; covering six hundred feet took the best part of another hour, zigzagging up and down the slope to either side of the walkway, inching forward any way that was clear.

About three in the morning he got back; he dozed on and off for an hour, then Eli Pearly jolted him awake again. "Chris," she said, "I just remembered. The staff bunker. They're burning kerosene lamps in there, right?"

He told her they were. So?

"It's sealed," she said, "that bunker's airtight. Those people have no air."

Chris looked at her and thought wryly, Why are you remembering these things one at a time?

Alice Norris watched her husband of two months loop the climbing rope around his wrist for the second time that night. She didn't want him going out there again, but she knew she couldn't stop him, either. Chris said later, "Each time you go out, you have your doubts if you're going to come back. But look, you've got thirty-five people who maybe might suffocate, one of them's a one-month-old baby—you've got to go, don't you? If I didn't at least make the attempt, I would never have been able to live with myself."

Besides, as he readily admitted, he was an adrenaline junkie; being out in the middle of a Category 5 hurricane was an experience most people might prefer to do without, but this guy viewed it as the rush of a lifetime. Certainly, he said, "it was better than being in that bunker."

There was a moment on the crawl back to the clubhouse when he did briefly revise that point of view. He saw a gust coming; he managed just in time to sling the rope around a tree trunk and get the knot through the loop— then the gust picked him up off the ground as if he were no more than a scrap of paper. It was like being a cartoon character, strung out and hanging horizontal in the air, his feet flapping on the wind as he clung for his life to that strand of rope. He said simply, "If I hadn't been roped up, I wouldn't be here. To be hanging in the air like that—that was the one time when I thought, I shouldn't be out in this. Excuse my language, but I thought, Oh *fuck*."

The gust passed, and he fell to earth. He was halfway to the staff bunker so he kept going, ducking and pushing through the debris. When he got there and opened the door he found the air stifling, he couldn't breathe in it, and the room was strewn with unconscious bodies. Four lamps were burning; he wedged the inner door open with a chunk of two-by-four, then blew out the lamps. Mercifully, the people were still breathing; he couldn't tell how much longer it might have been before the room became a morgue.

He waited for them to come round and recover—then the mutiny began. Heading for the door, he found himself confronted by a group of black and Hispanic islanders; terrified, dangerously frantic, they pushed him against the wall and surrounded him, shouting, shoving at him, demanding to know when the airlift was coming. Losing their heads in the endless storm, they'd convinced themselves that the American military were going to fly in and rescue the gringos, and leave the islanders there to die. Chris was thinking, Look outside, you fools—no one's flying in here anytime soon, can't you see that?

He managed to calm them down, and started edging back up the side of the bunker beneath the clubhouse. In the crawl space behind it he saw a woman lying on the earth, an empty vodka bottle rolling by her side. He tried to persuade her to get inside, but she wouldn't go; before the endless rage of the storm many of the staff, it seemed, were having a collective nervous breakdown.

Chris got back to the guest bunker, and told Don Pearly what had happened. Don had missed out on the previous expedition because he'd been upstairs in his cabin shoring up the walls with his furniture; the bathroom roof was gone, and he wanted to do all he could to try to save his cats and his parrots. Now he went back upstairs again, and returned with a Smith & Wesson .38.

Chris wondered if that wasn't a shade extreme—then Don pointed out that there were four more handguns in the safe, complete with ammunition. The safe was in the clubhouse, on top of the staff bunker—and the key to the safe was on a chain around the neck of the vodka-sodden woman in the crawl space.

Don tucked the revolver in his trousers, under his jacket, and set off with Chris back to the clubhouse. It was getting well into Wednesday morning by now, but the storm continued unabated; in the sea spray driven on the screaming wind, they couldn't see much more by daylight than they could in the dark. Don was sixty-one, a slim, wiry man probably not weighing above 140 pounds; Chris would get a bit ahead, then look back and see no sign of him, lost in the murk and the tangled mess of the ruined resort.

Together they made it to the clubhouse; unobtrusively armed, Don went to calm the staff while Chris retrieved the other firearms from the strongbox. It took two hours to defuse the situation and get themselves and the weapons back safe to the other bunker. Each journey was different from the last; the terrain was changing by the minute. They'd pause under the remnants of a cabin, get their breath, plan the next move, and push on. When they finally made it back they collapsed, Don on the floor, Chris in a chair. It was Wednesday afternoon, and Chris had had no sleep to speak of since he'd got up on Monday. He passed out, and woke up on Thursday morning.

Outside it was absolutely quiet, absolutely still, and the barometric pressure was so low that their ears were popping. Looking out to sea, they saw a towering wall of gray cloud over the reef. It was featureless, perfectly smooth, and it climbed from the sea as high into the sky as their eyes could see. It looked, said Don Pearly, like a wall of stuccoed concrete. Sometimes it shifted like a living thing, bulging and swelling, rocking toward them or backing out to sea. They were in the eye of the storm.

Staring at the eyewall in that eerie silence and stillness, they called Tom Fouke on the satellite phone. Straightaway he yelled at them to get everybody back inside the bunkers.

Normally when you go through the eye of a hurricane, the second hit is the worst. The first one builds up over at least several hours, but the second pitches you abruptly from the storm's inner calm into its maximum ferocity. Worse, that new blast is coming at you from the opposite direction—so everything that's been blown one way is now violently flung back on itself. Any structure that's been sufficiently weakened can, at this point, quite literally explode.

Don Pearly and Chris Norris understood this; they had, however, a more immediately pressing problem. Their guests had been quite frightened enough already—but now the woman who'd drunk the vodka was telling anyone who'd listen that there was going to be a landslide, and that the guest bunker was going to tumble beneath the rockfall down the hill into the sea. The gully by one corner of the guest bunker was indeed now filled with a raging stream, chewing dirt off the slope, lapping against the concrete.

Pearly didn't know whether this was a real danger or not, but he didn't believe it was, and he didn't want anyone else believing it was. Above everything, he wanted to keep people calm. So, while they listened in on his call to Tom Fouke, Pearly asked his boss how secure the footing of the bunker was. In Fort Lauderdale, Fouke asked him how the hell should he know? He'd built it sixteen years ago. . . .

Pearly didn't relay that answer. Instead, improvising, as if repeating what he was hearing, he said, "OK—the footing's twelve to fourteen inches thick. It's got steel pins every twelve inches . . . the walls have rebar every twelve inches in both directions . . . the foundation's poured around boulders so it's integral. OK."

That seemed to work. Then—partly in case Mitch should come back on them as bad as it had been before, but mainly as a further reassuring placebo—he and Chris cut lengths of rope like Chris had used on his earlier journeys for everyone, and they assigned each person a number. It might or might not be any use, but it made it look as if they were on top of things.

Alice Norris, meanwhile, was looking about herself in awe. The scene was surreal; devastation lay everywhere, as if the resort had been bombed. Where before they'd been hidden in dense trees, now the hillside was gouged open to the sea and the sky, and the forest lay in bare and shattered pieces around their feet. The cabins, reduced to little more than splintered sticks on buckled foundations, gaped from the wreckage.

We sold everything, Alice thought. We came here five days ago to start a new life. And now it's all been blown away.

Happily, it didn't turn out that way. First, continuing perverse as ever, Mitch was in dramatic decline; after wreaking havoc on Guanaja, the hurricane started edging away south toward the mainland, with wind speeds falling fast as it went. Friday was still gusty, as the tail of the storm moved over them, but it was nothing compared to what had gone before.

Second, Tom Fouke wasn't ever going to give up on the Bayman Bay, no matter how badly the place had been hit. With a ready American mix of determination and insurance, he started rebuilding, and by Easter five months later he had cabins back up, guests to stay in them, and Chris and Alice Norris still working with Don Pearly to look after them.

Pearly said proudly that throughout the whole experience, he and other members of the staff had still managed to keep the guests in meals and coffee. That allowed Fouke to smile and say, "The service at the Bayman Bay is unparalleled, of course"—but it was a pained and ironical smile. Financially, he'd had a whole year written off. He said, "I do still wonder sometimes, Why me? But then, nobody died here—and next to that, what else matters?"

On Guanaja as a whole, only a handful of people died. The number's not exact—it depends whether you count islanders only, or people over from the mainland during the storm as well—but I was given death tolls varying from seven to twelve. Given the force with which Mitch struck Guanaja, and the duration of the strike, this was astoundingly low.

But Mitch was far from finished. As far as Mitch was concerned, Guanaja was just the beginning.

ZCZC MIATWOAT
TTAA00 KNHC 012105
TROPICAL WEATHER OUTLOOK
NATIONAL WEATHER SERVICE MIAMI FL
530 PM EDT TUE JUN 1 1999

FOR THE NORTH ATLANTIC . . . CARIBBEAN SEA AND THE GULF OF MEXICO

TODAY IS THE FIRST DAY OF THE OFFICIAL ATLANTIC HURRICANE SEASON WHICH
CONTINUES THROUGH NOVEMBER 30TH.

DURING THIS TIME . . . THE NATIONAL HURRICANE CENTER WILL ISSUE A TROPICAL
WEATHER OUTLOOK AT 530 AM . . . 1130 AM . . . 530 PM . . . AND 1030 PM
EASTERN TIME. THE OUTLOOK WILL BRIEFLY DESCRIBE SIGNIFICANT AREAS OF
DISTURBED WEATHER AND THEIR POTENTIAL FOR DEVELOPMENT. IT WILL ALSO LIST
TROPICAL CYCLONES FOR WHICH ADVISORIES ARE BEING ISSUED.

ON AVERAGE . . . THERE ARE 10 NAMED TROPICAL STORMS OF WHICH SIX REACH
HURRICANE STRENGTH . . . WITH 3 TROPICAL STORMS OR HURRICANES HITTING
THE UNITED STATES. LAST YEAR THERE WERE 14 TROPICAL STORMS . . . OF WHICH
10 BECAME HURRICANES. HISTORICALLY MOST TROPICAL STORMS AND
HURRICANES OCCUR DURING AUGUST . . . SEPTEMBER AND OCTOBER.

HERE ARE THE NAMES FOR THE 1999 TROPICAL STORMS AND HURRICANES:

NAME	PRONUNCIATION	NAME	PRONUNCIATION
ARLENE		LENNY	
BRET		MARIA	MA-REE-AH
CINDY		NATE	
DENNIS		OPHELIA	O-FEEL-YA
EMILY		PHILIPPE	FE-LEEP
FLOYD		RITA	
GERT		STAN	

NAME	PRONUNCIATION	NAME	PRONUNCIATION
HARVEY		TAMMY	
IRENE		VINCE	
JOSE	HO-ZAY	WILMA	
KATRINA	KA-TREE-NA		

FRANKLIN/GUINEY

... TROPICAL STORM FORMATION IS NOT EXPECTED THROUGH WEDNESDAY.

NNNN

2

BRET

Your evacuation and preparation times are diminishing. This is a very, very serious situation. You need to take it seriously right along the Texas coast. In Cameron, Willacy, and Kenedy counties, if you live in a mobile home, leave it and go inland *now.*"

It was ten months after Mitch; it was the evening of Saturday, August 21, 1999, and the Weather Channel wasn't pulling any punches. Veteran forecaster John Hope told his viewers that if they were given an evacuation order, "the reason is to save your life. That's it, really. You do not want to be there."

Bret, the first hurricane of the 1999 Atlantic season, was twenty-four hours from making landfall in West Texas, and quite possibly less. Along the threatened coast, either Brownsville by the Mexican border or Corpus Christi 120 miles to the north of it could easily be targets as the storm came ashore; together, the cities were home to some 300,000 people. Bret was a small system but a ferocious one, a Category 4 hurricane with maximum wind speeds reaching 135 miles an hour. On the Saffir-Simpson scale, it was one grade shy of the worst a storm can be; it's a safe bet that a fair proportion of any urban area hit by winds like these would be reduced to rubble.

At 1:30 in the afternoon of the day before, a team of scientists from the federal government's Hurricane Research Division had taken off from

MacDill Air Force Base in Tampa to fly in this storm. They'd arrived just as it was becoming a fully fledged hurricane, as the maximum sustained winds accelerated past seventy-four miles an hour. Since then, those winds had nearly doubled in speed in less than twenty-four hours—and when storms are strengthening like that, when the winds are spiralling inward ever faster and stronger, they virtually always fill with unpredictable turbulence and disorder.

The plane was hit by lightning in a thunderstorm complex on the way out from Tampa across the Gulf, and again in the hurricane itself; the second strike snapped one of the UHF antennae. These are two half-inch-thick wires running along the top of the fuselage, from a point above the front of the cabin to midway up the tail fin. The wire broke off at the tail end, so that it was flapping along the right-hand side of the plane, whipping against the window by the rearmost bank of instruments. The two scientists by that window left their seats pretty sharply; at 16,000 feet, above the freezing level, depressurization would not have been a comfortable experience.

The lead pilot was Captain Gerry McKim. He brought them down a couple of thousand feet, worried more about the wire snagging in an engine intake. They flew home with it snapping about the plane, and after nine hours they came into MacDill with their fingers crossed that it wouldn't tangle in the landing gear. That had been Friday; at 1:30 in the afternoon on Saturday they'd got in another plane, and they'd gone straight back out there.

What sort of person does this? Mike Black was the lead scientist on both flights, a quiet-spoken man of forty-four, a dry character with a sharp wit and an acute consciousness of the human impact of the storms he studied. With his father in the armed forces he'd grown up nomadic, but he counts himself a Virginian, and he recalls being in high school there when a dissipating tropical storm rolled over that state, depositing spectacular quantities of rain.

There was a threat that a local dam was about to burst. Black had just gotten his first car and, enthralled by the tumult of the elements, he drove up to have a look at the dark waters teetering against the lip of the curtain wall. There were two patrolmen there, and they told him to get away from the place; a lippy teenager, Black retorted that he didn't see the policemen leaving, so why should he? He still remembers the change in the officer's face, the stern firmness with which he was advised to stop being a young idiot and to leave when he was told—but the raw power of the wind and the downpour, the threat and the violence of it, had him hooked from that moment.

He studied meteorology at the Rosenstiel School of Marine and Atmospheric Sciences in Miami, and joined the Hurricane Research Division in 1985; he'd been flying hurricanes for a living for fourteen years. In 1992 he'd flown in Andrew, even as that storm bore down on South Dade to trash his house.

He said, "It's hard. We love to study these beasts, but you have to remember what they do. I didn't really realize until it hit my own home—people don't. Like Hugo hitting Charleston in 1989—you fly it, you land, you go home and turn on the air conditioning, and you go out to your favorite restaurant. After Andrew, all of a sudden you can't do that. I couldn't live in my house for six months; I almost quit this job then. I was tired of it; they do too much damage. Then a month later, we flew Tina in the east Pacific. It was a Cat 4 headed west, affecting no one, and it was a beautiful storm. Then I thought, I can do this. Because if we can help improve the forecasts, it's worth it."

Earlier, on Saturday morning, Bret's winds were climbing past ninety miles an hour, and the storm was creeping slowly north-northwest. At that point, at the National Hurricane Center in Miami, the forecasters still reckoned on a landfall in Mexico, maybe sixty miles south of Brownsville; like all forecasts, however, this prediction had acknowledged fallibility attached. Pete Black, one of Mike Black's research colleagues (related by name and trade, but not by kin), said, "This is one of the most difficult forecasts for them to make. It's going parallel to the coast, and all the computer models want to turn it left and onshore—but it's showing little inclination to do that."

As things stood, landfall was set for the early hours of Monday morning. In a cramped little office in the back of the Hurricane Center, the research team juggled with the implications of that. The experiments they wanted to do had two principal objectives, two large questions they badly wanted to answer: How exactly does a storm strengthen over the ocean? And when the storm makes landfall, how does the wind field behave as it leaves the sea to come onshore?

Answer these questions, and you can warn people more precisely of the dangers they face—but hurricanes don't yield their secrets easily, and the timing and logistics of flying in them are fraught with unsettling choices.

The scientists had two planes to work with, known in shorthand from their call signs as 42 and 43. 43 had flown yesterday, on Friday, and was now having its antenna repaired. 42 would fly today to monitor the storm's explosive evolution and its interaction with the sea in the course of that process; if they could learn what particular conditions in the Gulf were letting Bret build so rapidly, maybe in future storms they'd be able to spot such a dangerous strengthening earlier and give people in the path of it better warning.

Logistically, this was the easier of the two problems; Bret was intensifying over water so they'd fly out there, study it, and try to see why that was happening. The main difficulty arose over how to catch the landfall later on—because this involved planning for an event whose precise timing and location were both far from certain.

Bret was the best part of three hours' flying time out of Tampa; that gave them a shade under five hours that they could spend actually working in the storm before their fuel ran low. So did they send a mended 43 out on Sunday afternoon, in case landfall came earlier than expected? And did they put 42 on alert for a midnight takeoff, to follow on and catch landfall in the small hours of Monday if Bret held off for that long?

Where landfall would happen was as much of a problem as when. Observing how a hurricane's winds behave as they pass on to land was a vital experiment, at the heart of these scientists' raison d'être; it was about understanding and thus accurately defining the true extent and severity of the threats people face.

To do it right, however, they needed radar on the ground as well as on the plane. The plane's Doppler beam would sweep vertically, the ground station horizontally, then they'd mesh the two to build a composite 3-D picture of the wind field—so if Bret crossed the beach before it got to the border the experiment was off, because the Mexicans had no ground radar. Besides, it was bureaucratically awkward seeking clearance to overfly their territory.

The storm chasers from Texas Tech toting portable radar to the coast to play their part in this dangerous dance wouldn't want to take their instruments over the border, either—so if the storm hit Mexico, there was no point flying in it. On the other hand, if it stayed on its northerly heading long enough to hit Texas . . .

This is not to say that these men sit quietly hoping for horrific tempests to obliterate convenient stretches of American coastline just so they can successfully pull off their experiments. They know more than anyone what hurricanes can do, both professionally and personally, because most of them lived through Andrew. Many of them, like Mike Black, saw their homes extensively damaged; at the time, Black's wife was six months pregnant; she went into premature labor as the wind roared and the air pressure plummeted, and today Black cites Andrew as a contributory factor in the breakup of that marriage. Two of his colleagues had it even worse; they had their houses literally blown to pieces around them, and are simply lucky that they and other members of their families are still alive.

In consequence, no one could be less inclined to take hurricanes lightly; their situation is, rather, somewhat like that of pathologists. Pathologists don't want people to die, but seeing that they do and that it isn't desirable, it makes sense for someone to study it. Similarly, tropical meteorologists don't want hurricanes to happen—but they do, so it's reasonable to try to understand how they work.

The director of the Hurricane Research Division is a theoretician named Hugh Willoughby, an affable character with no airs and a sly, impish wit. While his colleagues toiled over flight patterns and forecast tracks, he made the analogy explicit:

"There's a sign in many autopsy rooms that reads 'This is where the living learn from the dead'—and that's what we do. So if Bret does hit Texas sometime late tomorrow and we fly in that event, we get one more case of ground truth onshore, and that helps us to tell people how the wind's going to blow in their backyards in future landfalls. Will there be flooding? Will your roof blow off? Should you leave? We won't know next week or next year, maybe, but these are the questions to answer—because weather, like politics, is ultimately local, and this is squad level meteorology. This is about what we can provide to the sergeants on the ground out there, to the emergency managers in the local communities."

Back in the forecast center, senior hurricane specialist Miles Lawrence decided to extend a hurricane warning north up the coast and across the border in his next advisory. A watch was already in place up to Baffin Bay, Texas, meaning that hurricane conditions were possible in that area within the next thirty-six hours. When they upgraded the watch to a warning, that meant they were narrowing the window; it meant this storm could now be onshore within twenty-four hours. It was time to up the ante, and put people on the dime; it still might not happen, but it looked more likely by the hour.

Far away, enormous computers were chewing through mountains of data. Besides the scientists' research missions, the hurricane hunters of the Air Force Reserve's 53rd Weather Reconnaissance Squadron fly round-the-clock surveillance of any threatening system out of Keesler Air Force Base in Biloxi, Mississippi. Regular updates on the storm's strength, its direction and speed of motion, its moisture content, and on conditions in the surrounding atmosphere that are acting to steer it, all flow back to be processed through mega-machines packed with epic equations.

On a Cray C90 supercomputer at the National Centers for Environmental Prediction in Suitland, just across the D.C. line into Maryland, on the U.S. Navy's equivalent machine in Monterey, California, and at Great Britain's Met Office in Bracknell outside London, a dozen different models of the atmosphere are constantly shifting and evolving. Approximations of climatic flow and structure composed out of deep physics and mathematics, these models try to figure what each storm aims to do—and as that Saturday progressed, the tracks they produced as they studied Bret were all fanning closer and closer to the Texas border.

The hurricane was accelerating, making a Sunday evening landfall more likely than Monday morning—and it was nudging north ever nearer toward Brownsville. Offshore from that town lay the southern end of Padre Island, a slender waft of sand and marsh then hosting over 2,000 residents and vacationers—who were now crawling in a choked clog of traffic over the bridge to the mainland.

The authorities were glad to see them leaving, and leaving early. Too often in response to crisis, said Willoughby, "unreflective lethargy is replaced by paralyzing panic. But if you don't leave, don't go looking for help at the last minute. When the wind's blowing at 150 miles an hour, there's no civil authority then."

He ran through flight patterns and landfall prospects with his old friend and colleague Frank Marks, the director of the Research Division's field program—the man charged with finding the most fruitful use for the 190 hours of plane time they'd been allocated this season. Their planning just then, said Marks, came down to blind reliance on the forecast tracks. "All the models hook the storm west, but it still hasn't done that. And computers are computers. . . ."

Meanwhile, Mike Black and his team were setting off from Tampa on 42. For a second day, they spent five hours inside Bret—and though the day before they'd observed its birth as a hurricane, now they witnessed its supercharged development. Bret grew from a Category 1 storm at dawn to Category 4 by dusk. To use the terms of the Saffir-Simpson scale, it matured from minimal to extreme in the course of one day.

I left the Hurricane Center, and set off to drive from Miami to Tampa. As I left, a conference call was in progress with local emergency management teams in Texas. The last voice I heard crackling over the speakers said simply, urgently, "We need all the help we can get."

By dawn on Sunday Bret was 110 miles due east of Brownsville, and swinging northwest as the computer models had suggested—if somewhat later than they'd thought it would happen. All major roads toward the coast were closed; the first drenching rainbands were coming onshore, and 90 percent of southern Padre Island was evacuated. Anyone who stayed, said the mayor bluntly, risked drowning in the storm surge.

Sucked upward by barometric pressures so low in the storm's center that people who've been through it describe their lungs being vacuumed clean of breath, the sea rises in a great dome of water. Driven forward by the winds, this dome hits the shallow reaches of the continental shelf and builds into a series of waves that, in a major storm like Bret, can reach fifteen feet or more above normal high tide. One single cubic meter of water weighs three-quarters of a ton—so when a storm surge piles many millions of cubic meters of ocean against the shore, neither people nor buildings can withstand such an awful force and mass.

On the far side of the Gulf from the storm, in the Wyndham Westshore in Tampa, the HRD crew loaded their bags and cases in their rental van;

Mike Black was embarking on his third flight in three days. En route to MacDill they stopped for supplies at Whaley's Deli on South Howard, and discussed the merits of Bern's Steak House down the road as a post-flight dinner venue. There would be no dinner, of course, when you landed at eleven o'clock at night.

Peter Dodge asked, "Dinner? What's that? When you eat two or three meals a day?"

Dodge was today's lead scientist now that this flight had become a land-fall observation; he and Mike Black would be working with two other HRD men, Joe Cione and John Gamache, and they had a fast-developing situation on their hands. If Bret kept going as it was, by the time they got there the hurricane might well be on the beach already. As for the second flight that night, designed to catch landfall if it happened later on, that looked likely to be canceled. If it did go, said Cione, "it's mop-up duty. Like a 14–3 base-ball game."

These four would be doing everything in the hurricane that time, turbu-lence, and the interplay of their instruments would allow. Radar would examine the wind field, together with ingenious little devices called GPS dropsondes launched from a chute in the belly of the plane. Not much larger than a thick, rolled-up newspaper, and falling on a streamer through the body of the storm, these devices would send back many detailed mea-surements of wind speed and direction, air temperature, barometric pres-sure, and moisture content. Besides these, another string of instruments called AXBTs would be dropped, and their role was to take the temperature of the sea.

AXBT stands for Airborne Expendable Bathythermograph. These are cylinders four feet long, eight inches in diameter; packed in their launch containers, they weigh about sixteen pounds apiece. From 12,000 feet, the planned altitude for today's mission, they take about four minutes to fall to the ocean on miniature parachutes. When they hit the surface the salt water activates a battery, a float collar pops out, and a plumb-bob starts unwinding down into the sea.

On the end of this wire tether, as it descends to a maximum depth of 1,500 feet, a temperature sensor radios the heat of the water back up to the plane. Meanwhile, the float collar's slowly deflating; the scientists get their readings over a couple of minutes as the wire plays out, and the buoy then sinks. That way, the signal from buoy A doesn't interfere with the signal from buoy B that's dropped next.

The goal is to discover how deep the "mixed layer" is, that is, to what depth the ocean's temperature stays warm. Hurricanes are fueled by hot water; over the tropical sea, sun-cooked air full of evaporated vapor rises, creating low pressure that sucks in wind around and beneath it. As it lifts into cooler high air, the vapor condenses into water droplets; gas becomes liquid, the water molecules congeal into less agitated structures, and the energy of their previous agitation is released as heat. That's how a thunderstorm is built, and (at least in part) a hurricane is built in turn out of a whole brood of maybe thirty thunderstorms circling ever tighter together around the central warm column of rising moist air.

At certain places in the sea, the water stays hotter, deeper. In the Gulf Stream, or in the Loop Current that snakes up between the Yucatan Peninsula and the western tip of Cuba, then turns east through the Straits of Florida to join up with the Gulf Stream, there's a rich fund of hurricane fuel. As it turns, the Loop also spins off giant eddies of deep warm water that slowly separate from the main current, then ponderously migrate north and west through the Gulf of Mexico. Normally, the sea is warm for only thirty feet or so; at the heart of an eddy, however, the water can stay as hot as 27° centigrade down to 600 feet.

It follows that if a hurricane crosses one of these deep warm features, it will—other conditions permitting—get a massive extra kick from that increased source of heat lying beneath it. It will thus become the most dangerous kind of storm, a rapid intensifier—a storm that becomes a monster very quickly, very near land, and gives you very little warning that it's doing that.

Andrew crossing the Gulf Stream in 1992 was one of these. Camille hitting the Mississippi coast in 1969, one of only two category 5 hurricanes to make a U.S. landfall in the twentieth century, and Opal in 1995— both erupted from nothing to nightmare far faster than people could safely evacuate. So did they cross over Gulf warm eddies? Almost certainly. And had Bret crossed the remnants of last year's eddy off the Mexican coast yesterday, helping it to boil up suddenly into the brute now bearing down on Texas?

AXBTs could help to find the answer; the answer in turn could help forecasters to predict storm intensity more accurately in the future. Yesterday's instruments would yield data on how much deep hot water might have helped Bret to grow in the way it did; today's would try to discover how much energy Bret had sucked from the sea to become such a storm, by seeing how much cooler the water had become in its wake.

What mattered more right now, however, wasn't where Bret had been, but where it was going. "Seeing it's a strong storm," said Joe Cione grimly, "it's bound to hit where the poorest people with the most mobile homes live. They should use that as a predictive technique."

Bret looked like Andrew; the eye was bigger, some twenty miles across, but overall the system was compact. The worst of the winds were crammed tight into the eyewall, the dense ring of cloud packed close around the heart of the vortex. It was now 110 miles south of Corpus Christi; the worst scenario had the eye crossing overland just south of Corpus, because the fiercest winds in a hurricane are in the front right-hand quadrant of the eyewall—in this case, on the northeast side.

That's where the worst of the winds have the direction of the storm's motion added to them, because they're blowing the same way as the hurricane's traveling. In Bret's case, you were adding fifteen miles of forward motion per hour to winds already raging at 135 miles an hour—and if that hit Corpus Christi, said Mike Black, "It's a major disaster."

MacDill Air Force Base is effectively a town within a town, with its own clubs and stores, its own housing office and cinema. It covers about ten square miles, occupying the entire southern end of the peninsula jutting down from Tampa between Old Tampa Bay and Hillsborough Bay. From the main gate at the end of Dale Mabry Highway, the road into the base describes a long curve past a standing area lined with a dozen giant, dark gray KC-135 tankers for airborne refueling. Beyond these lies a row of massive hangars, painted in neutral shades of brown and cream, and identified only by single numbers.

Hangar 5 is the home base of the National Oceanic and Atmospheric Administration's Aircraft Operations Center. It's so huge that 42 and 43, the two Lockheed P-3s used by HRD on their research missions, can both comfortably fit inside it, though each is 111 feet long, with a wingspan of nearly 100 feet. It's so huge that when you've parked those two planes inside it, there's still room for the Gulfstream G-IV jet that HRD and the forecasters also use, as well as a Twin Otter, two Shrikes, and a pair of McDonnell-Douglas helicopters.

That Sunday morning, 22 August 1999, both P-3s stood in the sun outside the hangar; a trolley hummed back and forth toting AXBTs to 43. The full call sign was N43RF; informally dubbed Miss Piggy, the plane had a brightly painted image of the Muppet in flying jacket, scarf, and goggles on the fuselage, and a checklist ticked off in flags and storm logos beneath it. In nearly a quarter of a century's worth of research missions, 43 had flown to thirty-two countries from Norway to Mexico to Kiribati, and in fifty-six hurricanes. Her first storm had been Anita in 1977; her most recent was Mitch over the island of Guanaja ten months ago.

Lockheed built the first of these planes in the fifties as commercial airliners; seating eighty to ninety people, they were called Electras. Then they shortened them by sawing a ten-foot chunk out of the fuselage and turned them into submarine hunters called Orions. They have four turbo-prop engines and a fine look to them, with the Florida sunshine on their fresh cream and gray paint job; they have something about them of the classic fifties car, glossy, heftily crafted, stoutly functional.

Maintaining them was evidently a labor of love. Flight engineer Greg Bast told me, "They're almost empathic. If one has a problem, you can bet within a week the other one'll have the same problem too. It's happened so often it's almost scary."

Phil Kenul, one of the pilots, chipped in to say, "42's the neater plane. 43's more of a slob."

Mock-affronted, Bast told him sternly, "Don't say that. Don't even say that." He turned to me and went on, "They're very temperamental. You've got to keep 'em wiped down and clean, 'cause if you don't they'll turn on you. They'll keep you in a few extra hours."

Outside the hangar, the ground crews prepared 43 to fly in Bret. Inside, a first-story walkway ran past a line of offices in the side of the building. In the hallway that led to it, a glass cabinet displayed souvenir T-shirts. One was captioned "Mercenaries for Science," and showed a crew of hairy-faced techie longhairs crawling about the wings of a P-3 in a black stack of storm clouds, trying to fix the burning engines while clutching whirling wind gauges and being skeletonized by lightning strikes.

HRD scientists don't really look like that cartoon image of the reckless geek brainiac (or not much), but for obvious reasons, a certain degree of ironic bravado is necessary to this terrain. The safety record's reassuring— especially bearing in mind that in the early days, before a hurricane's wind structures were as well understood as they are now, many more flights went into storms at altitudes as low as 1,500 feet, or lower. Looking back, HRD director Hugh Willoughby, who recorded his 400th visit into the eye of a hurricane during Danielle in 1998—more than any other man now flying—says of going in that low, "It was crazy. It was badly thought out. It was a miracle we didn't lose more."

The navy lost a P-2 Neptune during a low-level penetration in the fifties; the air force lost two C-130s in the seventies. In one case, the storm was almost certainly an assist on a mechanical problem; the other plane went down in the South China Sea, and (though it was kept quiet at the time) the North Vietnamese were fingered in some quarters for that loss.

As for NOAA's flight crews and their research scientists, they've not lost a plane in over forty years. Nonetheless, there have been flights on which people have known that they faced death; on several occasions, brave men have disembarked from a Lockheed P-3 and vowed never, ever to fly in a hurricane again.

The worst was on 15 September 1989 in Hurricane Hugo. The plane was 42; both Willoughby and Frank Marks were on it. They took off from Barbados with the storm four hours away in the mid-Atlantic and still, as far as they knew, just a Category 2. What they didn't realize was that it was intensifying extremely fast; it was on its way to Category 5. All around, however, it was one of those days when a sequence of small errors, omissions, and mechanical problems would add up imperceptibly until the danger they were in was suddenly and most alarmingly obvious.

One leg of the flight pattern required that they drop down to 1,500 feet. They wanted to get a close look at the inner core winds at that level; it was an experiment they'd been trying to do for several years but it had kept misfiring, with an instrument malfunctioning, or some problem with the plane forcing them to turn back. There was a distinct sense that it was something about which they'd started getting frustrated; something that might help you toward a mood where maybe you took your eye off the ball.

One of the pilots was Gerry McKim, the same man who'd brought 43 out from Bret with its snapped antenna trailing along the fuselage, and who was preparing to fly back into it now. Ten years earlier, he'd just transferred to NOAA; he'd flown P-3s for twenty years in the navy, but Hugo was only his fourth hurricane, and he readily admits that he was inexperienced.

As they approached the storm, he said that flying down at 1,500 feet was the hardest, most physically demanding part of the job; he was keen to do that leg first and get it over with. Not knowing how bad Hugo was becoming, they all agreed to this; no one thought to point out that they'd be doing it still heavy-laden with fuel in the fuselage. Having fuel in the wings is fine, because that's where the lift is; having weight still centered in the body of the plane, on the other hand, means more stress on the wing spars. But no one spoke up.

No one was quite on the button with the radar, either; the most experienced guy had a headset whose microphone wasn't working. "Knowing what I know now," says Willoughby, "if I'd been sitting at the radar, I'd have said, 'Folks—this looks like a Cat 5. I don't think we should be at fifteen hundred feet. That's what would happen now. I, or Frank, or hopefully anyone at all qualified to take a plane out would say, 'This is not a fifteen-hundred-foot hurricane.'"

Hindsight, of course, is twenty-twenty. Besides, Willoughby wasn't looking at the radar; his part of the day's work wasn't due until later, and he was in the back of the plane. Then, at a crucial point on the approach when someone else might have spoken up, they had a data system crash. Another thing they didn't know, meanwhile, was that there was a problem with the fuel injector in one of the engines. So they just drove on in.

Willoughby was looking forward to it. "We thought we were going into a hundred-knot hurricane," he says, "and a hundred-knot hurricane's about the prettiest there is.° You get stronger than that, the water's all white. You

°100 knots = 115 mph.

get below eighty knots, the streaks and ripples and blowing spray are less spectacular. But at a hundred knots, the sea has this kind of turquoise color, and it's layered. There's a filigree of foam on the surface, long streaks of glowing foam with long streaks of greenish bubbles beneath that, and between the disturbances there's a deep navy blue. I once tried dabbling with oil paints but I never could paint it, and there's been very few successful photographs. It just has something about it; anybody that's seen it wants to see it again. So I slid into one of the window seats and"—he shrugs—"I was going to have this aesthetic experience. Then it started to get bumpy."

They went down to 1,500 feet a hundred miles from the center, then the radar failed. They circled for a while; in the front of the plane, Frank Marks and the others were preoccupied with getting the data system fixed. Marks remembers, "Everybody was thinking about the instrumentation. We got it back up, more or less, and as we started going in, the storm looked pretty strong. There was a good tight doughnut of an eye on the radar as we approached—but it hadn't dawned on anybody yet.

"We were still trying to get over the instrument problems and the wind wasn't too strong, it was sixty, seventy knots—then it climbed really rapidly. It got rocky real fast. The wind went up to about 120 knots in four miles, in about a minute, and it just kept on going up. We had 180-knot gusts and we started hitting these up and down motions, the plane was going all over the place, we got into this rock and roll, we were lurching from side to side. . . ."

"Severe turbulence," says Willoughby, "definitely gets your attention. Turbulence comes in four flavors. There are three that you're likely to experience and live. Light turbulence, you're flying over Florida here and you bump around a little bit. Moderate turbulence, you're on a commercial airliner, the lady in the seat behind you is going to gasp when the plane jolts, and the flight attendants should really be sitting down. Severe turbulence, you're strapped in, and you're thrown hard against the straps. Things that are unsecured in the aircraft come loose. The pilot loses control of the aircraft intermittently. Then extreme turbulence is where the airplane's absolutely out of control, you have structural damage . . ."

And probably you die.

"If the wings come off, you probably do."

A twenty-man life raft strapped to the deck in front of Willoughby's seat broke loose and flew to the ceiling, denting the metal handrail along the top of the walkway through the middle of the plane. The galley at the back was completely trashed, reduced to a flying pulp of coffee, soda cans, peanut butter, and paperwork. The toilet was flowing all over the floor. Willoughby saw his laptop flying through the air. He worried about what would happen if it hit someone, but his memory of what he did next is unclear, as if it happened in a dream. He believes he undid his straps, stood up, caught the laptop, sat down, and strapped himself back in again. He talks of this as if mystified by the memory—probably because there's a piece of him that can't believe he didn't end up with broken limbs at the very least.

Behind him, one of the engineers was strapped down flat on a bunk, saying over and over, "Oh shit, goddamn, oh shit," just swearing and swearing. Willoughby looked out of the window, and saw that they were dumping fuel. Well, he thought, we're in an emergency now.

In the cockpit, Frank Marks was warning the pilots about the updraft they'd hit when they reached the inside edge of the eyewall. As they broke through, the wind dropped almost instantly from 150 to 50 miles an hour, the updraft heaved the plane skyward at twenty meters a second—that's 45 miles an hour—then there was another monster lurch back down again. Clipboards and Coke cans and headsets careened through the air all about them.

Worse, there was a flame thirty feet long shooting from the back of the inboard starboard engine. The governor on the fuel injector had failed and it was out of control, pouring gas onto hot metal. The engine shut down automatically—so now after they'd survived the turbulence they had three engines, at an altitude of maybe 1,200 feet.

There was another problem. When you pop out from the eyewall into the eye of a hurricane, to all intents and purposes you're flying sideways; to stay in a straight line against the wind swirling around the eye you have to travel crablike against that wind. When the wind abruptly falls as you break through into the calm center, therefore, that means the plane veers into a sudden curve—straight back toward the eyewall. So now they had two bad choices. They could either slide right back into the worst of the winds, or they could try to stay in the eye by turning—but that meant turning into the wing that had only one engine.

McKim made a split-second decision to go for the latter. He made a three-sixty circle out and away from the eyewall, losing another 400 feet of altitude in the process. Another thirty seconds, Marks reckons, and they'd have been in the water—but McKim made the turn, and slowly they started climbing. It took them an hour to get to 5,000 feet, straining upward, lamed inside the eye. All the while they didn't know if they'd damaged the plane, or how badly, or what had caused the flame-out on the engine.

"It's a little strange," says Willoughby, "to be going round and round in the eye thinking, This may be the afternoon that I die. But look—you've known you might die from the first time you fly in a hurricane. It's not likely, and I'd certainly prefer it not to happen. As we used to say in the navy, I'd like to be shot by a jealous ensign when I'm seventy-three. But the fact is, it's worth it."

The next time he was in church (it's somehow not surprising to learn that, in one faith or another, a fair number of HRD's people are believers) members of his congregation asked Willoughby if he'd prayed. He told them he hadn't. He said, "We got ourselves into that situation. Asking God to get us out of it seemed a little presumptuous."

An air force plane was flying reconnaissance on a high pattern above them; it broke off, came into the eye, looked for a quiet way out, and led the shaken P-3 back home to Barbados. Onboard with the scientists and air crew that day was a journalist from the island, a young woman who'd stayed extremely quiet throughout. Eventually someone realized she must have thought it was like that every time.

One of the pilots said, laughing, 'Man, she must have thought we eat lead and spit bullets. She must have thought we have balls of steel. So someone had to tell her that day really wasn't normal. Someone had to point out the window and say, 'Ma'am. You see that propeller there? It's supposed to be *turning*.'"

Willoughby flew every other mission they undertook into Hugo, the same way you want to get back in a car after you've had a wreck. He'd been flying storms for twenty years at that point already, since he was a young meteorologist in the navy working out of Guam in the Pacific, but he readily admits he was nervous for several years after Hugo all the same. Every time the plane bounced, he'd break out in a sweat.

"The storm can kill you," he says. "That kind of flying, inherently it's not real safe. It's not overwhelmingly dangerous, either—it's just that if you do it for a long while, you roll the dice a lot of times. But then"—and he shrugs—"as any flying instructor will tell you, landing's a maneuver that you'd also tend to avoid, if it weren't absolutely necessary."

As for Frank Marks, when I asked him what it had been like, he said without hesitation, "It was probably the most incredible data set I've ever seen."

He said that what happened to the aircraft was of course frightening, "but I was of two minds. I was overwhelmed by what I was seeing as well, by what we were flying in. I was subdued all the way back to the ground—then I said, 'Damn, why didn't we turn the data system back on once we got the plane righted?' So it had taken me four hours to get over the shock."

Marks has a sign on his door announcing, "God put me on earth to accomplish a certain number of things. Right now I am so far behind, I will never die."

Peter Dodge ran through his flight pattern for the landfall experiment with flight director Barry Damiano, pondering whether they could fly the full pattern if Bret was already crossing onshore when they got there. Then, at midday, it was time for the preflight briefing.

Gerry McKim was the lead pilot; fifty-five years old, he was a short, broad-shouldered man with the stocky, triangular build of a pit bull, and a rather better sense of humor. He looked at the pattern and said thoughtfully, "That northeast quadrant is dangerous as hell."

They planned to go in at 12,000 feet. The forecasters at the National Hurricane Center had an air force C-130 working recon for them at 10,000 feet, and going lower than that in a Category 4—especially a Category 4 shaken up by the friction impacts of wind over ground at landfall—was an option you'd avoid if you could. Then Dodge and Mike Black told McKim they didn't want to pass in and out of the eye in a straight line as they normally did. When they got in the eye they wanted instead to stay there, flying around the edge of it.

McKim raised an eyebrow, laughing. When they got in there, he asked, "You want me to turn left?"

For some time the HRD scientists had been wrestling with a problem. They didn't feel that they were truly sampling the maximum winds, and this had led to a certain order of controversy.

How do you measure the true maximum surface winds in a major hurricane? Any instruments on the ground aren't in the eyewall, or if they are, they get blown away. When HRD used their plane-launched dropsondes to fall into the storm and call a surface maximum that way, however, and when the forecasters then broadcast what they'd found, the process had led some in the hurricane community to charge that they were over-warning.

Generally speaking, the wind speed increases as you rise away from the friction of the storm against the earth's surface; the argument therefore ran that HRD was taking flight-level speeds and extrapolating them downward to arrive at artificially high surface winds. Given the evidence, quite why anyone should want to argue (in effect) that hurricanes *aren't really as bad as you say* rather escapes me—but it was true that with the old, more cumbersome sondes that they'd used until recently, the low-level measurements (if the sondes survived that far at all) had been patchy at best.

Taking many more measurements, however, and using the Global Positioning System to attain a higher order of accuracy altogether, the new sondes were reaching farther down more often, and more clearly. They were, indeed, producing such a fecund and startling mass of data that from the moment they were first deployed—in Hurricane Guillermo in the east Pacific in 1997—HRD scientists could be observed excitably waving their arms about and shouting at each other in the corridors of their laboratory in Miami and, shall we say, *productively disagreeing* as to what all this data truly meant.

It did seem clear, however, that in a major hurricane, flight-level winds really could extend a long way down toward the surface. They didn't know how spread out those worst winds at ground level might be, but as Mike Black put it, "If there's one spot getting 140 miles an hour, that's one spot too many. People need to be warned, and warned correctly. A Cat 4 like Bret's a lion, and you don't want to say it's a mouse."

The trouble was, however, that more often than not their dropsondes weren't finding the kind of winds which, from every other indicator, they expected to see. By late on Saturday afternoon in Bret, for example, they were flying in a hurricane that looked horrendously potent, and yet the worst winds they were recording were barely topping 100 miles an hour. So if they were right that the eyewall had pockets within it that were dangerously more extreme than that, all the way down to the surface—that Bret was indeed the Category 4 storm it appeared to be—then how did you prove it?

In 1998, Black and a colleague named James Franklin came up with an idea. The eye of a hurricane isn't a perfect cylinder; it's not a straight tube plugged through the storm's heart from sky to sea. It's more like an inverted cone; the eyewall slopes down and inward toward the center, banked like the stands of an enormous stadium. In the past, they'd flown into this on the perpendicular, and either carried on clean through the eye, or turned in the middle to head straight out on whatever other heading the next leg of the pattern required.

The trouble with this was, it only gave you a very brief, one-time chance to get a sonde dropped accurately into the inside edge of the eyewall where the worst winds are. What Black and Franklin therefore proposed was that the plane should instead turn once it got inside, and fly around the inner edge of the wall; it should circle around at least a portion of the eye's rim.

Doing this at ten or twelve thousand feet, they'd be in clear air. If they then dropped their sondes while flying that circle, they'd take advantage of the tilt in the wall, and the sondes should fall beneath them right into the area of maximum wind. Moreover, they'd be curving over that area long enough to drop more than one instrument, with a correspondingly better chance of finding and confirming how bad (or not) the storm really was.

They had the idea on paper, and the Aircraft Operations Center agreed to it in theory. Normally, you'd then brief on it before you flew; you'd all know you were going to try it. By August 1999, they hadn't done that yet—then, late on Saturday, flying 42 through Bret with Captain Dave Tennesen at the helm, on their fourth and final pass into the eye Black called into the mike on his headset, "Hey. How about it?"

They were, literally, winging it—but here they had this storm, they couldn't find the true maximum winds, they believed them to be there, they wanted to prove it, and they wanted people to know about it. So, for the first time, they popped into the eye and turned to make that deliberate circle. Going upwind, the pilots could see what they were headed into—and they needed to.

Bret's eyewall had hook-shaped protuberances bulging inward. No one knew what they were—maybe the tips of spiral rainbands ripping in through the wall—but Tennesen didn't like the look of them. Another feature was the phenomenon dubbed "miniswirls" by tornado expert Dr. Ted Fujita; the HRD people called them "mesovortices," and they looked like billowing, cylindrical smokestacks spiraling up and around the inside edge of the eyewall, twisted, spinning columns within the larger whole.

Maybe it was one of these that threw the plane up and down so violently in Hugo. Maybe it was these that caused the "damage streaks" gouged out through the paths of major landfalls, or led people who survived Mitch on Guanaja to speak of that storm being "full of tornadoes." But whatever they were and whatever they did, if you hit one—and Tennesen grinned—"it'd make the guys in the back wake up fast." At the bottom line, "You don't want to fly in one."

If you steered clear of these, that didn't leave you free of risk. Consider that your left wingtip is a mile, perhaps only half a mile, from the eyewall. Traveling at five miles a minute, that leaves you between six and twelve seconds from grazing it. If you did, and the left wing slipped into the wall, it'd be hitting the storm's worst winds even while the right wing was in relatively motionless air.

This could result in what Mike Black euphemistically defined as "control problems." The control problems in question might well involve the winds in the wall flipping the plane over on its back, whereupon you roll, fall, and die. "This," said Black, "is something you want to avoid."

In Allen in 1980, a P-3 caught a wingtip in the eyewall; snagged, the pilot couldn't pull out of the wind, and had to travel two-thirds of the way around the inside of the wall before he found a way loose from it. It was one of HRD's horror rides; two of those onboard had never flown a storm since.

By now, Dave Tennesen had joined the briefing for this third flight into Bret; a lean man forty-eight years old, tanned, craggy-jawed, and neatly fitted as they all were with the aviator shades and the nonchalant manner. Of flying around the eye the afternoon before, he told the other pilots, "It's really cool. You've got to fly level a bit to get maybe two radar swipes, then turn, level, turn, and you can go round and round in there forever."

Another pilot, Ron Phillipsborn, looked sideways at the scientists. He smiled and said, "Don't give these guys ideas"—but it was too late to stop them trying it again now. On that final circling pass through Bret's eye on Saturday afternoon, they'd thrown sondes into the sloped wall beneath them, and found winds near the surface at 135 miles an hour. The National Hurricane Center had the news inside ten minutes and it was then that they upgraded Bret to a Category 4, at least twenty-four hours before the expected time of landfall. Needless to say, as Mike Black observed contentedly, "this has practical implications."

Fortunately I'm not superstitious, as the time on my watch when Barry Damiano called us to board 43 was 13:13. In the cabin the air conditioning vented clouds of chill vapor; the air crew zipped up their flight suits. The interior was an open space lined with workstations, each stacked with mostly miniature, hand-sized computer screens in beige-painted metal cabinets. A small galley at the back had a fridge, a microwave, and a coffee urn; a printer sat incongruously amid piles of cookie snacks and loaves of bread, ready to churn out hours' worth of flight data.

The walls, the lockers, and the toilet cubicle all about the galley were decorated with stickers and decals celebrating bars, research projects, and other air forces around the world. Fore of the sticker zone, two metal tubes jutted at an angle from the floor behind the station where the electronics engineer would work; these were the chutes for launching dropsondes and AXBTs. Some instruments were preloaded in pods in the plane's belly; the rest went out by hand and were tied down in stacks between the workstations.

Also between the workstations as you went forward toward the cockpit were racks of electronics, and another rack packed with thick files. Taped to this rack was a forty-three-title publications index concerning this one single plane; *Integrated Flight Station Wiring Data*, for example, or *Airframe Illustrated Parts Breakdown*. The volume of *Structural Repair Instructions*, I devoutly hoped, was not intended for use inflight.

A payment of $2 each granted all onboard "unlimited foraging rights" in the galley. I contemplated the mounds of Little Debbie's Fudge Rounds and Oatmeal Creme Pies. "Amazing," said a mechanic, looking up from his Tom Clancy, "what $2 will buy." The airsick bags, I noted, were located strategically close at hand.

Gerry McKim gave a graphic briefing on emergency disembarkation. If you're down in the sea and the life raft's gone out the door, a slender lanyard leads from inside the plane to where the raft's in the water. McKim said, "It's very unlikely that I'd ditch in a hurricane, but if I do and you don't hang on to the lanyard, you won't make it. You get to the life raft and if nobody else is in it, that means they didn't make it. So if you have to inflate it yourself, be careful; there's an eighty-pound oxygen bottle and if that thing hits you in the head, you're gone. Now, anyone get sick in amusement parks? Take two airsick bags, I never seen a guy fill only one. If you do only fill one, fine, take the other one home and you've got a souvenir."

We were in the air at 13:40, climbing slowly to 18,000 feet; the Gulf below was a gently rippled, sunlit gray-blue, flecked here and there with the shadows of small clusters of cloud. When we leveled off, Ed Walsh, a NASA-funded scientist from Colorado, asked if he could run a quick test on a new tool he hoped to try out on the landfall. It was a scanning radar altimeter capable (in theory) of measuring wave heights to an accuracy of ten centimeters—equipment with many potential uses, among them increased accuracy in the prediction of storm surge.

"For our visitors," came a voice on my headset, "we're going to do a ten-degree wing roll left then right, over and over a few times."

"We won't do it too hard," chipped in another voice, "we don't want people getting sick already."

The plane dipped smoothly one way, then the other. Unconcerned, McKim sat in the galley reading *Sports Illustrated*. Flying landfalls, he said, sometimes presented unusual problems; landside, you could find your options a shade restricted. Friction as the storm went ashore threw up tornadoes and wind shear, and you didn't want to drop too low and meet up with that. But then, you never knew what any given storm might throw at you anyway.

"They all look different," he said, "and any one of them can reach out and bite you. Gilbert in '88 was the strongest we've ever flown in, but it was really well organized, it was classic, and it was one of the easiest rides of them all. Then Hugo kicked the crap out of us—so you can never really say what it's going to be like."

He'd done around 225 eyewall penetrations; when he first started, he couldn't believe what he was being asked to do. He'd spent twenty years in the navy trying to avoid bad weather, so it was a surprise to find himself actively seeking out the worst weather on the planet; it went against the grain of everything he'd been taught. He remembered his first penetration, thinking, What the hell am I doing here? Then Hugo showed him what it was all about. He said, "I was kind of naive. Basically, I did not have control of the airplane." He shrugged and said, "Lesson learned."

The lesson was to fly gentle and not to fight the storm. If you tried to fight it, all you did was max up the stress—stress which, in Hugo, measured six positive G's and three negative, twice the plane's design limit. But unless a storm was actually trying to turn you upside down, or throw you in the sea, you didn't start engaging in "abnormal stick controls."

In essence, he said, "in an eyewall situation, anyone who thinks they're really flying the airplane, they're being silly. Just the volumes of water, the plugs are shorting out, you've got so much noise you can't hear each other— so you let the storm do what it wants, and you correct when it's done."

One of the worst experiences had been Andrew—not because that storm was especially violent to fly in, but because five people on the plane had families going through it on the ground. They landed in Jacksonville, and the next day they all bought water, chain saws, tarpaper, anything they could think of. Two guys managed to get word that their families were safe; a third received the same message from the control tower as they came into Miami International, and there were tears in his eyes as they rolled down the runway. The other two didn't find out that their wives and children were all right until they got back to their homes.

McKim's family had left two days before Andrew hit. He said, "People worry that their house will be destroyed, or looted—but if the storm's going to destroy it, or the looters are going to loot it, then OK. Better to get out— 'cause there's nothing but bad can happen to you if you stay. I'm amazed at the number of people who stay, when we see over and over what hurricanes can do. You can replace your house—but you can't replace a human life."

It was his last season flying; he was looking forward to retirement. He said, "I won't miss it. I've done it a lot, and I don't need to do it anymore. I'm going to go fishing. Sure, when I see the TV and I know the guys are going out, I'll feel a little bit of longing, but I've done my bit. See, the air force can go out all they want and tell you where the storms are, and that's fine—but you need these scientists going in there to find out how they work as well. Every time we fly, if we help to refine those computer models only one-thousandth of one percent, that's good. And that's why these planes need to fly."

A t 15:45, half an hour out from the edge of the storm, whitecaps were beginning to scurry and crest over the sea far below. Above us spread a huge shield of cirrus, the storm's exhaust flowing outward for hundreds of miles all about. The sky to our north and south was still clear blue, but ahead lay a thickening bank of cumulus towers, merging imperceptibly as we approached into a solid gray wall, growing ominously darker.

Word came from the air force plane already in the storm that Bret was accelerating closer to land; HRD's second mission, planned for later that night, had been canceled already. In his seat behind the pilots, Peter Dodge sat anxiously poring over his flight patterns, hoping Bret would cooperate and stay offshore until we got there; obviously enough, to learn how landfall changes a hurricane, you have first to capture the state of it before the landfall occurs.

The scientists readied their instruments. Onshore, tornadoes were reported sprouting from one of the outer rainbands near San Antonio. From the cockpit at 16:04, McKim announced that he had the eye on radar, 125 miles ahead; the screen showed a double eyewall and the inner eye contracting, the classic signature of a fully matured storm.

The sea below was churned into a racing turmoil, streaked white, laced all over with wide trails of breaking spray. Unhurried and meticulous, navigator Dave Rathbun plotted bearings and range with ruler, pencil, and compasses on a detailed chart; he had the eye a shade over twenty miles from land, bearing down on Padre Island National Seashore, and Kenedy County across Laguna Madre behind it.

The people of southwest Texas could not have been more lucky; if they had to be hit by a Category 4 hurricane, they couldn't have been hit in a more sparsely populated area, exactly midway between Corpus Christi and Brownsville. With evident relief Mike Black said, "There's nothing down there but cows and rattlesnakes. It's the absolute best place it could go. Sixty miles north, and Corpus Christi would be lunch meat."

The scientists were lucky, too. They could still fly their full figure 4 to get the landfall profile; the far end of one leg would take them over the coast, but not so much as to wreck the experiment. As they made their final preparations, the sky ahead of the cockpit was now a solid wall of deep gray, and the sea below a morass of heaving white foam. At 16:20 McKim's voice came through the headset, saying calmly, "OK, everybody, let's get ready to rock and roll. We're going into the hurricane. Let's clean up the cabin, get everything stowed away. First pass especially, get ready for the hurricane."

We vanished into a sudden milky whiteness. Tiny droplets of water started racing across the windows; the plane began gently to jolt and bump. McKim swapped coordinates with the air force plane 2,000 feet below us, forty-five miles ahead, making sure no instruments would be released when they were passing beneath us. Barry Damiano cut in, alerting the electronics engineer that he had six and a half minutes to the first drop.

The cloud outside remained a surprisingly radiant, pristine white; the flight stayed smooth, with only the occasional mild shudder to remind us that we were now flying virtually sideways, angled against the wind.

"One minute to drop."

The headset muffled all noise; the droning hum of the engines and the rattling of the steel lockers and cabinets was a dim, steady background to the even crackle of the air crew's voices. We were closing fast on the eyewall.

"Stand by to drop, one, two, three."

There was a loud hissing, and a solid double thud.

"Sonde and BT away."

"Make sure you're holding on," said McKim—and then, abruptly, we broke into the eye of the storm. The cloud parted around us, there was a sudden blinding brilliance of sunlight, the plane banked to start circling around the wall, and as my sight grew accustomed to the glare, I began slowly to realize the astounding vastness and beauty of the place we had entered.

Blurred here and there with drifting wafts and tendrils of wispy, blue-gray vapor, the eyewall was an enormous bank of whiteness sloping steeply upward to 50,000 feet or higher, and curving sharply beneath us down to the sea. It seemed to be built of roll upon roll, coil upon coil of bundled cloud, like a massive pile of folded towels—except, when you looked again, you could sense that this soft, piled solidity of cloud was spinning.

It had an eerie blend about it of impassive poise and furious motion, a titanic stillness containing terrible energies. It soared up to a clearly delimited rim, and within that lay a blazing, spotless hole of sunlit blue sky. Below, patches of sea boiled in a seething mayhem of broken water. It wasn't a *perfect* eye—very few are—and patchy drifts of cloud were just beginning to fill in the base as Bret, fading a hint past its peak, began to weaken near shore. But it was God's stadium nonetheless, an almighty bowl of tranquillity surrounded by epically vast stands of wind-packed white cloud climbing all about us, unbroken, smoothly towering taller than mountains. The sea writhed beneath it, spume-streaked, and the sky stared down blank and empty above.

"I must say," came a quiet voice from the cockpit, "this is definitely impressive."

Can we measure the winds over land?"
"You want to drop a sonde over land?"
"If you're willing."
"There's nothing out here but marsh."
If there was anybody down there, another voice observed dryly, 43 dropping sondes would be the least of their problems. As the plane passed up and down the coast, in and out of the eye while Bret rolled toward land, glimpses of the shore beneath were bleak and disturbing. Mercifully unpeopled, Padre Island lay dun and waterlogged, with giant breakers raking against the dunes. The first sonde, falling just inside the eyewall, had reported winds of 148 miles an hour at 500 feet, 138 at 400, and had then fallen silent, pulped by the storm.

We passed over farmland and isolated homesteads, then turned back toward the driven white sea. Ten miles south of the eye we made a sharp turn north, then ran a straight leg back through the center, heading 105 miles to Port Aransas. The electronics engineer had a busy time of it here, dropping three sondes and an AXBT on either side of the eye; the first set of four instruments fell away in quick succession, the eyewall loomed, and McKim called sharply, "OK, let's sit down."

"I need a different channel for the next BT. The first one's stuck in the mud, it's still transmitting."

"So we've got a weather station on Padre Island now."

"Only giving sea surface temperatures."

"Mud surface temperatures."

"Everybody *sit down.*"

We lurched into the eyewall again, the plane bumping and sliding—not violently but steadily, persistently, held for those few moments in the worst of the winds until again, with that dazzling abruptness, we were out in the eye. For four minutes the blue sky glared down, the banks of whiteness rose all about, the flight was smooth, then we were across it and back into pale grayness and murk, the rain streaming along the windows, with that insistent juddering starting up again straightaway.

Apparently oblivious to the turbulence, the scientists batted their options back and forth. They ran a triangle around the back of the storm, dropping AXBTs in the wake to see how much Bret had cooled the sea— then Ed Walsh wanted to try running a leg between the coast and the eyewall to measure the waves in the storm surge.

There was a question whether the wall wasn't on the beach already; Mike Black and Peter Dodge, meanwhile, discussed with mild irritation the fact that they were supposedly budget-limited to twenty sondes per flight. They'd dropped twenty-four already, they badly wanted to throw out more, and they plainly weren't going to stop. How often, after all, do you catch a Category 4 making landfall?

I stared down at the Padre Island beach through a break in the clouds, trying to imagine how huge the waves must be if you could see each one individually from 12,000 feet. We were turning to do the run that would try to measure that; we passed into a stack of blue-gray cloud and the worst jolting so far started up, suddenly pressing bodies against harnesses.

McKim ignored the call for a heading parallel to the coast; we were slipping toward the northeast quadrant of the eyewall, and he'd seen something in there that he didn't much like. He tried to pass around it instead, crossing over the mainland coast, and as we bucked and thudded against the wind someone mildly inquired, "See anybody sunbathing down there?"

"Nope. See anybody skinny-dipping, maybe?"

"If they are," said Mike Black quietly, "it's 'cause they've had the clothes blown clean off them."

He was running through the data from the instrument drops; he thought a couple of the sondes that had gone out over land looked interesting, and now he ventured a suggestion that they might try dropping another. In the cockpit the pilots had other things on their minds, and asked him to wait until they'd found a way back to the beach. They were trying, as one of them put it, "to scootch left to get around this stuff. There's a couple of cells coming up ahead. Can we slip through the gap there?"

"We're over by Kingsville, right? We're definitely over land, I can see a house. We're definitely not going to throw a sonde out here."

"There's no city here."

"Is it OK by you?"

"Yeah. Some farmer'll find it."

"Is that a first?"

"No."

We hit more bumpy air, still hunting the beach. It looked as if we were due north of the eye, in which case Bret had either crossed by now onto Padre Island, or was on the brink of doing so. With the storm changing and moving the way it was, finding the shoreline was hard; from the back Ed Walsh at the radar altimeter tried calling out directions, using topography off his readings. Absorbed in his instruments, his voice was remarkably, incongruously tranquil. "Maybe a hair left," he mused, as the plane tilted this way and that to find the right track, still ducking and slipping all the while in the wind and rain and cloud.

Now we were flying on the cusp of beach and eyewall—but again McKim could see the northeast quadrant looming, and again he cut away to avoid it. Water streamed by the windows as he said firmly, "Let's make sure everybody's strapped in on this run, OK, folks?"

"I'm sorry, Barry, how long till the next drop again?"

"Three minutes."

"Scientist time? Or navigator time?"

"Where's the air force?"

"Closing fast south to north, they should be in the eye now. Call 'em. Can we drop a sonde in the north eyewall?"

"We're about three minutes out. . . ."

"OK, hold the drop. Hold the drop."

The plane lurched, the rain flooded past, and beneath the crackle of voices metal all about seemed quietly to be creaking and rattling. It wasn't really much worse than you might get on a commercial flight, but it didn't stop—until, in another flash of sudden light, we were back in the eye. The plane tipped from side to side, McKim dipping the wings to try to spot the C-130 eleven miles away, 2,000 feet below. In that moment I caught my best sight of the wall yet, this colossal, radiant cliff of cloud leaping skyward all about us. Joe Cione knelt on the floor by an overwing window and said quietly, "We got lucky today. That's a real pretty wall."

"Heads up, people in their seats. It's your game, Ed."

"How close are we to the beach?"

"I think we're over land now, go five degrees left."

"Wings are level, Ed."

There was a moment of silence; Walsh was lost in his altimeter again. "Hey, Ed," McKim told him mildly, "we get real insecure up here when nobody's talking to us."

"Well," he said contemplatively, "I don't see any waves."

"We got an inshore breeze here, Ed, I can tell you that."

We were running out of time. Dodge and Black scribbled patterns, trying to figure out the most productive way home. They stared into the radar screen; Bret was a spiraled mass of dense green precipitation, veined through with curling orange strips of thunderstorm, and trailing a fat, flared, ragged-edged sash of inflow beneath it to the south. On the west side, a curved talon of dry air snagged in toward the center; Black and Dodge wondered if they could throw a sonde in there, to try to see how much rain that air had lost before it circled back offshore from the hurricane's leading edge. At that moment we were thirty miles south of the eye, heading straight in.

During the last penetration a few minutes later, the effect of a stadium roof arching high above us was clearer than ever. The top lip of the wall had a shadowed, deep blue overhang on it, as if the storm were consciously sculpted, a monumental piece of climatic architecture planned and built to be just exactly this way. There were those precious few minutes to admire it, then . . .

"Strap in, folks. Last eyewall, might be a little rough." We slid once more into the harsh embrace of the cloud, and were instantly rocked from side to side. Someone called a wind speed measurement near 140 miles an hour. "Hold on, guys," said McKim calmly—then, as things eased up, he added calmly, "Well, children, I count five penetrations today."

That put Ron Phillipsborn past 200, and gave another member of the air crew his first hundred. The scientists, on the other hand, weren't counting just yet; thirty miles ahead there lay a vivid orange rainband, and they fancied dropping one last sonde to see what was in it.

"Looks ugly," said someone.

"What we just went through was ugly."

"No it wasn't."

McKim took us in there, and the few seconds it took to cross it were the worst shake yet; still nothing genuinely traumatic, but certainly enough to have you clinging to your armrest. A series of ragged kicks and we were through, Ed Walsh in back still scanning his radar for the wave heights along the coast beneath us. Someone reported more thunderstorms in a second rainband farther ahead; on the radar they looked tight and dense, coiled bundles of red-centered orange. Again we plunged into them; this time the convection threw us up and down, left and right, tossing the plane through a sharp series of sudden blows as McKim called a warning of lightning ahead.

As if from some alternative zone of monastic calm Ed Walsh announced at this moment, "The dune line's on a heading about oh-fourteen degrees."

"Yeah," said one of the pilots through gritted teeth, "we're not too worried about that right now."

There was a moment more of bucking and lunging in rain so thick on the window that you couldn't see through it, and then we were out the far side, slipping finally away after four and a half hours inside Hurricane Bret.

"Who needs eyewalls," a voice asked mildly, "when you've got stuff like that?"

In the darkening evening, we turned east across the Gulf.

Bret had probably peaked sometime in the early hours of that Sunday morning. What 43 had flown in was still a major hurricane, but over shallow, cooler water it was just starting to fade, and after landfall it broke up in a matter of days. That landfall, meanwhile, had taken place in an area so thinly populated that the principal casualty was the local cotton crop. Cotton doesn't like heavy rain; after six years of near-continuous drought, however, sugar cane, bell pepper, and citrus fruit farmers were in many cases heartily glad of Bret.

There was one other impact. Flying back over the Gulf that night revealed the startling quantity of oil rigs now at work in those waters; the sea was bejeweled with their lights, a whole galaxy of steel villages strewn across the waves. Lying ahead of the storm, many of them had shut down production; consequently, the day after Bret made landfall, the price of oil rose.

For the scientists, meanwhile, it had been a perfect storm. Above all, there had been no human calamity—but beyond that central fact, they'd assembled the best data portrait of a major landfall ever drawn. Within twenty-four hours, sixteen different wind field analyses were available to all comers on the Web. Moreover, two notions of significant practical import looked to have been granted healthy backing.

First, Bret had rapidly intensified over a deep pool of warm water, just as Pete Black and others had been hoping to document. True, whatever the ocean was doing, there'd been other important factors in play in the atmosphere as well; most vitally, the winds at different altitudes around the storm had all been blowing in pretty much the same direction, a condition highly conducive to hurricane development called "low vertical shear." Which of these two factors had played the greater part in this particular storm's evolution remained to be determined in months, probably years of study that still lay ahead—but the point was that a dangerous air-sea interaction had happened, and they'd recorded it.

The second idea that gained good supporting evidence came from taking a chance; the chance Mike Black took when he called out to Dave Tennesen at the last moment on the second day to try circling in the eye. The outcome was new ground truth about the worst winds in the base of the eyewall; two dropsondes had been launched in quick succession, and graphs demonstrating wind speed against altitude as they fell seaward were dramatic, showing striking double peaks at 5,000 feet, and again near the surface. Thus was Bret shown to be a Category 4—and if Miami, Houston, or New Orleans had lain in the path of such a storm (to name just a few significant potential targets) millions of people would have needed to know that.

On the way down, one of those sondes had also hit a huge bubble of warm air bursting upward in the wall. Though they were only a thousand yards apart, one sonde was plummeting, and the other one was bouncing. At that point, Mike Black said later, "It wasn't a dropsonde anymore. It was an upsonde."

Flying back from Bret on Sunday night, he didn't know that yet; he only knew that in the course of three days, they'd documented a nascent hurricane through explosive growth to landfall. He looked out of the window across the rig-sparkling sea and said wearily, but with evident satisfaction, "It's a done deal. So now let's turn our eyes east and see what's developing out there." Tropical Storm Cindy, as it happened, was already on the march in the mid-Atlantic.

We landed at MacDill at 22:50. Cold beer was waiting in an ice-packed cooler in the hangar doorway; Pete Black and Eric Uhlhorn, whose night flight on 42 had been canceled, were waiting with it. Mike Black told his namesake that he and Dodge had dropped thirty-six sondes, nearly twice their supposed budget per flight; Pete whistled through his teeth, feigning shock. "Well," Mike told him, "we knew you weren't flying. So we used yours."

Gerry McKim described the feature he'd been so careful to avoid in the northeast part of the eyewall; the two Blacks told him it sounded like a mesovortex. McKim laughed. He said, "I hear the second time you fly one it's real easy."

Out on the standing area, the ground crew made ready to tow 43 back into the hangar. Behind them in the blue-black Tampa sky, lightning flared through thunderstorms parked all about the horizon. As people stood watching and talking in the vast, echoing doorway, the sense of unwinding tension was physically palpable.

They would, however, have plenty more of this to come; Bret, as they knew all too well, was only the B storm. If 1999 turned out anything like the last few years, there was a lot of the alphabet to be worked through yet.

ZCZC MIATCPAT3 ALL
TTAA00 KNHC DDHHMM
BULLETIN
TROPICAL STORM BRET ADVISORY NUMBER 21
NATIONAL WEATHER SERVICE MIAMI FL
4 PM CDT MON AUG 23 1999

. . . BRET CONTINUES TO PRODUCE HEAVY RAINS . . .

TROPICAL STORM WARNINGS ARE DISCONTINUED FOR THE SOUTH COAST OF
TEXAS. ALL INTERESTS SHOULD EXERCISE CAUTION UNTIL WINDS AND SEAS
SUBSIDE.

AT 4 PM CDT . . . 2100Z . . . THE CENTER OF TROPICAL STORM BRET WAS LOCATED
NEAR LATITUDE 27.8 NORTH . . . LONGITUDE 99.1 WEST OR ABOUT 30 MILES . . .
45 KM . . . NORTHEAST OF LAREDO TEXAS.

BRET IS MOVING TOWARD THE NORTHEAST NEAR 6 MPH . . . 9 KM/HR . . . AND A
TURN TOWARD THE WEST IS EXPECTED IN THE NEXT 24 HOURS.

MAXIMUM SUSTAINED WINDS ARE NEAR 40 MPH . . . 65 KM/HR . . . WITH HIGHER
GUSTS. BRET IS EXPECTED TO WEAKEN TO A TROPICAL DEPRESSION TONIGHT.

TROPICAL STORM FORCE WINDS EXTEND OUTWARD UP TO 115 MILES . . . 185 KM
FROM THE CENTER . . .

. . . THERE IS A RISK OF ISOLATED TORNADOES TONIGHT OVER PORTIONS OF SOUTH
TEXAS . . .

. . . THIS IS THE LAST PUBLIC ADVISORY ISSUED BY THE NATIONAL HURRICANE
CENTER ON THIS SYSTEM. THE HYDROMETEOROLOGICAL PREDICTION CENTER WILL

BEGIN ISSUING STORM SUMMARIES ON THIS SYSTEM AT 6 PM CDT . . . 2300Z.

LAWRENCE

NO STRIKE PROBABILITIES ARE ASSOCIATED WITH THIS ADVISORY.

NNNN

3

BE CAREFUL
OUT THERE

On 17 June 1527, Admiral Panfilo de Narvaez set sail with a fleet of five ships from Sanlucar de Barrameda on the Gulf of Cádiz. After crossing the Atlantic, Narvaez picked up a sixth ship in Santo Domingo on the island of Hispaniola, and went on from there to Cuba. At Cabo de Santa Cruz he sent two ships ahead to Casilda, a small port halfway along the southern coast.

The settlement of Trinidad lay a league inland from the harbor, about three and a half miles; a shore party of thirty men was sent there to gather supplies. It was a Saturday morning; on one of the ships, Alvar Nuñez Cabeza de Vaca noted that the weather was worsening, with torrential rain and a rising sea. Luckily for this voyager he was needed onshore, and a canoe came out to fetch him. About an hour later, as Cabeza de Vaca described it, "The sea commenced to come very rough, and the north wind was so strong that not even the small boats dared to land."

Through Saturday night and into Sunday, "the rain and the tempest began to increase so much, that the storm was not less in the village than on the sea, because all the houses and churches fell down. It was necessary for us to go about seven or eight men locking arms at a time, to prevent the wind from carrying us off; going among the trees was not less dangerous than among the houses, for as they were blown down we were in danger of being killed beneath them. In this tempest and danger we wandered all night, without finding any part or place where we might be safe for half an hour."

It was Monday morning before they were able to get back to the harbor. Both ships were lost, without any sign of wreckage or survivors. The men followed the shoreline; still finding nothing they turned into the forest, and nearly a mile inland they came on one of the ships' small boats, blown into the tops of the trees. The only other remains were discovered thirty-five miles along the coast. There were a few broken pieces of crates, a cape, a tattered quilt, and two bodies "so disfigured by striking against the rocks as to be unrecognizable."

Sixty men and twenty horses had perished. The shore party lived, but they were left in dire straits. Virtually all food and supplies in Trinidad had been lost, many cattle had been killed, and it was two weeks before any help arrived. "The country remained in such a way," wrote de Vaca, "that it was pitiable to look at; the trees fallen, the woods blighted, all without leaves or grass."

His story was published at Zamora in Spain in 1542. According to Cuban meteorologist José Carlos Millas, it was the first eyewitness account of a hurricane, though by then many Spanish colonists and adventurers had experienced these storms. What especially marked out de Vaca's tale, however, was his eerie description of the noise of the wind.

"While wandering," he wrote, "we heard all night, especially from the middle of it, a great uproar and the tinkling of little bells and flutes, and tambourines and other instruments, that lasted until morning when the storm ceased."

De Vaca's story was translated into English. When Shakespeare came to write *The Tempest* (itself inspired by the story of English mariners shipwrecked by a hurricane on Bermuda) it is hard not to believe that the bard had read or heard some version of de Vaca's image, of the storm's wind filled with this haunting, unearthly music. But how to explain it? Other writers reached again and again for the obvious; these storms, they averred, were nothing less than the work of the devil.

Writing of the hurricane that destroyed Santo Domingo in 1508, Spanish historian Gonzalo Fernando de Oviedo said, "It was of such nature that many that saw it will testify and declare firmly that it was the most frightful thing that the eyes of men could behold . . . as if all demons were loose."

The word *hurricane* derives from the name of an evil deity, the Carib god Hunrakan. This malign spirit craves human life; it is reliably estimated that, in the five centuries since Columbus first arrived in the Bahamas, at least a quarter of a million people—perhaps a third of a million—have been killed in the Atlantic tropics by hurricanes.

It follows that if you live in this region, you need a well-built house and good insurance coverage. Unfortunately, if your home's a plank-and-tin shack on a denuded hillside in Haiti or Honduras, those options aren't available. At least in the United States, however, where forty million souls now dwell on hurricane-prone shoreline, people can be better warned, better prepared, and better protected. Indeed, many tend to think that today's technology makes forecasting Hunrakan's behavior—where he'll go, how fast he'll get there, and how evil his temper will be when he arrives—an exact and reliable science. Unfortunately—as many have found out in the past, and as many more will find out in the future—it isn't.

Colin McAdie works on computer models at the Tropical Prediction Center in Miami; naturally, he can argue a close and forceful case for the increasing worth and sophistication of the guidance those models provide to the hurricane forecasters. But he also readily accepts that there's a limit to their precision, for the obvious reason that in a chaotic system like the atmosphere, you can't measure everything accurately everywhere at the same time.

McAdie says, "There's always going to be white noise. The error can't ever go to zero. Just given the size of the phenomenon, if the core's a hundred miles across, there's always a margin of error even in saying exactly where the center is. So can we get better? Yes, we can. But there's a theoretical error bar that you can't get below—and the thought in this game always has to be that you really can't see into the future."

*H*urricane is the term used in the Americas for a storm system more correctly known by meteorologists as a tropical cyclone. These systems develop over seven distinct areas of the earth's oceans, called cyclone basins, of which the busiest region by some margin is the northwest Pacific. Across a vast expanse of warm water stretching westward from the international date line to Asia, and including the South China Sea, major storms occur virtually all year round. This is Cyclone Alley, semantically and actually the home of Joseph Conrad's *Typhoon*.

The world has eighty-five or ninety tropical cyclones a year, and twenty-five or thirty of them happen in the northwest Pacific. No country on earth gets hit more often than the Philippines; even as Mitch set his sights on Honduras in 1998, Babs and Zeb were crossing the island of Luzon in rapid succession. In the Philippines, Vietnam, Taiwan, China, Korea, and Japan, large populations both urban and rural stand annually vulnerable before the worst storms in the world.

The first record of a tropical cyclone in written history comes from this region. In 1274, Genghis Khan's grandson Kublai Khan made ready to invade Japan with a war fleet commanded by Korean admirals—then a typhoon blew in, sinking hundreds of ships and drowning thousands of men. Seven years later the Mongol emperor tried again; he established a beach-head with the largest invasion force then known, reportedly two hundred thousand warriors borne on a thousand vessels.

Again, a typhoon thwarted the Khan's dreams of conquest. The fleet was crushed against the shore, half the men were drowned, and the dazed remainder were put to the sword. By this quirk of history, therefore, while the Tainos, the Arawaks, and the Spanish in the Caribbean came to think of cyclones as the work of the devil, the Japanese by contrast credited their national salvation to the *kamikaze,* "the divine wind."

Although the northwest Pacific gets the largest absolute number of storms, the most concentrated area of cyclone activity is instead the eastern Pacific off the west coast of Mexico. This basin gets fewer storms, perhaps fifteen or twenty a year, and not many of them come ashore; they're mostly steered away from land by easterly wind flows to dissipate over colder water between California and Hawaii.

Nonetheless, as a smaller area of tempest-prone ocean, this is the one spot on earth statistically more likely to hear the devil's music than any other. Spend six months from May to late October sailing in circles a few hundred miles southwest of Baja California, and there's a good chance of three major storms passing close by you—which explains why California gets good surf.

The other five regions of the world that fall victim to cyclones have smaller areas of unbroken water over which the storms can develop; in some cases, they also have climatic conditions less favorable to that development in the first place. Consequently, all five see fewer such storms. It only takes one storm, however, to make a disaster—and in terms of human fatality, the North Indian basin has been visited by some of the worst natural calamities in history.

About midnight on 13 November 1970, the people living along the shores of the Ganges Delta on the Bay of Bengal heard a low rumbling sound. The estuarine islands and mudflats of what was then East Pakistan, and is today Bangladesh, are home to a multitude of impoverished farmers and fishing people packed across channel-laced deposits of alluvial soil. None of the islands stands more than a few feet above sea level. Perhaps some of the people there heard warnings of the storm that night, if they had a radio; in the absence of cars or roads, however, few who knew about it could have left quickly enough anyway.

Peering out to sea in the wind-torn darkness, the people of the delta saw a cloud in the distance hanging low over the water. As they watched, it grew closer, and the roaring noise grew louder until their shacks and hovels shuddered on the doomed wet earth. In what must have been moments of unimaginable terror, they realized that the glistening cloud was the crest of a titanic storm surge, a tidal wave forced up by the cyclone across the shallow sea floor beyond the Ganges' outflow.

It was the last thing they'd ever see. No one knows how many perished; in the aftermath there were too many bodies to count, and no dry land in which to bury them. Officially 200,000 died, with another 100,000 missing— and this is far from the only such major disaster in a hopelessly vulnerable region. The Bay of Bengal is a region of serial catastrophe; from the destruction of Calcutta in 1864 to the obliteration of the east Indian state of Orissa in 1999, tropical cyclones claim lives here with profligate rapacity.

Unfortunately, when large numbers of uninsured small poor brown people die, it tends not to be much noticed in the Western media. Besides, in places like these, there are more urgent matters than counting the dead after a cyclone has done its work. In a brave and moving report in the London *Guardian,* from Paradip in Orissa on 3 November 1999, Suzanne Goldenberg found a wealthy man named Nidhi Behera who'd opened his house to homeless victims of the storm. He told her, "Do not ask me now about dead persons. The question now is: How will the others live?"

Besides the Atlantic, three other basins produce major storms. From the East African coast across Madagascar, Mauritius, and the Reunion Islands, and on either side of the vast emptiness of Australia, cyclones are irregular but sometimes massively destructive visitors—as in 1974, when the city of Darwin in the Northern Territory was leveled by Cyclone Tracy.

Around the world, these storms have different names. They're called cyclones in India and Australia; they're called typhoons in the western Pacific, and baguios in the South China Sea. In the east Pacific and the north Atlantic basins, they're hurricanes—and from June to the end of November, in a handsome concrete bunker on Virginia Key across the Rickenbacker Causeway from downtown Miami, the men and women of the Hurricane Research Division meet daily to discuss what those hurricanes are doing.

The HRD unit in Miami has some thirty scientists and support staff; it's one of four research outfits known collectively as the Atlantic Oceanographic and Meteorological Laboratory. Built by the Navy Corps of Engineers in 1973, the building is a substantial, weatherproof white fortress, set on heavy stilts in a mangrove pond. It has an airy atrium beneath a high glass roof; a dropsonde, installed by Hugh Willoughby in a playful moment, the green handkerchief of its streamer open above it, hangs on wires in the dim wide space.

On the fourth floor, in a pokey little corner by the tables where they eat their lunch, the HRD scientists gather at 12:30 before two monitor screens. On these, you can key into satellite images of any cyclone in progress in any part of the world. Visible imagery shows the cloud patterns, and infrared shows the temperature of the cloud tops; the colder the tops, the more energy is being released as heat underneath them.

The daily maps discussion centers on these images. Depending how many scientists and students are in the building on any given day, and how immediately threatening the tropical weather might be on that day to the United States—to South Florida in particular—the discussion might be attended by anywhere from a dozen to forty or more people. If time and an inactive Atlantic allow, they might rarely consider any actual or potential cyclones in the Indian or South Pacific oceans; more often, they'll look at what's happening in the west Pacific.

On most days during the hurricane season, however, the greater part of their attention is naturally given over to events nearer home—to the eastern Pacific, and above all to the Atlantic cyclone basin into which Florida so brazenly projects itself. North America's big toe, rashly dipped deep into the sweltering tropic seas, Florida is a hurricane target 400 miles long; storms make landfall here more often than in any other state of the union.

The scientists meet at 12:30 for a simple reason. If there's a hurricane active or imminent, they have to decide whether it'll be fruitful to fly in it the following day—a collegial decision arrived at under the cheerfully chivvying oversight of Frank Marks. If they do decide to fly it—or to go on standby to do so, with a final decision to be taken at seven o'clock the next morning— the deadline for alerting AOC in Tampa to get an airplane ready is 13:00.

In June and July, the first two months of the Atlantic hurricane season, it's normally a quiet and routine process. Ordinarily, nothing much happens during those two months, and 1999 was typical—just a tropical storm named Arlene that fizzled briefly and faded in midocean. Then, in August, the tension starts ramping up; the peak of the season looms, and the tropical waves over West Africa start forming into a train of thunderstorms—discrete, bundled clusters of rain and lightning, fiery balls of red and orange infrared reaching one after the other back across the continent toward Chad and the Sudan.

As the waves roll out into the ocean, it's a matter of statistical certainty that some will become hurricanes; on average, the Atlantic basin has nine or ten named storms a year, with six becoming hurricanes, and two of them major ones. Everyone standing in front of the monitor screens knows what that involves—they know more than anyone.

A few of them won't fly inside storms—they're motion sickness victims, or they've had bad flights—in each case, it's a personal decision that Willoughby genially respects and accepts, describing it with a dry smile as eminently rational and intelligent. But most of them can't wait to fly; they hover on a strange cusp between anxiety and anticipation, knowing that sleep, weekends, family life will all go by the board once the hurricanes begin.

Frank Marks makes the final call on which storms they'll fly, and what experiments they'll try to do in them. Forty-seven years old as the 1999 season began, keeping the arthritis in his hip at bay by swimming prodigious distances daily, he's revered by the students who come into his orbit as an inspirational teacher; he's an open, thoughtful character with an unruffled manner masking a steel-firm decisiveness. He grew up on a farm in upstate New York—where, like many of his colleagues, he caught the weather bug as a young boy.

He doesn't remember which storm it was; it was one of the spate of hurricanes that tore through the Carolinas and New England in the fifties. He'd have been six or seven years old, they'd had a family holiday on the coast, and warnings were posted on the day they were driving home. He only remembers the power of the event, the thrilling force of it, even as his parents filled with fear and worry, and from that day forth he wanted to know how the weather could do such things.

It was the same for his old friend and colleague Pete Black. Black's a tall, lean, patrician New Englander; he has a quiet, courteous demeanor, belying a creative inner absorption in matters cyclonic so complete that there are almost certainly days when he forgets his own name.

In 1954, growing up outside Boston, he was twelve years old when Carol tore into Massachusetts. That hurricane had winds reaching 130 miles an hour and a ten-foot storm tide; it killed sixty people, it caused nearly half a billion dollars' worth of damage, then the worst economic impact of any natural event in U.S. history—and Pete Black ran out into his garden to get a closer look at it. "My mother"—he grins—"near beat the hell out of me."

Their awe remains undimmed. Each time you go into the eye of a major storm, says Marks, no matter how many times you've seen it, "you realize how insignificant you really are."

That sense of wonder is matched by a healthy respect. At the beginning of August, as the peak of the 1999 season approached, HRD had an all-hands meeting to prepare for it. Opening the session Hugh Willoughby told them, "As the boss, I need to say the same thing I say every year. This is not a normal thing to be doing. Most people are screened out by survival instincts—but those of us who've done it a few times know it's

conducive to health, and stimulating to the adrenal glands. Nonetheless—
be careful out there."

The peak of the Atlantic season is the three months from August through
October, but at the National Hurricane Center they go fully operational
a lot earlier than that. The east Pacific season opens on May 15, two weeks
before the Atlantic; this is the day when NHC's six hurricane specialists go
on twenty-four-hour shifts. Half an hour's drive across Miami from Virginia
Key, the center's on the campus of Florida International University, housed
in a steel and concrete bunker designed (in theory) to withstand a Category 5
storm; it was built after Andrew trashed their previous offices in Coral
Gables in 1992, ripping the radar dome clean off the roof.

The Hurricane Center's at the sharp end of a large bureaucracy fielding
an onerous responsibility; these are the people charged with issuing storm
advisories, forecasts, watches, and warnings. Get it right, and you save lives
and property; get it wrong, and the potential consequences are horrific. In
this regard, the people at HRD have an easier life; they pursue the pure science of understanding hurricanes, and they apply that science to seeking
ways of improving forecasts in the future. The six specialists at NHC, by contrast, have to make a forecast right now.

Early in 1999, James Franklin left HRD to become one of these specialists. Franklin knows personally the consequences of making a mistake,
because he made one himself in 1992.

That year, he and his wife had just bought a new house; his mistake was
to spend money first on buying new furniture to put inside it, instead of hurricane shutters to put on the windows outside. Knowing the climatology,
knowing there hadn't been a direct hit on Miami since Cleo in 1964, he
decided he'd rely on what meteorologists call persistence—on the general
inclination of the climate to go on doing the same thing. The market in storm
shutters, he reasoned, was a seasonal thing, so he'd put off buying them until
winter came around; he thought, let's make the house nice inside first, and
buy the shutters when they're cheaper. This in a house of which the whole
east side was glass sliding doors giving onto a patio . . . and then Andrew hit
the patio before winter did.

There were five people in the house—Franklin, his wife, his father, his uncle, and his brother-in-law. It's in Kendal, a little north of the worst-hit area, but they were still well within the eyewall; the anemometer on the house pegged out at 120 miles an hour, as high as the instrument could read, so they certainly had winds stronger than that.

The winds came from the east; long before the worst of it, they'd retreated to the main bedroom on the west side of the house. Then, says Franklin, "we started hearing glass break. Just this constant crashing of something breaking somewhere in the house, one thing after another for hours. We were all sitting there with water coming in under the door, knowing we couldn't go to any other part of the house because it was all blown open—so you're just listening to things crash. You're thinking, you want the house to stay together. In moments of optimism you start wondering, what was *that* that just broke? What part of my life was *that* that's just been destroyed? Those are the moments of optimism. The moments of pessimism, it's just, the whole house is going to fall apart and we're going to die."

Only thirty-six hours earlier, Franklin had been flying in Andrew. Now forty-one years old, he's a short, bespectacled figure whose unobtrusive manner conceals a sharp cast of opinion and a firm way of expressing it; he'd gone to HRD straight out of MIT in Boston, and flown storms for sixteen years. There is, he says, "a contrast between the sense that you're out there doing something good, and the exhilaration of flying, just for the *fun* of it—because it *is* fun. But when you're involved in that, you can forget what it's like for the people who are experiencing it on the ground."

He was born in Miami; like many of the others, he was drawn to meteorology after going through a storm in his childhood. He was six years old when Cleo passed over his family home in 1964, "and Cleo was a blast. It was maybe a Cat 2 and my parents' house had shutters, it was one of those big houses in Coral Gables built in the twenties, it had withstood all kinds of storms down the years, so my parents had no great concern—and when you're six, you don't have any concern anyway. The lights go out, you get to play in the dark with flashlights, then the next day the trees are all down and it's like, oh boy, this is *neat*. Big balls of roots fifteen feet across sticking up in the air—and you're not the guy who has to take a chain saw to it and clean it all up.

"So I think that's what got me into this field, and working in it just went on being neat—until you experience it as an adult, and you see what it can really do, and how frightening it really is. After that, whenever I would fly again, it was always in the back of my mind what it really means for people. Because what's stayed with me over the years is hearing things break—just this endless sound of things smashing and breaking."

Now, seven years later, he'd moved to NHC to become a forecaster. So why (apart from the money) would a person exchange the intellectual pleasures and aeronautic excitements of HRD's research for the emotional and mental stress of this new job?

He paused to think about it, then he said, "When you're flying research, you know some of the things you do are going to have a concrete impact on the forecast and warning process, and I enjoyed that; I got a great deal of satisfaction out of it. But you can only do it for a few days a year—so I'm hoping I'll get that same level of satisfaction several months a year here."

Nonetheless, the pressure . . .

"To come over here was the hardest decision I've ever had to make. To give up something I loved for something that might be more satisfying, but might be so pressure-filled that you just can't take it, and you don't want to deal with it . . . I was very nervous about that. And I'm still somewhat nervous about it."

He knew he had people with plenty of experience around him; he had plenty of experience himself. All the same, as his first season as a hurricane forecaster began, he readily admitted, "you're scared to death you're going to make the wrong decision."

The first man of the modern age to grope successfully toward an understanding of hurricanes was a remarkable Cuban priest named Benito Vines. Vines published his *Investigations Concerning the Cyclonic Circulation of Hurricanes in the Antilles* in 1895, at which time the Belen Observatory where he worked probably had more practical insight into the subject than any other place in the world.

Across the Straits of Florida, meanwhile, early attempts to forecast hurricanes were largely stimulated by the requirements of the military. The

United States Signal Service had started collecting tropical cyclone data in 1871; during the Spanish-American War, President McKinley worried more about hurricanes than he did about the Spanish navy, and that led directly to increased investment in at least a rudimentary warning system. America's success in the war, however, resulted in an idiotically vainglorious suppression of Cuban wisdom—with disastrous results for Galveston in 1900.

The storm that killed some 9,000 people in and around that city in September of that year was the worst natural disaster in the history of the United States. Most of the victims drowned in the storm surge; along a mile and a half of oceanfront, nothing was left of any house three blocks back from the shore but the foundations. Before it arrived, the Cubans knew better what the storm was doing than the Americans did—but the Americans didn't listen, and Galveston wasn't warned as well as it might have been.

When the American Meteorological Society was founded twenty years later, forecasting still remained a patchy, rough-and-ready business. It was dependent on in situ reports from ships at sea, and on observations from a flimsy network of surface stations scattered through the tropical and subtropical regions. Behind this system, there lay little understanding of a storm's structure, mechanics, or formation. Scientists knew what a hurricane looked like, but they couldn't tell how or why it came to be so; as a result, forecast warnings were limited to twenty-four hours at best, and often rather less.

The hurricane that hit Miami on 18 September 1926 was first detected a week earlier, 1,000 miles east of the Leewards. A few days later, moving fast, it passed northeast of Puerto Rico—but matters were confused by another hurricane south of Bermuda, and a tropical storm moving north over central Cuba. Eighteen hours before landfall, at noon on September 17, the Weather Bureau in Washington warned, "This is a very serious storm"—but they didn't follow that up with explicit hurricane warnings until midnight, leaving Miami essentially ignorant. Most people had gone to bed; the first many knew of their danger was when the wind and the water started destroying the city around them in the small hours.

Miami had been growing at a fevered pace since Henry Flagler's East Coast Railway arrived in 1896; by the mid-twenties, the city was in an explosive frenzy of property speculation. The mangrove swamps of the shoreline fell everywhere before an unbridled rush of construction; hotels, casinos, and luxury housing sprang up behind manicured lawns sewn down into pumped-in sand. Behind the city, the Everglades retreated as "communities" were dreamed up out of thin air and thick sawgrass, subdivided, and hectically marketed to the flood of new settlers.

Some new arrivals became millionaires; many more lived in shanty camps, marooned there by the bottlenecks induced by too much demand, too few materials, and too little labor. When the hurricane arrived, these people would have nowhere to hide.

That morning, an anemometer on the roof of Allison Hospital on Miami Beach recorded a top wind speed of 138 miles an hour; winds consistently blew above 120 miles per hour for forty-five minutes, before finally blowing the instrument away. Eight inches of rain fell on the city before the rain gauges were also destroyed. A fifteen-foot storm surge swept into Coconut Grove; at least 150 ships were sunk or grounded in Biscayne Bay.

As described in *Florida's Hurricane History* by Jay Barnes, the eye passed over Miami Beach at six in the morning. In the eerie silence, few knew what it was—like so many of Florida's residents today, most people had only arrived last year, last month, last week—so they spilled from their shelters to see what was happening.

> *Some were seen kissing the earth and praying aloud with their faces turned upwards towards the boiling grey skies . . . within minutes, a stream of cars began racing across the causeway from Miami Beach. But Gray* [Richard W. Gray, Miami's Weather Bureau Officer] *knew the coast was not clear. According to the* Miami Herald, *he threw open the door of his office and shouted to those in the street, "The storm's not over! We're in the lull! Get back to safety! The worst is yet to come!"*

The back half of the storm struck at 6:45. People were caught in the street with no protection from an abruptly renewed hail of flying debris; cars were trapped on the causeway, their occupants doomed. Houses damaged in the first onslaught now collapsed around their occupants. When it was over at last, a local man named L. F. Reardon penned a vivid account of how it was to emerge in the aftermath:

Few people were to be seen. Are they all dead? Those we did see were either laughing hysterically or weeping. One grocer stood calmly back of his cash register, his entire stock naked to the lowering Florida skies. There were no customers . . . whole sides of apartment blocks had been torn away, disclosing semi-naked men and women moving dazedly about the ruins of their homes. Houses, stores, and shops lay sprawled. How many dead are under them? Everybody was looking for a drink of water—and there was none to be had . . . there's a boy covered with blood running blindly across the street. Where are his parents?

No downtown building survived unscathed. The business district was under four feet of water. Yachts and barges weighing hundreds of tons lay on their hulls along Biscayne Boulevard. There was no food, no electricity, no communications, no windows, no trees, no landmarks.

Miami Beach was worst hit; much of the island was flooded with six feet of seawater or more. The mansions of some of the wealthiest in Florida lay in ruins. As the ocean receded, the streets were left scattered with broken statues and splintered pianos amid a carpet of dead fish. Ocean Drive was buried under two feet of sand.

Inland at Moore Haven, Lake Okeechobee burst over and through its retaining dyke under the weight of the wind and the rain, sending a fifteen-foot wall of water ripping through the settlement to drown scores of men, women, and children; no one knows how many for sure, but certainly a couple of hundred. Bodies were washed far into the Everglades; vultures drifted in the hot sky for days afterward.

The Florida East Coast Railway offered free tickets to any who wanted to leave; many did. For those who remained water was rationed; the city management took control of all food supplies. Eleven looters were shot. In Miami the Red Cross reported 373 dead, 811 missing, 6,381 injured, and 43,000 homeless—this from a population at the time of only 300,000.

The damage was set at $159 million. With a group of his colleagues, Chris Landsea at HRD has recently calculated that another storm like that of 1926 hitting Miami today would cost $80 billion.

Unsurprisingly, the Miami boom collapsed overnight. Land that had sold for $60,000 a year before now changed hands for $600. Seventy-three years later, Hugh Willoughby described how an old house he'd once lived in had plummeted in value like that at the time; since then the lot had been redeveloped, and a fine urban residence built there. He said, "It's probably worth $250,000 now. Until the next hurricane comes, anyway."

Statistically, the time span for a return event of this magnitude in or near the city is about thirty years; if you wait long enough, says Willoughby, "a replay of the 1926 hurricane in Miami is inevitable." Today, however, there are twelve times as many people living in the path of that storm—and though the skill of the forecasters has improved out of all recognition since then, the average margin of error in any track prediction looking twenty-four hours ahead is still a hundred miles.

In other words, James Franklin and his colleagues may dread getting it wrong—but by definition, if they ever get it exactly right, that's not just science. It's also inspired intuition, bordering on a miracle.

In 1928, a Category 4 hurricane made landfall at West Palm Beach, leaving the streets there shoulder-deep in debris. Inland, Lake Okeechobee's a shallow body of water forty miles across; in the preceding years, as the Everglades were drained for farmland, "tractor towns" sprung up all around it with supply stores and juke joints for the agricultural workers. For irrigation purposes, the water level in the lake was maintained a little higher than the land, behind a growing system of dikes and canals.

The lake was already full with summer rains; the hurricane dumped another ten inches of water in it. Low pressure combined with winds touching 150 miles an hour picked all that up, and heaved it southward in a huge wave spilling across forty miles of inland shoreline. Over 1,800 people drowned; it was the second worst natural disaster in United States history, exceeded in horror only by the Galveston hurricane. Exact numbers of dead can't be known in either case; six weeks after the Okeechobee storm, they had to give up looking for bodies.

As memorably recorded by Lawrence E. Will:

One word describes it. It was Hell! A raging inferno of rolling, swirling waters, of shrieking, demoniac winds, of lashing rain and of darkness, black and absolute. There were no atheists that night on the shores of Okeechobee! Then, for those still living, came the second phase of hell; the phase of desolation and despair; of searching in the flooded woods and marshes, in elder clumps and sawgrass for the horrible remains of family and friends and neighbors; of loading them into trucks by unending scores; and finally of burning them in heaps of dozens when they could no longer be transported. It is hard to know which hell was worse.

According to Jay Barnes, "This calamity occurred within a few miles of a large city and of a world-famous resort, yet so isolated was the location that not until three days later did the state's own governor learn of its enormity."

Like communications, forecasting also continued to be an uncertain business. In August 1934, with a tropical storm approaching the Texas coast, the U.S. Weather Bureau issued a hurricane warning on a Sunday morning. Understandably nervous after what they'd suffered in 1900, the Galveston Chamber of Commerce wired Washington for an update that afternoon. The message came back, "Forecaster on golf course—unable to contact."

Happily, that storm didn't make landfall. Meanwhile, from New Orleans to Jacksonville, from Puerto Rico to Boston, a growing chain of observation stations at least meant that by the thirties, storms didn't get "lost" out at sea for days at a time. Scientific understanding was also advancing, and it was greatly helped by the establishment of the upper-air network.

This involves regular launches of balloons, now called rawindsondes, to monitor the behavior of the atmosphere. It began thanks more to Pan Am's desire for reliable forecasts, so they could fly safe on their expanding route network, than to any academic or governmental institution—but by the late thirties, this observation system was widespread. At intervals of 2,000 feet, up to an altitude of 14,000 feet, the flow of the winds started to be mapped as a matter of routine.

Scientists began to understand the mechanics of tropical cyclones. They recognized that they weren't just low-level systems but titanic structures climbing ten miles into the atmosphere. They started to fathom as well how storms formed, grew, and dissipated, and how (as Benito Vines had intuited forty years earlier) they were fed by the release of heat from condensing moisture in the ring of thunderstorms around the eye.

In 1942, as this scientific understanding increased, a meteorologist named W. F. McDonald posited a hypothetical top range of intensity for hurricanes. In theory, said McDonald, the limit to a hurricane was a minimum barometric pressure in the eye of 880 millibars—which turned out to be a pretty good estimate. The lowest pressure observed to date in the Atlantic basin is in fact 888 millibars, in Gilbert in 1988—though on 12 October 1979, in a monstrous system named Supertyphoon Tip in the west Pacific, a pressure of just 870 millibars was recorded.

When the air around you is as light as this—when the humid central column in the storm is vaulting so giddily skyward—you'll feel as if you've been abruptly relocated to high altitude. Your ears will pop, your lungs will empty, and pregnant women risk going into premature labor. The 870 millibars inside Tip was the lowest sea-level pressure ever recorded on earth; in achieving it, the typhoon grew until it was 1,400 miles across. Centered in the Gulf of Mexico, that would cover everything from Guatemala to Kentucky, from Mexico City to the Bahamas. If Andrew had had a wind structure like Tip, the worst of the inner core would have pulverized everything from the Florida Keys to West Palm Beach.

Luckily, by the time Tip emerged from the vast reaches of the Pacific between Guam and the Philippines, it had weakened to a tropical storm. Even so, making landfall at Honshu in China, it dumped enough rain to kill 42 people, with 71 others missing and 283 injured.

The Atlantic hasn't room to brew up giants like Tip. By contrast, like Andrew, some of that ocean's worst storms are instead small, intensely localized systems—and no landfalling storm in the United States has been more intense than the Labor Day hurricane of 1935.

That summer, in the depths of the Depression, hundreds of World War One veterans had been sent to the Florida Keys to restore Fort Jefferson in the Dry Tortugas and to help build the new Overseas Highway to Key West. Of these men, 684 were living in tented camps on Lower and Upper Matecumbe Keys; that Labor Day weekend many went to Miami, but several hundred stayed behind on the low-lying coral islands.

On September 2, late in the day, the eye of the storm passed over Long Key and Lower Matecumbe. It was only eight miles across; in the tightly packed vortex around it, across a radius of fifteen miles from the eye, some estimates had the wind speeds gusting up to 250 miles an hour. The barometer fell to 892 millibars, less than twenty-seven inches of mercury—the lowest until Gilbert, and the lowest ever seen in a hurricane on American soil. The pressure gradient was so steep, the fall in the barometer as the center approached so dramatic, that only in a tornado could you expect it to be more abrupt.

There was next to no warning. This wasn't just because forecasting in 1935 was still a loose and imperfect art; it was also because the storm had intensified so rapidly. The only surface observation before it reached the Keys had been south of the Bahamas, and that had indicated this wasn't too much of a system at all. It grew, however, from being barely a hurricane into a Category 5 in thirty hours.

Between the absence of any sound forecast and a woeful catalogue of delays, the rescue train sent out along the East Coast Railway from Miami to the Keys arrived too late—arrived, indeed, at the worst possible moment. At Islamadora on Upper Matecumbe, residents and veterans waited by the tracks, drenched in the rain, their hands and faces bleeding from the scouring impact of the windblown sand. Now and then as they waited, they found themselves illuminated in the dark by a strange, unearthly light; grains of sand flying through the air were generating flashing charges of static all about them.

The train pulled up at 8:20 in the evening and people started boarding—then the storm surge arrived. The sea rose nearly twenty feet. The track was "turned on its side like a fence"; ten train carriages were swept a hundred feet away from it. Later, twenty-five clocks would be found all over Upper Matecumbe, all of them stopped between 8:25 and 8:35. The island had been drowned in ten minutes.

Many perished in the water; others were decapitated by strips of sheet metal roof become "flying guillotines" or impaled on hurtling lengths of lumber. Bodies were found afterward sandblasted out of their clothes, with nothing left on them but belts and shoes. All the skin was flayed off them; they couldn't be identified because they had no faces left.

Ernest Hemingway lived on Key West, and went from there to help in the rescue effort. He described what he saw in a letter to his publisher, Maxwell Perkins: "Max, you can't imagine it, two women, naked, tossed up into the trees by the water, swollen and stinking, their breasts as big as balloons, flies between their legs. . . . We located sixty-nine bodies where no one had been able to get in. Indian Key absolutely swept clean, not a blade of grass, and over the high center of it were scattered live conches that came in with the sea, crawfish, and dead morays. The whole bottom of the sea blew over it."

The Red Cross counted 252 veterans missing or presumed dead and 106 injured; 164 civilian residents were dead or missing. Thirty-five miles of Flagler's railway through the Keys was washed away; already bankrupt and in receivership it now became, in the title of Pat Parks's book, *The Railroad That Died at Sea.*

The Depression deepened in the Keys, parts of which were cut off for three years until the Overseas Highway was finished in 1938. There were few jobs, little food, and some of those who didn't leave went mad.

James Leo Herlihy wrote in *The Day of the Seventh Fire:* "Many people had taken to eating grass and weeds, boiling the stuff with nothing to flavor it but a bird shot out of a tree with a BB gun. . . . An old man took off all his clothes, ran into the swamps and died there a week later, stark naked and alone; a middle-aged teacher surprised her students and colleagues one Monday morning by walking into the grade school dead drunk, her hair freshly dyed the color of ripe tomatoes and twirling a loaded pistol around her forefinger; and so on. Nothing made sense anymore."

In the sixties, a seventy-two-hour prediction for landfall could be 500 miles wide of the mark; since then, the average error looking three days ahead has halved. In the case of a rapid intensifier like Labor Day, however, the fact that track forecasting has significantly improved doesn't necessarily help, and it's a moot point whether today's forecasters could have done too much better with that storm.

The problem isn't to judge where the hurricane's going, but how bad it'll be when it arrives. In the Florida Keys especially, a botched intensity forecast could be deadly; surrounded by water, mostly standing only a few feet above sea level, the Keys are one of the hardest places to evacuate in the United States. There's only one road in and out, and all too much of it has only one lane each way; one accident or breakdown and thousands of people could be caught exposed on the bridges and causeways in the path of the storm.

The forecasters would dearly like to see that stretch of highway upgraded—because even if it were easier to get away, a storm like Labor

Day doesn't give you much time to do so. Forecasting intensity is markedly more difficult than forecasting the track; when the specialists say that a storm at landfall will be in one or another of the Saffir-Simpson categories, therefore, they always want a rider attached that they could be wrong by a category either way.

In 1995, their worst nightmares very nearly came true with Hurricane Opal. Opal started life as a tropical wave, leaving Africa on September 11; nineteen days later, she started getting organized over the Bay of Campeche. For a couple of days she sat there, neither moving much nor strengthening unduly—then she became a hurricane on October 2, and started moving north-northeast.

At midday the next day she was a Category 2; people on the Gulf Coast went to bed that evening knowing she was out there, but it didn't seem she was too much to worry about. Unfortunately, the O. J. Simpson trial verdict had just come in and a lot of people weren't paying too much attention to this apparently minor hurricane anyway.

During its original development, this "minor" hurricane had in fact already killed thirty-one people in Guatemala and nineteen more in Mexico. Now, overnight, Opal turned into an intense Category 4, with winds rocketing up to 150 miles an hour; worse, she picked up speed as well, and started racing toward the coast at over twenty miles an hour. It happened so fast that people in the Florida Panhandle woke up to find a frantic evacuation going on all around them; the roads leading away from the sea turned into parking lots, until the hurricane was traveling faster than the traffic.

It was very nearly the disaster that's only waiting to happen—a late, chaotic evacuation provoked by a suddenly deepening hurricane marooning thousands of Americans in their cars on low-lying coastal highways—and there's simply no place worse to be caught than that. Category 4 winds can throw cars down the road like so many tin cans, yet it may well be that people can't leave the road, because the land all around it will be getting flooded— so, sooner or later, a storm like Opal will turn a traffic jam into the meteorological equivalent of the road to Basra.

Mercifully, Opal weakened even faster on her final approach than she'd previously intensified, probably because she crossed colder water on the continental shelf. Nonetheless, making landfall just east of Pensacola as a

Category 3 hurricane, she still produced a ten-foot storm surge, with waves in some places washing debris twenty-five feet above sea level.

The coast was battered from Destin to Panama City; flooding continued inland into Alabama and Tennessee, and the storm spawned a dozen tornadoes. One of these killed one person in Florida; eight others in Alabama, Georgia, and North Carolina were killed by falling trees; and the total damage tally topped $2 billion. The National Weather Service's report on Opal concluded that "NOAA must continue aggressive research into tropical cyclone intensity change and acceleration."

HRD scientists call Opal their "poster child" for the theory that hurricanes can intensify rapidly when they pass over deep pools of warm water (other conditions permitting) and they would indeed love aggressively to pursue their research into that notion. Unfortunately, despite the extremity of the threat to people's lives and property and an average annual damage bill from hurricanes hitting the United States of nearly $5 billion, their research is conducted on a budget so impoverished that some of the instruments they were using in 1999 to map the Gulf warm eddies were second-hand cast-offs from the U.S. Navy.

They'd been sitting around the base at Subic Bay in the Philippines; when they arrived in Miami, the crates still had volcanic dust on them from the eruption of Mount Pinatubo. The sell-by date on the batteries inside these instruments had, in some cases, expired several years ago—so when the scientists threw them out of the plane, they did so with no guarantee that these things would even work.

F ear is healthy, preparation is essential, and neither may be enough." These striking words come from a report in the *Fort Lauderdale Sun-Sentinel* on the aftermath of Andrew's rampage through southern Dade County. The report is on one of several front pages framed on the walls of the corridor running past the offices of the top men at the National Hurricane Center—director Jerry Jarrell and his deputy Max Mayfield.

Mayfield said, "The message has been clear for decades. Everyone, every individual, every family, every business, every community, needs to have a hurricane plan, and they need to have that plan in place in good time. A lot of this is not meteorology. It's land use, it's building codes, it's communication, it's education. If you know your vulnerabilities and you have a plan, you can act. If you don't and you haven't, you put yourself and your family at risk."

As a storm approaches, multiagency conference calls based out of NHC connect every relevant state and local emergency service to the weathermen. The forecasters provide their best predictions of who stands most at risk; emergency management directors act accordingly, and the toughest call they have to make is the evacuation order.

Given the margin of error, every hurricane forecast has an element of overwarning to it. In consequence, two out of three times that people are warned, nothing too bad actually happens to them or their property. This can draw those who've been through an evacuation into dangerous complacency: "Hey—I moved out last time, and for what?" Clearing and closing long stretches of American coastline, moreover, is horribly expensive.

The figure usually mentioned is an average of a million dollars per mile evacuated—but it depends, obviously, which mile you're talking about. David Berri and Christopher Adams at Colorado State have therefore produced some more precise numbers. When Bonnie hit North Carolina in 1998, Adams and Berri calculate that the average cost of evacuation to the average business was $17,593. On the Mississippi coast, if you were to shut down the casinos and the rest of the summer tourist trade there, they estimate a daily loss in revenue of nearly $4 million.

In the Galveston-Houston area, meanwhile, you have the eighth largest port in the world, and three hundred chemical, petrochemical, and petroleum plants—half of all U.S. production is in those industries. Shut that down, and the bill's nearly $300 million. As for many islands in the Caribbean, a hurricane warning can bring the entire economies of several small nations to a complete dead stop.

The authorities do not, therefore, issue evacuation orders lightly—yet all too often when they do, people don't leave anyway. In 1998, as Georges left Puerto Rico and the Dominican Republic with 600 dead in its wake, and started bearing down on the Florida Keys, Monroe County's Emergency Management Director Billy Wagner made a bold decision. Three days ahead of time, he called for evacuation.

Wagner's a feisty little Cajun who was, at the time, in his eighteenth hurricane season; he's also a little hard of hearing. As he started closing the state parks and shifting people out of their mobile homes, Max Mayfield told him on the phone, "Billy, if you're wrong, you're going to lose your job."

Wagner misheard him; he thought Mayfield was telling him he was doing a good job. He said, "Thanks very much"—and as it turned out, he was doing an excellent job because Georges went right by Key West. For all Wagner's efforts, however, and all the warnings from NHC that this storm was a dangerous Category 3, something over 30,000 people *didn't leave Key West.*

As it so often can be, the intensity forecast was wrong; Georges was a Category 2 when it came through the Keys. If the intensity forecast had erred the other way, however, and if Georges had instead been a Category 4, then hundreds, maybe thousands of people could have drowned.

For obvious reasons, people at both NHC and HRD are profoundly reluctant to criticize the public—but frustration bordering on anger isn't hard to detect: "People haven't seen a major hurricane because they've moved here in the last few years," says one staffer, "so they don't know what's coming. Or they say, 'The damn federal government says the water's gonna be this high, and it ain't *never* gonna be that high.' But the thing is, it will be. One day, no doubt about it, it will be."

When they call for evacuation, therefore, they mean it. Max Mayfield says simply, "I'd rather have people mad at me than dead. But everybody in this building knows it's only a matter of time before we have a real disaster in the United States. It's absolutely possible. The misperception is that with satellites, radar, aircraft, computer models, people think we do a lot better job forecasting than we really do. People think we can do a perfect forecast—and I can assure you *we cannot do that.*"

One of the forecasters put it more bluntly. He said, "There are times when, no matter how well you do your job, people are going to die. And you just have to accept that."

ZCZC MIATCPAT5 ALL
TTAA00 KNHC DDHHMM
BULLETIN
TROPICAL STORM DENNIS INTERMEDIATE ADVISORY NUMBER 3A
NATIONAL WEATHER SERVICE MIAMI FL
2 PM AST TUE AUG 24 1999

. . . AIR FORCE RECONNAISSANCE PLANE FINDS THE FOURTH TROPICAL STORM OF
THE SEASON . . .

A TROPICAL STORM WARNING IS IN EFFECT FOR THE TURKS AND CAICOS ISLANDS
AND FOR THE SOUTHEASTERN BAHAMAS AND A TROPICAL STORM WATCH FOR THE
CENTRAL BAHAMAS. RESIDENTS ALONG THE SOUTHEAST COAST OF THE UNITED
STATES SHOULD MONITOR THE PROGRESS OF THIS SYSTEM.

DENNIS IS STILL IN FORMATIVE STAGE AND IT DOES NOT HAVE A WELL DEFINED
CENTER. AT 2 PM AST . . . 1800Z . . . IT WAS ESTIMATED NEAR LATITUDE 22.7 NORTH
. . . LONGITUDE 71.2 WEST OR ABOUT 85 MILES . . . 140 KM . . . NORTH OF THE
TURKS ISLANDS.

DENNIS APPEARS TO BE MOVING TOWARD THE WEST NORTHWEST NEAR 9
MPH . . . 15 KM/HR . . . AND THIS MOTION IS EXPECTED TO CONTINUE DURING
THE NEXT 24 HOURS.

MAXIMUM SUSTAINED WINDS ARE NEAR 45 MPH . . . 90 KM/HR . . . BUT CONFINED
TO THE EAST AND NORTH OF THE CENTER. A GRADUAL STRENGTHENING IS
EXPECTED TODAY AND WEDNESDAY . . .

. . . THE NEXT ADVISORY WILL BE ISSUED BY THE NATIONAL HURRICANE CENTER AT
5PM AST.

AVILA

STRIKE PROBABILITIES ASSOCIATED WITH THIS ADVISORY NUMBER CAN BE FOUND
UNDER AFOS HEADER MIASPFAT5 AND WMO HEADER WTNT75 KNHC.

NNNN

4

PROJECT
STORMFURY

The first man to fly deliberately into the eye of a hurricane was Colonel Joseph P. Duckworth. He'd started flying with the army in 1928 and then become a commercial pilot; during World War Two, he was made a flying instructor. At the time, hardly anybody knew much about instrument flying—about flying blind in clouds or darkness, or both. Duckworth's flying school at Bryan, Texas, was supposed to address this.

On 27 July 1943, Duckworth heard about a hurricane making landfall between Bryan and Galveston. As described by David E. Fisher in *The Scariest Place on Earth*, "He grabbed a young navigator who didn't have the sense he was born with, Lieutenant Ralph O'Hair, and together they set out in a single-engine trainer, a North American AT-6, to take a look. Stupid, stupid . . ."

Stupid or otherwise, Duckworth evidently enjoyed the ride—so much so that when he got back to base and a local weatherman said he envied him the experience, Duckworth promptly invited him into the rear seat of his little plane, and flew straight back into the storm.

The navy and the air force both began regular missions the following year. Grady Norton, the first meteorologist in charge at the forecast center when it moved to Miami at this time, would later say, "No forecaster can do much at hurricane forecasting unless he knows where his hurricane is and how intense it is, and there is no quicker way to find out than with aircraft."

In those early days, "quick" may not have been an entirely apt word. Before satellites, aerial reconnaissance was a difficult, drawn-out, and costly business, for the simple reason that to fly into the storm and see what it was doing, you had first of all to find it. Matters were so primitive that at one stage, once the pilots had found their way into the eye, they'd then take celestial fixes with a sextant to figure out exactly where it was they'd got to.

Between these pioneering hurricane flights and the development of radar, however, postwar science started making considerable progress in understanding how a tropical cyclone works. Radar in particular began to reveal the complex structure of the inner core, and of the spiral rainbands spinning in around it; the vertical motion that helps to power the hurricane was also located, lining the narrow band of the eyewall around the center.

Influences on the motion of a storm came to be better understood as well. The analogy most often used is that of a log in a stream; the hurricane's the log, bobbing along in the steering flows of the atmosphere all around it. Usually it'll have a fairly smooth path overall, determined by large features of pressure and wind flow; locally, rocked by its own internal processes, it'll wobble a shade to either side of that track as it goes.

By 1954, Hurricane Hazel showed how forecast methods were gaining in reliability. Planes started tracking Hazel off the coast of Venezuela on October 5; the storm moved west for five days, then turned north above Colombia. Passing over Haiti it killed nearly a thousand people, mostly in floods and landslides, before finally curving northwest to strike at the border of the Carolinas on October 15.

The impact at landfall was devastating. An officer of the Raleigh Weather Bureau described the beaches:

All traces of civilization on that portion of the immediate waterfront between the state line and Cape Fear were practically annihilated. Grass-covered dunes some ten to twenty feet high along and behind which beach homes had been built in a continuous line five miles long simply disappeared, dunes, houses, and all. The paved roadway along which the houses were built was partially washed away, partially buried beneath several feet of sand.

The greater part of the material from which the houses had been built was washed from one to two hundred yards back into the edge of low-lying woods. . . . some of this material is identifiable as having been parts of houses, but the greater portion of it is ground to unrecognizable splinters and bits of masonry. . . . in most cases it is impossible to tell where the buildings stood. Where grassy dunes once stood there is now only flat, white, sandy beach.

Aerial reconaissance had made it possible for the forecasters to start issuing warnings twenty-three hours before Hazel came ashore. Nonetheless she was such a brute of a storm, and produced so much freshwater flooding inland, that on top of the slaughter in Haiti she also killed thirteen people in Virginia, twenty-six in Pennsylvania, twenty-one in New York, and seventy-eight more in Toronto after she'd crossed Lake Ontario.

No matter how improved the forecast, this was a calamity. Hazel ripped a battleship from her moorings and ran her aground, it spilled a six-foot tide into the streets of Baltimore, it blew gusts nearing 100 miles an hour through Washington, D.C.—and it was only one among six hurricanes to hit the eastern seaboard in the course of two years.

Hazel was preceded in 1954 by Carol and Edna, and followed the next year by Connie, Diane, and Ione. The cumulative damage was horrendous, and in total nearly 400 Americans were killed. Between those hard facts, the direct impact on the nation's capital, and some efficient lobbying by Bob Simpson and other meteorologists, Congress was therefore persuaded in 1956 to start funding the National Hurricane Research Project. In time, the NHRP would become the Hurricane Research Division; first established in West Palm Beach, and moving to Miami shortly afterward, this allowed scientists to start regularly flying storms in planes loaned to them by the air force.

Like the forecasters, however, research scientists can also make mistakes—and for nearly three decades, one of the principal official motives behind their work was arguably the biggest mistake in the whole history of the hurricane business. It sounds bizarre today, but what they set out to do was to try to weaken hurricanes, to dissipate them and break them up—or, failing that, at least to steer them away from land.

A good-sized hurricane contains enough energy to power all the electrical requirements of the human race *for an entire year*—and these people dreamed that they could stop such a thing . . . but it was the Age of Optimism. America was the most powerful nation in history, responsible after World War Two for fully 50 percent of all humankind's economic activity. What was there, then, that God's country couldn't do? What force of nature was there that couldn't be tamed? How long could it be before America found a way to balk the hurricane? And thus was Project Stormfury born.

The name of the game was "weather modification." By 1973, it was the principal occupation of several hundred American scientists and engineers. Some $20 million was spent on their research annually, and a couple million more on operations. The gung-ho attitude of those involved is well expressed by R. Cecil Gentry, a director during this period of HRD's forerunner: "For scientists concerned with weather modification, hurricanes are the largest and wildest game in the atmospheric preserve . . . there are urgent reasons for hunting and taming them."

It began in the late forties, when Vincent Schaefer and Irving Langmuir ran a series of experiments seeding water vapor with dry ice at General Electric. Schaefer found that he could produce snow in a box, if he filled it with droplets of supercooled water, then added dry ice. W. N. Hess, editor of a collection of essays on the subject published in 1974, wrote in his preface that Schaefer's success generated "considerable enthusiasm for seeding everything in sight."

This wasn't completely daft, by any means. It's since been reckoned that seeding clouds in the right conditions can increase precipitation by up to 15 percent—which, if you're a drought-stricken farmer, might well mean the difference between getting a crop and going bankrupt.

Applying this to hurricanes, however, pushes science to the outer limits of the plausible. "The initial enthusiasm about large controllable effects," wrote Hess, produced "a group of practitioners of the art, not all of whom were well based technically, and maybe a few of whom bordered on charlatanism."

The idea that human beings might find a means to change the weather has, of course, been with us since the first shaman did a rain dance. Plutarch observed 2,000 years ago that rain often fell after battles, and the notion that detonations spark rain continued to be mooted ever after. In 1871, a book titled *War and Weather* by Edward Powers stimulated debate among scientists, engineers, and politicians that eventually led to a series of rainmaking experiments in the early 1890s.

The object was to promote rain by means of "airquakes," these to be caused by explosions set off with rockets and balloons. The experiments got nowhere; according to Horace R. Byers's contribution to Hess's volume of essays, however, they did lead to "a rash of rainmakers who, armed with crude pyrotechnics and a convincing sales pitch," proceeded to gull farmers for years thereafter.

In 1924, a professor of physics at Harvard named E. Leon Chaffee tried to produce rain by spraying clouds from above with electrically charged particles of sand. Rather than raining, some of the clouds disappeared instead—prompting Chaffee, with a notably unscientific contrariness, to declare the experiment a success.

With equally unimpressive results, a Frenchman named Henri Dussens tried using controlled brush fires in what was then the Belgian Congo to generate rain for the colony's planters. At Lannemazan near the Pyrenees in southwest France, further experiments with "controlled heat generators" (burning 100 metric tons of fuel in thirty minutes) did at least manage to produce a small tornado.

No one, however, could accuse Irving Langmuir of being a climate nut or a mountebank. He wasn't a meteorologist, but a highly respected Nobel laureate in the field of cloud physics; he moved into weather modification after a series of research projects into precipitation and icing in clouds atop Mount Washington in New Hampshire.

In time, in his newly chosen field, Langmuir would come to infuriate many of those who'd worked on the weather all their lives. Horace Byers was a professor of meteorology at Texas A & M University; if his account of the subject has an occasional edge of tart skepticism to it, that's because he was, in Hugh Willoughby's neat phrase, "Starbuck to Langmuir's Ahab. A rational person, drawn into something pretty bizarre."

Byers wrote, "That Langmuir was not familiar with the existing literature, and had not talked to knowledgeable meteorologists (he rediscovered several meteorological facts during these years) was evident." His repute was such, however, that politicians and bureaucrats would readily lend him their ears and their research grants all the same.

In essence, what Langmuir found on Mount Washington was that in wintertime, if you had clouds that weren't snowing, even if temperatures inside them were well below freezing, that was because they didn't have any snow in them. They consisted instead of droplets of water, supercooled to very low temperatures. It didn't matter that meteorologists had known this for twenty-five years already; the difference was that Langmuir and Schaefer did something about it. Meteorology was an infant science, after all, whereas physicists had built the bomb. People listened to them. This, as Byers notes with an almost audible sigh, "is what set them apart from the rest of us, and brought them fame."

Schaefer crystallized water droplets into ice in the summer of 1946. He used a home freezing unit (then so rare and precious a commodity that influence peddlers in Washington were said to use them as bribes, alongside more familiar inducements like cash and fur coats) and he breathed into the unit at −23°C. All he got was supercooled droplets until, by accident, trying to cool the unit, he introduced dry ice, and before his eyes the water crystallized.

Schaefer was jubilant. Reporting his results in *Science* in November 1946, he concluded, "It is planned to attempt in the near future a large-scale conversion of supercooled clouds in the atmosphere to ice crystal clouds, by scattering small fragments of dry ice into the cloud from a plane. It is believed that such an operation is practical and economically feasible and that extensive cloud systems can be modified in this way."

Two days before the article appeared, Schaefer flew through a cloud above Mount Greylock, to the east of Schenectady, New York; he scattered three pounds of dry ice in a three-mile line at 14,000 feet. Within five minutes, the whole seeded cloud turned to snow; it fell about 2,000 feet, then evaporated. In his notebook Schaefer wrote, "While still in the cloud as we saw the glinting crystals, I turned to Curt [the pilot] and we shook hands and I said, 'We did it.'"

Meanwhile, another scientist at General Electric's Schenectady labs, Bernard Vonnegut, found that silver iodide worked even better, getting ice to nucleate at temperatures only a few degrees below zero. As their work garnered ebullient press coverage, Langmuir became an evangelical prophet of "weather control." Desert wastes would become fertile farmland; all manner of possibilities lay within their grasp. A December snowstorm in New York and New England, he claimed, had been triggered by one of their seeding experiments—disregarding the fact that the U.S. Weather Bureau had forecast the snowstorm anyway.

Thus began a string of conflicts with the weathermen. In a paper in the *Journal of Meteorology* in 1948 Langmuir wrote, "It becomes apparent that important changes in the whole weather map can be brought about by events which are not at present being considered by meteorologists."

"Published comments of this type," notes Byers wearily, "and even more challenging informal comments, started years of heated arguments."

The Weather Bureau tried to restrain Langmuir; they had enough of an uncomfortable problem on their hands trying to reassure people that nuclear tests didn't change the weather, without someone trying to do it deliberately. With his reputation going before him, however, Langmuir was now proselytizing for weather control with an undimmable fervor.

General Electric had supported the initial research; now the U.S. Army Signal Corps, the Office of Naval Research, and the U.S. Air Force all got on board. As the bandwagon gained momentum, the Weather Bureau people found themselves reluctantly compelled to join the team, and together these agencies commenced Project Cirrus. They found that they could indeed produce snow in clouds, making paths a mile wide from a single plane. So, on 13 October 1947, the first attempt was made to modify a hurricane.

The storm was 350 miles east of Jacksonville, traveling away from land to the northeast. The plane flew along a spiral rainband, dropping eighty pounds of dry ice along a track 100 miles long. The flight crew reported that the cloud did appear to change; whether or not it had, and whether or not that had anything to do with the seeding, was rather less clear than the observable fact that the hurricane changed course and slammed into the Georgia coastline.

Langmuir proclaimed the experiment a success. People living where the hurricane made landfall would, one imagines, have taken a different view. General Electric's legal counsel, perturbed about the potential for lawsuits, strongly warned Langmuir not to ascribe the hurricane's change of direction to the seeding experiment, but the man was indomitable. "The stakes are large," he declared, "and, with increased knowledge, I think we should be able to abolish the evil effects of these hurricanes."

Langmuir expounded his views to all who would listen. "The chance that a given hurricane between latitudes 20 and 40 North will change its direction in any given six-hour period is only about 1 in 110. Therefore, the fact that the 1947 hurricane did change its direction within six hours after seeding has a significance factor of the order of 100, so there is considerable evidence that seeding hurricanes does tend to change their behavior."

Rebutting criticism from F. W. Reichelderfer, chief of the Weather Bureau, Langmuir grandly stated, "I pointed out to him . . . that the larger the storm, and the more energy that is stored within it, the easier it should be to get widespread effects. To assume that a hurricane could not be successfully modified by even a single pellet of dry ice is like assuming that a very large forest could not be set on fire by such a small thing as a single match."

We know today, to put it politely, that this is unscientific; to put it frankly, we know that it's nonsense. We should, however, temper any sense of incredulity with a recognition of what was and wasn't known at the time. On Virginia Key Frank Marks shrugs and says, "In those days there was a lot of uncertainty. So while it seems almost ridiculous to believe that stuff now, it probably wasn't so unreasonable at the time. And I think Langmuir believed . . . well, there's something about these people who do weather modification. Most of us who know the business realize that it's futile, but I've known people who really have a very firm belief that they're doing something. I mean, it's unshakeable. They become almost religious about it."

The Weather Bureau would have preferred to do without Langmuir. They were, however, beset by a whole range of interests eager to pursue grand dreams of weather management, from agriculture to the military, and Langmuir's following in the press and among politicians made a potent lobby. There was no solid proof of any kind that seeding could either deflect or dissipate a hurricane, but Langmuir continued forcefully to argue the case until his death in 1957, at the age of seventy-six.

His last paper was titled "Freedom: The Opportunity to Profit from the Unexpected." This was, as Horace Byers observed, "a fitting philosophical close to the career of a man who, while in his sixties, climbed Mount Washington with Vincent Schaefer in the middle of winter" to study clouds.

More than a hint of exasperation, however, is evident in Byers's other conclusions: "Langmuir made some great contributions to weather modification, and perhaps if he had comprehended fully the magnitude of atmospheric phenomena, he might have been discouraged from the start."

It was true that dry ice could initiate the crystallization of water droplets—and hence the precipitation of snow and/or rain—and silver iodide even more so. "But beyond that," Byers wrote, "the effects of seeding became more a program of advocacy than of proof. . . . This writer has heard colleagues say that the overly enthusiastic advocacy impeded the orderly progress of the science."

Langmuir was far from the only proponent of weather modification; this was a period when other reputable scientists were even seriously suggesting that hurricanes should have hydrogen bombs dropped into them. By the time Horace Byers was voicing his skepticism in 1974, however, it was too late; the ambitions of the weather modifiers had gained an unstoppable momentum. In theory, the government's new hurricane research agency had a fourfold mission: to study the formation of hurricanes, to study their structure and dynamics, to seek means for hurricane modification, and to seek means for the improvement of forecasts.

In practice, through the sixties and seventies, says Hugh Willoughby, "it was hard to justify anything but weather modification in this organization."

Project Stormfury," says Willoughby, "was the HIV of meteorology in the sixties. It was really visible. People with only modest levels of insight could publish in *Science* on the subject. People with very great levels of insight could publish on it, too—but it was the hot topic, and it was well supported. And the difficulty was, there were political problems with doing the experiment, and there were scientific problems with doing it. Because"— he laughs—"we had no reason to expect a positive result."

It's obvious enough that if you could find any way to weaken a hurricane, you'd surely get out and do it. The damage caused by a hurricane's winds increases exponentially; that is, the force of the wind is proportional to the square of its speed, so if the speed gets only a little higher, the impact jacks up dramatically.

Imagine that at 50 miles an hour, the wind has a force equivalent to one sixteen-pound bowling ball crashing into each square foot of your wall. If the wind goes up to 80 miles an hour, you double that. At 110 miles an hour, you double it again; now you have the weight of four bowling balls pounding into each square foot. By the time you get into a Category 5, therefore, every ten square feet of your wall is taking repeated impacts equivalent to about a thousand bowling balls at a time.

Now add in the way that wind flows around a structure—the structure in question being your house. The wall facing the hurricane is experiencing what's euphemistically termed "positive pressure"—many, many bowling balls. As the wind goes past the other walls and the roof, however, the wind balloons outward around them, and—much as an airplane's wing is given lift—this exerts a negative pressure. While one wall's being pounded, in other words, the other walls and the roof are being vacuumed away from it. Breach the structure in any way, and the consequent change in pressure will be abrupt and explosive; in a Category 5, the house will not so much fall down as fly apart in many pieces.

Working the other way, if you could somehow reduce the storm's wind speeds by 10 percent, you'd reduce the damage potential by twice as much—and there are two ways in which people have thought they might do this. One is cloud seeding, to make the heart of the storm spread out and weaken; the other is to spray some kind of film on the sea, blocking the evaporation of hot water and thus cutting off the fuel supply.

Apart from the environmental impact of whatever chemical that might be, however, there is as yet no substance known to man that's going to stay intact on top of waves churned forty or fifty feet high by a hurricane—and if there were, how would you get it there? Exactly how many ships and/or planes would you dispatch into the middle of a storm to distribute this material?

There are people still dreaming of going this route, in pursuit of what Willoughby drily terms the "miracle active ingredient." He is, he says, always reminded of Dr. Seuss's story *Bartholomew and the Oobleck*, in which a bored and whimsical king instructs his wizards to get something new and more interesting to fall from the sky than rain, with predictably disastrous results. But then, as HRD director, Willoughby is not infrequently beset by all manner of people keen to tame hurricanes. Early in 1999, one fellow called to ask if he could go out and throw cluster bombs at them. "They can get pretty antsy," sighs Willoughby, "when you tell them it won't work."

Project Stormfury was going to tame hurricanes more scientifically altogether. The working hypothesis was that when the supercooled water high in the clouds near the eyewall got turned to ice, this would release extra latent heat outside the eye, and the eyewall would therefore migrate outward into the disturbance you'd created. The eye would get bigger and sloppier; the winds racing around it would go more slowly around that larger circle. Looked at another way, by heating the outer area you'd reduce the temperature gradient toward the core of the storm; the pressure gradient would fall accordingly, and the wind speeds with it.

In 1947, when Irving Langmuir first seeded a hurricane during Project Cirrus, the experiment had been done pretty much on the basis of "let's try it and see what happens." Despite Langmuir's claims at the time, subsequent analysis made it clear that the experiment hadn't involved equipment reliably able to measure the state of the clouds either before or after the seeding. Moreover, because some of the navigation aids failed, the plane hadn't seeded an area close enough to the eyewall anyway. Overall, the seeding appeared to have had no effect whatsoever; the hurricane had gone ahead and done what it was going to do anyway, and that was bad luck for Georgia.

When the National Hurricane Research Project decided to try again in 1961, therefore, they approached the task in a somewhat more rigorous fashion. To test their theory properly, they needed first to find a particular kind of perfect storm—one that was at least fairly intense, with a well-defined eye, and a rapid fall in wind speeds as you moved away from the center. Once you'd found that storm, of course, you then needed to drop your silver iodide in the right place.

On 16 September 1961, Hurricane Esther provided just such an opportunity, and eight canisters of silver iodide were sprayed into the eyewall. Before the drop, Esther had been deepening; afterward she stopped intensifying, and the winds fell instead by about 10 percent. When they tried again the following day, the canisters were dropped too far outside the eyewall, so when this second seeding produced no effect, that failure, together with the verified weakening the day before, was taken to mean that the hypothesis was viable and that the experiment could be deemed a success.

Stormfury was formally established the next year as a joint project of the U.S. Navy and the Department of Commerce (who still, through NOAA, run HRD today), and it was, obviously, a fantastically ambitious thing to try to do. Quite apart from the grandiose objective itself, there was the practical difficulty of finding the right kind of hurricane in the right kind of place.

Too far away, and you couldn't fly it. Too close to land, on the other hand, and you couldn't risk it in case you got sued or worse in the event of a destructive landfall. It would be bad enough if it transpired that you'd steered a storm into Florida, but what would happen if you steered one into some other country altogether? At the height of the Cold War, Cuba might well have considered such an outcome to be an act of war.

Consequently, 1962 produced no suitable storms. In 1963, however, experiments on cumulus clouds made it look as if seeding did produce the desired results, and then Hurricane Beulah came along. Beulah had a disorganized eye and wasn't too much of a storm, but on August 23 the planes flew out and dropped 220 kilograms of silver iodide anyway. They missed what there was of an eyewall, and nothing happened, but the next day Beulah intensified, and this time the seeding hit the target.

Ten planes flying in and around the storm reported that the eyewall disintegrated, re-forming with a larger radius so the maximum winds were farther from the center and had correspondingly diminished by between 14 and 20 percent. In R. Cecil Gentry's phrase, like Esther two years earlier, this was "encouraging but nonconclusive."

In the following five years, no eligible storm came within range. While they waited, experiments continued on individual clouds, improved seeding methods were developed, and a new strategy was devised. The idea now was to seed the first rainband outside the eyewall with repeated drops of iodide over a period of hours, trying to get a second, larger eyewall to form so that the original inner one would have much of its heat and moisture supply cut off. It would then fade away, choked, leaving lesser winds in the new and expanded wall.

Hurricane Debbie finally offered a chance to test this approach in 1969. On August 18 and again two days later, a fleet of thirteen aircraft flew out to seed and monitor the storm; five of them dispensed over a thousand silver iodide pyrotechnics each time, while the others watched what happened. On the first run, the winds fell by 30 percent. The next day, Debbie grew stronger again; after a second seeding on August 20, the winds again fell by 15 percent. On the face of it, the experiment was a spectacular success. Gentry reported, "These results were so encouraging that a greatly expanded research program was planned."

To no avail. In 1970, no appropriate storm showed up. Ginger wasn't suitable in 1971, either; it was diffuse, with no well-defined eye. They tried seeding it twice anyway, with no discernible effect. In 1972 all the storms were too feeble, too far away, or too close—and other problems were beginning to stack up in the meantime. The navy pulled out of the project; the planes were getting old and worn out while, as Gentry wrote in Hess's volume of essays two years later, it remained hard to be sure of the apparent successes they'd had so far.

"The most difficult job in hurricane modification," Gentry said, "is determining whether the seeding causes changes in the storm. . . . The natural variability of hurricanes is nearly the same magnitude as the changes expected to be induced by the seeding." In other words, they might well be making no difference whatsoever.

The researchers pressed on. At a cost of around $30 million, they ordered the two Lockheed P-3s and planned to move the project into the Pacific where they'd have more storms to work on, over more open water. With a third plane of their own, and two more operated by the U.S. Air Force and NASA respectively, from 1976 the intention was now to run Stormfury out of Guam. The objective, however, remained the same; according to a chronicle of the project published in the *Bulletin of the American Meteorological Society* by Willoughby and three others in 1985, the goal was to "establish an operational hurricane modification technology within a few years."

To do that, Stormfury needed five things to happen. First, it had to be politically viable; the risk of a seeded storm making landfall remained ever-present, and the government had to be ready to wear that risk. It was both a legal and a PR danger that existed whether the seeding actually worked or not; be it Tampa or Taiwan, the inhabitants of a flattened coastline weren't likely to pause and inquire too deeply into the contentious and uncertain science involved in this project.

Second, you needed planes, people, and instruments in constant readiness. Then you needed a cyclone with enough supercooled water in it, and with the right sort of inner structure. Finally, you needed a lot of them—enough that the experiment could be statistically proven to work.

All in all, these five prerequisites added up to an order as tall as the troposphere—as it turned out, an order too tall altogether. By the late seventies, nearly ten years after Debbie had been seeded, the international political agreements necessary for Stormfury to relocate into the west Pacific hadn't materialized. Scientifically, meanwhile, the new P-3s were proving to be wonderful platforms for the observation of hurricanes—from which platforms, ironically, the scientists were beginning to discover that the entire hypothetical basis for Stormfury had been questionable from the start.

It was emerging that the large quantities of supercooled water required for the seeding to work didn't often seem to be present in hurricanes in the first place. It was also beginning to look as if a fair few unseeded hurricanes did exactly what Esther, Beulah, and Debbie had done—that concentric eyewalls often developed as part of a storm's natural evolution, whether you threw silver iodide at it or not.

No more storms were seeded. Behind a slow-grinding facade of bureaucratic and scientific face-saving, Project Stormfury was finally laid to rest in 1983. In the blunt conclusion of Willoughby's postmortem report two years later, it had had "two fatal flaws: it was neither microphysically nor statistically feasible."

Looking back on the project today, Willoughby is sanguine about it. "There was," he readily admits, "a *really* big loss of credibility when we said, 'Oh! This thing we've been spending a couple of hundred million dollars on? Making the hurricanes go away? Well, that doesn't work.'" With a rueful laugh, he says, "That doesn't do much for an institution."

Bureaucracy has a long and vengeful memory. When Willoughby first went to work for what's now HRD, the base funding in 1975 money was $4 million, and the agency employed around one hundred people. When they came clean on Stormfury, killing the goose that had laid all their golden eggs, they lost 10 percent of that funding. Today the agency has a staff of thirty, and base funding of $2.6 million; regardless of inflation, it's been pretty much level funded for nearly two decades.

Any further money for HRD has to be proposal-driven, generated in collaboration either with academia or with private industry. They talk, for example, with the insurance business, which has a fairly direct interest in better hurricane science. As Willoughby puts it, "They don't like to pay claims, obviously. But they don't like their policyholders to become destitute or die, either."

If Stormfury ultimately proved an embarrassment—something of an institutional calamity, indeed—it would nonetheless be wrong to write it off as a total waste of time. On its own terms, the idea of man standing before the storm and striving to tame it certainly reeks of hubris, but there are plenty who have been guilty of that. Out of Stormfury, meanwhile, a great deal of good science did emerge along the way—including the science that showed it wasn't viable, this very often being the way that science works.

Not least, the project had motivated the acquisition of the Lockheed P-3s, which have been busy gatherers of data ever since. Even during the Stormfury years, after all, the great majority of flights never seeded anything; they continued throughout, as they do today, to be exercises in the observation of hurricanes. This helped to bring advances in many areas, from understanding the storms themselves to the development of new instruments, computer models, and a steadily improving forecast system.

"So as a bureaucrat trying to put the best face on things," says Willoughby now, "the investments we made in the early years of hurricane research developed opportunities that we're still exploiting today. Because"—he smiles—"we planned all of this very carefully."

Stormfury was the child of a different age, when all science was good science, and all goals were attainable. Partly because of the project itself, and partly because of something more general in the tenor of the times, one effect was a period of some divergence between the interests of the researchers and the forecasters. While the specialists in the Hurricane

Center wanted to know what a real storm was really doing right now, some researchers were roaming off into wondrous realms to pursue such fine-sounding beasts as CISK—Conditional Instability of the Second Kind.

In a world grown wiser and humbler, the approach today could not be more different. In terms of pure science, HRD still has a mission to pursue the basic physical understanding of tropical cyclones—but maybe 75 percent of their work is now directly applicable to improving forecasts of track, intensity, and rainfall.

In essence, says Willoughby, "the bureaucrats have said we have to plan a lot more. The downside is, it generates a lot of paperwork, and people who like to arrange the dominoes neatly on the table don't always contribute to the effort. It can be forgotten that science is a creative endeavor, and that things nobody thinks are important can turn out to be vital. But all the same, we never want to get so far out of the applied side of things as we were back in the Golden Era. Because the Golden Era wasn't all that golden. It was gilded, and there was brass underneath."

"You have," says Frank Marks, "to understand the history of this place. It was formed in 1956 after all the big hurricanes tore up the East Coast, and it was designed to be a limited-term thing to figure out what we could do about hurricanes, and to *solve the problem*. So in the first few years they did fantastic science; almost all the stuff we were taught as students came from that era, up into the early sixties. Then things started getting weird. It was like, now they knew all this stuff, they got more and more into thinking they had to *do something* about these storms.

"But how can you get enough information in ten years to know everything there is to know, and to do something about it? People say to me today, 'Why are you still flying out there? You've been doing this for forty years now—don't you know what's going on yet?' And I say, listen—this is a *rare* phenomenon. First of all, we get maybe two a year that we can really study. A good year three or four, a bad year, one. So that's only seventy or eighty storms so far, out of a population of who knows how many—and we're only now getting enough information statistically to be able to say that something we see from time to time even has meaning, let alone 'solve the problem.' You *can't* 'solve the problem.' You've got to live with it, and find practical ways to do that."

Marks has worked at HRD since 1980, when former director Stan Rosenthal first started turning it away from the modification game. He works there because he loves it, obviously, because he really can't wait to get inside the next storm—but he works there for another reason too.

"I come from a generation where we've gone into our professions because we felt like we could make a difference. We come from an idealistic point of view, we're basically optimists by nature, and that's why we're in this business. It's not to make money, that's for sure. The money's not bad, don't get me wrong, I live comfortably—but if I wanted to make money the way the next generation seems to want to do"—he laughs, entirely without rancor or regret—"I wouldn't be a meteorologist working for the U.S. government, I'll tell you."

In 113 years, from 1886 to 1998 inclusive, 49 tropical storms sufficiently dangerous to merit being christened under today's criteria have developed in the Atlantic basin during the first ten days of August. During the second ten days of the month, that figure climbs to 74; in the final third of the month it climbs again, to 119. Statistically, therefore, it's better than evens that there won't be a hurricane early in August, and better than evens that by the end of the month there will be.

Apart from the unremarkable Alex early in the summer, 1998 followed that pattern. Bonnie didn't develop until August 19—and in the next five weeks, there were ten named storms. Again in 1999, Arlene was an early season blip—then, a year after Bonnie to the day, Bret was born in the Bay of Campeche. Even as Bret was growing, Cindy became a named storm far out in the Atlantic by the Cape Verde Islands, just twenty-four hours after Bret.

The anxious weeks of waiting were over, and the new season was under way. At their daily maps discussions, the HRD scientists watched tropical waves flare in an ominous line along the base of the Sahara. In the east Pacific, meanwhile, twin hurricanes named Dora and Eugene formed, very nearly identical, both with winds topping 100 miles an hour. On the satellite images they looked entrancing, 500 miles apart, rolling westward in majestic synch across the vast and empty ocean.

Infrared imagery presented them as spinning Catherine wheels of fierce red and orange with vivid green surrounds, casting spiraled plumes of vapor behind them. The main body of each storm was well over 200 miles across, yet both were dwarfed in the blue void of the Pacific. They were new children of the sky set loose to roam a waterworld entirely empty of islands, and very nearly so of ships; without satellites we might never even have known they were out there.

Dora and Eugene would send big surf to the southern shores of Hawaii, and eventually cause Johnson Atoll to be evacuated, but otherwise they harmed no one. On Virginia Key, Bret was a greater concern; HRD planned their missions into that storm, scanning Africa all the while with an uneasy mix of fear and fascination.

The tropical wave that would grow into Cindy moved onto the ocean by the Gambia, large, intense, heavy-laden with thunder, already beginning to spin. Another wave ahead of it looked less threatening; its chances of development were variously judged to be moderate to zero.

One of those regularly attending the discussions was Chris Landsea, a large, amiable character with a penchant for shooting hoops in the lunch hour, and a particular expertise in long-range climate forecasts. That wave ahead of proto-Cindy was, he declared firmly, "a dead wave."

While Cindy started growing into a Category 4 monster in midocean behind it, this wave by contrast was a dry and thunderless bone of a thing, idling to no apparent purpose across the sea—then, on Saturday, August 21, as all eyes still followed Bret erupting in the Gulf toward Brownsville and Corpus Christi, the dead wave slyly spawned a rotating disturbance just northeast of the Leewards. It still wasn't much, but it was over hot water, the wind shear was low, it was headed for the Bahamas, and beyond the Bahamas lay Florida.

By Monday evening, creeping northeast of Puerto Rico, it was upgraded to Tropical Depression 5. No longer a dead wave at all, at HRD it was renamed the Lazarus wave. Chris Landsea took it in good humor. After all, he pointed out, he was a long-term climate man, not a short-term forecaster—and he had indeed pinpointed the moment when all this action would start cooking well ahead of time. Mike Black said, "Chris told me a week ago, look out for Friday, August 20. And sure enough, it's like someone threw a switch over the whole Atlantic basin."

It was midday Tuesday; Black was preparing to lead the maps discussion, but he couldn't get the satellite loop to sit steady on the screen. As images of Bret stuttered and jumped Black said mildly, "Look at that. That thing's so strong it moved Texas." But Bret in fact had weakened rapidly over land; he tottered, spilling rain, toward Laredo.

Across Africa, a rolling train of new waves reached back as far as the Sudan. Cindy was in midocean, with a forecast track passing northeast of the Virgin Islands, and most likely then "recurving" back northeast and away to fade out over colder water beyond Bermuda. Black said, "I don't think this one'll be a player. Not for us to fly it, and not for any interests on the U.S. coast either."

Frank Marks laughed. "That's the kiss of death. It'll hit us now."

Two other systems nearer land were more troubling—harder to define, harder to forecast. One was an odd, tiny feature that, without direct observation from ships and planes, might easily have escaped notice altogether. Most likely it had broken off the bottom of the Lazarus wave; now, still unclassified, it was a little speck of a thing nudging west toward Barbados.

The latest guidance from the computer models on TD5, meanwhile, had it arriving over the northern Bahamas in seventy-two hours or less. The air force had found a closed circulation in it that morning, and falling air pressure; the official NHC advisory brought it not too far southeast of Miami by Thursday evening, and well on its way to being a hurricane by then.

"So," said Marks, "we'll be under a tropical storm watch by Thursday."

"We might be under a watch by tomorrow," said Black. "I see no reason why it shouldn't strengthen. It could maybe be a hurricane even earlier than they're forecasting, maybe even forty-eight hours from now. It could be a tropical storm by the five P.M. advisory today. That water's thirty degrees all the way to the coast."

It was hard to call because it was hard to tell where the center was, and it was hard to tell if it was moving. NHC was shifting the system northwest at ten miles an hour, but on the satellite imagery it looked pretty much stationary. It had a big bundle of thunderstorms strapped on its back, but the center of circulation didn't seem to be underneath that, it looked well out ahead of it—and when the bottom half of a nascent storm isn't co-located with the top half, it's difficult to know how fast it plans to move, how bad it aims to be, or where it's likely to end up.

A deep, V-shaped trough of low pressure was digging down across the central states from the Great Lakes. This had a southwesterly wind flow rolling up its eastern, forward side, a barrier of wind in the path of the storm—so if TD5 moved sharply enough, that trough would pick it up and shepherd it away north and east, keeping it away from Florida and out to sea.

If TD5 didn't move fast, on the other hand, the trough would push past to the north of it, leaving a gap beneath it in its wake that the growing system could slide into toward . . . toward Miami? West Palm Beach? Jacksonville? Who knew?

Frank Marks threw out options for the team to consider. The forecasters at NHC had tasked the Gulfstream jet to fly out around both new systems, TD5 and the midget by Barbados, on the following day; the role of that plane was to examine the steering flows around the two depressions, to see where the wider atmosphere might be trying to send them.

At the same time, 42 was going into the heart of TD5 to take a closer look at it. "So," Marks asked, "does 43 fly too? Do we follow on from 42 tomorrow night and try for genesis? Or if genesis has already occurred, are we interested in other things with this?"

In an ideal year, Marks would spend 20 percent of his flying time studying cyclogenesis—the unknown mysteries of how storms are born. Why should it be that one set of favorable conditions should produce a hurricane, when another apparently similar environment fails to do so? The answer is that we don't really know, and we'd like to—but it looked as though this system would have developed too fast before they could get to it and try asking that question.

Pete Black argued that they should fly 43 on Wednesday night and look at intensification instead. The heat potential, he said, was out there in the water for this system to spin up all the way.

Marks asked him, "Why go out at night when it could happen the next day?"

Black shrugged, champing at the bit. "To take the chance."

"I want to hear some good arguments why we should get real tired here. I mean, you guys can get as tired as you like. But why should we get the AOC guys tired too?"

It was 13:08; a computer modeler named Sim Aberson appeared in the hallway with the latest news. He said, "They just upgraded it to Dennis."

Once a system has become a named tropical storm the stakes start rising, and new issues start arising with them. Who wants to crew research flights out of Tampa when their families might be going under a storm watch in Miami? Whose wives and children move, and to whose house?

As the discussion progressed with a more urgent tone added to it, a younger scientist named Rob Rogers said quietly, "I think there's that element of dread in it now—when people realize things are really kicking in."

Whenever you hear people complaining of big government, think of the bus timetable pinned to the elevator wall in these labs on Virginia Key, and the little notices posted around the building seeking cheap apartments, and the front door at the National Hurricane Center that was broken when I first went there in May and never got fixed until late August. Think of Mike Black standing in the doorway of Hangar 5 at MacDill near midnight, after his third flight into Bret in three days, comparing the damage bill hurricanes do against the fact that when they fly in them, they have to count on their fingers how many $500 dropsondes they can use. But this, of course, is called value for money for the taxpayer.

One of the younger guys would on one occasion raise a wistful hope that they might lay their hands on some more free instruments like the batch of AXBTs they'd cadged off the navy. Willoughby smiled impishly and told him, "We can't budget in the hope of getting things for nothing. The prisons of this country are full of people who thought like that."

A fellow parishioner at his church was an assistant coach with the Miami Heat; he'd told Willoughby of basketball players who could fund his entire annual research budget out of their salaries, and still live very comfortably indeed on the remainder. "So what we need," one of the most respected and experienced hurricane researchers in the world told me, "is some tall people who like to play basketball to come and moonlight for us."

After maps, they ate lunch at two round tables on an open piece of landing by the discussion area. They had a little cubbyhole of a kitchen with a soft drinks machine, a fridge, a microwave, and a sink. If their circumstances sometimes seemed a little pinched, however, I'm not sure they were bothered, or even noticed; they only noticed if they couldn't get the instruments they wanted, or the flying time. Otherwise they were too busy discussing momentum fluxes, and boundary layers, and step-frequency passive microwave radiometers.

Lunch was enlivened by a battery of sauces brought back from past missions and seminars. They had Doc's Special Jamaica Hellfire, The Brutal Bajan, and Big John's Famous Mango Fandango. They had Colorado's Hotlips Ten Peppers Nectar, Outerbridge's Original Royal Full Hot Rum Peppers Sauce, and Dave's Gourmet Insanity. The latter was deemed to be silly, preposterously hot for the sake of it; this was a field low on funding, perhaps, but high on discrimination.

Depending on the behavior of Cindy, Dennis, and the third small system by Barbados, much discrimination would certainly be needed in the coming days—in resource terms, in scientific terms, and in human terms as well. At least in one way, however, they were in a win-win situation.

With three systems now active, the forecasters at the National Hurricane Center needed all the planes flying that they could get. If, therefore, one of the P-3s was tasked to fly on NHC's behalf, the HRD staff would still have to crew it and pull data sets while they did so, and it wouldn't come from their own flying budget. They might not get a free hand designing the flight patterns, but in whatever ad hoc fashion they could manage, they could still get inside these storms and do their work. It was, said Marks contentedly, a no-brainer.

So far, for the air-sea interaction experiment, Pete Black had spent two ten-hour flights mapping the warm eddies in the Gulf of Mexico, in case a hurricane should then pass over one of those features. With three more flights undertaken in Bret, that meant Marks had already used a shade under a third of his flying hours—so if he only had one plane free now, the question was how best to use it in concert with their flights for NHC. For example, as Pete Black had suggested, did they put it on a night schedule?

Marks was inclined to think they should, but there were two disadvantages. First, if he split up the P-3s, that wrote off any chance of doing the more complex experiments that required both planes flying in a storm at once. Second, an AOC crew needed twenty-four hours' notice to go on night hours, and the same amount of time was lost when they shunted their body clocks back to flying daytime.

On the plus side, with Dennis only 500 miles away, if they staggered the planes, they'd have a better chance of straddling landfall if it came to that. Also, with the storm so near at hand, they could fly in it hour after hour, one plane after the next; there'd be little time wasted ferrying to and fro, especially if the crews and planes could recover post-mission at Miami instead of Tampa. This degree of storm coverage mattered, because Dennis was potentially another rapid intensifier. Marks didn't really expect a Category 4 to come charging down Governor's Cut into downtown Miami in forty-eight hours' time, but it was certainly possible.

Furthermore, if they put 43 on nights, there was a theory they could test concerning the diurnal modulation of convection—the way thunderstorm activity varies through the course of each twenty-four hours. Unlike storms over land, it seems thunderstorms in tropical systems deepen more by night than by day, and they didn't know why. A messy system like Dennis, still packed in its early life with thunderstorms strewn here and there before an eye had properly formed, was a good case where night flying might illuminate that issue.

There were many other complications, of course. First, there were people's families to think of; Marks had an "away crew," mostly of single men, which he'd instituted after the Andrew experience, but it still needed working out who could fly with the least sum of personal concerns elsewhere. Then there was the issue of what happened if the storm crossed Florida toward the Gulf and put Tampa under a watch, thereby closing down MacDill. If that happened, and they wanted Pete Black flying as Dennis neared the biggest Gulf warm eddy, where did they base the planes, and how did the scientists get there?

Add to this the fact that if a South Florida landfall loomed, their own building would need to be shut down—just when, with immaculate timing, the Atlantic Oceanographic and Meteorological Laboratories' director had been called up for jury duty—and the in-tray was looking pretty full. With luck, it wouldn't come to that; the computer models had Dennis staying just offshore, creeping up the Florida coast toward the Carolinas. But as Marks said, "There's always something out there you don't know about."

That Tuesday afternoon, the system by Barbados was named Tropical Storm Emily. Cindy lay 1,200 miles east of the Antilles; a lot nearer Miami, storm watches were posted along Dennis's track in the Turks and Caicos Islands, and in the southeastern Bahamas.

Then Dennis stopped moving. If he stayed still, the trough to the north would scoot past before it had a chance to pick him up and keep him away out to sea. If he stayed still, NHC's deputy director Max Mayfield told the media, "all bets are off."

Flashlights, batteries, and bottled water started shifting off the shelves of the local shops; supermarkets and home improvement stores began busily running commercials for their hurricane perparedness wares. "Trouble in the Tropics," proclaimed the Weather Channel, and started listing survival tips.

Dennis was now forecast to be a hurricane in thirty-six hours' time.

ZCZC MIATCPAT5 ALL
TTAA00 KNHC DDHHMM
BULLETIN
HURRICANE DENNIS INTERMEDIATE ADVISORY NUMBER 9A
NATIONAL WEATHER SERVICE MIAMI FL
2 AM AST THU AUG 26 1999

. . . DENNIS BECOMES A HURRICANE . . .

A HURRICANE WATCH AND A TROPICAL STORM WARNING REMAIN IN EFFECT FOR
THE CENTRAL BAHAMAS . . . INCLUDING CAT . . . EXUMAS . . . LONG . . . RUM
CAY . . . AND SAN SALVADOR ISLANDS. A HURRICANE WATCH REMAINS IN EFFECT
FOR THE NORTHWESTERN BAHAMAS . . . INCLUDING ABACOS . . . ANDROS . . .
BERRY . . . BIMINI . . . ELEUTHERA . . . GRAND BAHAMA . . . AND NEW PROVIDENCE
ISLANDS. A TROPICAL STORM WARNING REMAINS IN EFFECT FOR THE
SOUTHEASTERN BAHAMAS AND THE TURKS AND CAICOS ISLANDS.

RESIDENTS ALONG THE SOUTHEAST COAST OF THE UNITED STATES . . . PRIMARILY
THE CAROLINAS . . . SHOULD CLOSELY MONITOR THE PROGRESS OF DENNIS.

AT 2 AM AST . . . 0600Z . . . THE CENTER OF HURRICANE DENNIS WAS LOCATED
NEAR LATITUDE 23.8 NORTH . . . LONGITUDE 73.1 WEST OR ABOUT 290 MILES . . .
465 KM . . . EAST-SOUTHEAST OF NASSAU IN THE BAHAMAS.

DENNIS IS MOVING TOWARD THE WEST NORTHWEST NEAR 5 MPH . . . 8 KM/HR . . .
AND THIS MOTION IS EXPECTED TO CONTINUE TODAY.

REPORTS FROM AN AIR FORCE RESERVE HURRICANE HUNTER AIRCRAFT INDICATE
MAXIMUM SUSTAINED WINDS HAVE INCREASED TO 75 MPH . . . 120 KM/HR . . .
WITH HIGHER GUSTS. SOME ADDITIONAL STRENGTHENING IS EXPECTED DURING
THE NEXT 24 HOURS.

TROPICAL STORM FORCE WINDS EXTEND OUTWARD UP TO 105 MILES . . .
165 KM . . . MAINLY TO THE EAST OF THE CENTER . . .

THE NEXT ADVISORY WILL BE ISSUED BY THE NATIONAL HURRICANE CENTER AT
5 AM AST.

BEVEN

NNNN

PAINTING
BY NUMBERS

Only one in ten of the tropical waves rumbling out of Africa through June to November will grow into a hurricane. The reason so few of them make it is that, mercifully, the hurricane's a complex system; to get fully organized, it needs a lot of things to fall in its favor all at once.

First, the wave needs to pass over hot water; it needs that fuel source of moist rising air. Then it needs the atmosphere into which the wet air rises to be unstable; when this parcel of steamy vapor starts lifting, conditions above it have to be loose enough to let it keep on climbing. The result is thunderstorms, and a broad central area of low pressure at whose base (because nature abhors a vacuum) new air starts getting sucked in.

Third, this seedling disturbance needs to be far enough from the equator—at least 300 miles—for the "Coriolis effect" to kick in. This is the atmospheric nudge that imparts the hurricane's spin; the original wave that's now starting to pack itself with incoherent thunderstorms probably had some shade of vorticity to begin with, but Coriolis speeds that up.

This happens because, as the planet rotates, winds traveling north across it seem to bend to the right, or eastward. In reality it's the world that's turning, not the wind—but to an observer on the surface, the effect when the apparently curving wind brushes past the root of an incipient storm will be plain enough all the same. It pushes the ascending column of wet air into the beginnings of a spin—and with these conditions in place, you have the makings of a hurricane.

The African wave is the seed, the hot sea feeds it, the unstable atmosphere aloft lets it grow, and Coriolis sets it turning. To build the storm to completion, you then need low vertical shear. If the larger windflows at different altitudes around the storm are more or less consistently the same both in speed and direction, this gives it a permissive environment; if they're not, the top of the system gets blown apart from the bottom, and it drizzles away into nothing.

On Tuesday, August 24, it was unclear how these conditions applied to the newly christened Tropical Storm Dennis—unclear how much stronger he might get, and unclear how quickly he might do it. At 315 miles east-southeast of Nassau he stalled, meandered, maybe shuffled a hint northwest. He continued messy, with the low-level center struggling to get snugly fitted beneath the main mass of thunderstorms—but he was beginning nonetheless to look impressive on the infrared. A ring of high-level cirrus blasted out from the top of the system in all directions, the storm's exhaust like the corona of light around a solar eclipse. Everything pointed to intensification; hurricane watches were extended into the northern Bahamas.

Overnight, one of the more reliable computer models had suggested that Dennis would make landfall over West Palm Beach; in the morning the model backed off, and held the hurricane a whisker away from reaching the Florida coast. Other models took it north, more likely impacting the Carolinas—but the problem for all the models was that they had no history on this storm.

Dennis was the zombie 'cane, crawling unexpected from the graveyard of the Lazarus wave. If you have a long track on a cyclone, you can feed a more trustworthy initial input to the models on the state of that system. If it emerges disheveled in your front yard from nowhere, on the other hand, you can all too easily give the models an inaccurate opening chapter to work with, and everything they write in the story that follows may well be misleading in consequence.

At NHC, a dapper Cuban forecaster named Lixion Avila said firmly that Dennis would stay off the Florida coast. Mike Black, who'd been a graduate student with Avila, was fairly confident his former classmate was right. On the other hand, holding a storm on a track only a shade over a hundred miles offshore was a narrow call. Black said warily, "At one point they said we'd be all right with Andrew as well. They said, 'Enjoy the weekend.'"

Farther out across the ocean, Cindy laid a heavy hand on her little sister Emily 600 miles to the south. Cindy was a substantial system, pulling in windflow from all sides, including the air that wanted to spiral into Emily instead. As a result, rather than moving west toward Barbados as she'd have done if left unhindered, Emily braked; she began to find herself sucked northward toward the larger storm.

Emily was a bizarre system in the first place. One set of satellite images depicted the ebb and flow of water vapor in the atmosphere; looking at the patterns of moist and dry air around Emily in these pictures, Mike Black said, "On this basis, no one could convince me there's a tropical storm out there at all—and the forecasters were surprised when the planes found one there too."

Born strange, it seemed Emily might also end in strange fashion. It was more than feasible that Cindy would swallow the smaller storm whole, becoming a cannibal sister to zombie Dennis. For millions of human onlookers this would, of course, be an entirely acceptable outcome; one storm eating another a thousand miles away from land meant one less storm to worry about. There was, however, a second scenario.

Cindy could move north, pulling Emily behind her, then releasing Emily like a rock from a slingshot over her shoulder toward the Atlantic seaboard of the United States. The possibility was both slim enough and alarming enough not to get a public airing, but some long-term models were starting to suggest that Cindy and Emily could follow each other onshore into North Carolina within a couple of days—and that this could happen not too many days after Dennis had arrived there himself.

Overall, a triple hit like that lay on the further fringes of improbability. Being hit three times in three years as North Carolina had already just been—by Bertha and Fran in '96, by Bonnie in '98—was quite bad enough without anyone raising the notion now of three hits in rather less than three weeks. It did demonstrate, however, the disturbing range of options that NHC's specialists must confront when three storms are in play all at once.

The principal tools they have to aid them in such a situation are both fabulously ingenious and yet only tantalizingly approximate. They're one of the

most remarkable creations of modern science; they use massed ranks of numbers arrayed into regiments of equations that paint fluid, three-dimensional
pictures of the planet's atmosphere in motion. On the other hand, given that
the atmosphere is fantastically more complex and chaotic than this painting by
numbers can ever hope to imagine, it's also fair to say that, in essence, computer models are just big smart machines that make guesses.

L ike any branch of modern science, meteorology has developed its own
private realms of dense and impenetrable theory. Amid a cloudy soup of
acronyms and equations, its practitioners speak an arcane language mixing
physics and mathematics, fluid dynamics and computer programming. Within
the science as a whole, tropical meteorology is itself so subspecialized that one
HRD man readily confessed, "Maybe two hundred papers come out every
year—and a lot of them are Greek to me, never mind the general public."

The field's small enough that if a plane crashed on the way to a major
international conference, you could lose half the best and brightest of the
hurricane community right there. Hugh Willoughby reckons there are
maybe two hundred "heavy hitters" worldwide, half of them American, with
a strong showing in Australia. Of the latter he says wistfully, "I look at their
successes, and I look at the American community's shortcomings, and I like
not only the fact that they're successful, but I like the *reasons* they're successful. They're aggressive, they're creative, and their bureaucracy doesn't
have quite the stranglehold ours does. It's a very vigorous community, full
of . . . well, not *nice* people necessarily, but admirable people who have
exciting ideas."

Among these few hundred souls around the world, they break down
(crudely speaking, because there's a lot of overlap) into theoreticians, computer modelers, physical meteorologists, and observationalists. The last sub-
divide into satellite people working with instruments and imagery, airplane
people like Frank Marks, and observers trying to get measurements on the
ground with wonderfully reckless tools like portable radar towers. Among
these subsets and factions, the computer modelers have tended in recent
years to be the flavor of the times, calling hungrily for ever greater quantities
of iron to power their ever more curlicued data engines.

The first "objective hurricane forecast models" started coming into use in the sixties; the first man to conceive of the principle of computer modeling, however, had done so thirty years earlier. He was an Englishman named L. F. Richardson, and he epitomized the notion of being ahead of your time about as perfectly as one can. For the idea to work in practice, you have to process a vast quantity of data; with computers not yet invented to help him, Richardson estimated that if he had dozens of people working shifts around the clock, all hunched over calculators, then he could probably give you a twelve-hour forecast . . . in about three weeks' time.

Thirty years later, the first practical models were based entirely on the statistical record; that is, if you knew everything every storm had ever done, that gave you grounds for saying what the next storm would do. The principle is called *regression,* and the basic idea is that you're looking for predictors. Let's say you study the height and weight of 100 people, and all the short people turn out to be fat, and all the tall people turn out to be thin.

When the 101st person then calls out from behind a wall that he or she is short, it's therefore reasonable to predict that when you set eyes on that person, he or she will be tubby. Similarly, if a storm develops off the western tip of Cuba, if you have nothing else to go on but what's happened in the past, it's reasonable to propose that the new storm will head north for the Gulf coast of the United States.

Now imagine that your hurricane is a marble on a board. Without any data, without any models, the marble can roll anywhere—whereas if you've got a statistical regression model, that's like etching grooves in the surface of the board. They're mostly faint grooves, and the marble is not necessarily going to stay in one of them, but it's at least a fair hint of a likely direction— so much so that one such model is still in use at NHC today. It's called CLIPER, short for Climate and Persistence, and it's a benchmark; if you want to sell NHC a computer model, the first thing it'll need to do is make better track forecasts than CLIPER.

Statistical models improve when, instead of using all past storms indiscriminately to judge the storm you've got today, you weight the data to focus on storms that started at the same time of year as yours just did, and on storms that started in the same general area. Even with those weightings factored in, however, the model remains so simple that you can run it on a PC (and they do).

In the early days, a whole roomful of whirring, clicking metal cabinets was required to do what a PC can do today—and like the space program, meteorology is one of the fields that has helped to drive computer speed and power so rapidly forward.

The next kind of model to come along was called "statistical-synoptic." This means that you don't just look at the tracks of past storms in isolation, but also at what those tracks imply about their environment. You don't have any close idea what the conditions surrounding a given storm were in September 1903, for example, but you can surmise that because it moved the way it did, then there was high pressure over here, or a low trough over there—you have at least some impression of the large-scale flow field.

With the storm you're considering now, therefore, you have both the past record and the present flow field. This is the equivalent of setting your marble loose amid the grooves on the board, then blowing on it to help it on its way, just as the larger weather pattern is blowing on the hurricane.

From this, the art moved on to "statistical-dynamic" models. In these you have the past record, the flow field, and some predictive knowledge as well not only of where the storm's going but also of how the flow field's moving around it. To pursue the analogy, you aren't just standing there blowing on your marble now; like the atmosphere, you're also moving around while you blow on it.

There is, however, a quantum leap in both concept and potential when you pass from these statistical models to today's numerical ones; it's like jumping from impressionist painting to high-resolution photography. The first successful numerical model was written in the late sixties by Katsuyuki Ooyama at the City College of New York, before he joined HRD—and the way they've evolved since, there's no possibility that you could ever run one of these on your desktop. Running these requires the massive number-crunching capabilities of the world's biggest supercomputers—because, in their fullest flowering, they're nothing less than mathematical representations of the planet's entire atmosphere.

While the functioning of these models is dizzyingly sophisticated, the basic principle isn't hard to grasp. Think of the atmosphere as a fluid—which most meteorologists do, most of the time—and then consider that at any given time, different parts of that fluid are heavier than other parts, and moving at different speeds, in different directions, at different heights. We know that the laws of physics apply to all the component parts and motions of this fluid overall—so if you're exceedingly patient, and equipped with a very large brain, you can represent these masses and motions, and all the forces involved in them, as a series of equations.

These equations are detailed, complicated ways of saying that heavy air will shunt lighter air out of the way, or that hot, wet air will rise. Now consider these equations, taken all together, as an engine waiting to run—and the fuel on which it runs is a giant mass of data.

The data are gathered from a set of points all over the planet; these data points between them construct a grid, or a three-dimensional starting line. Obviously, the places in real space and time where the information is originally collected are not themselves arrayed across a perfectly mapped out set of squares; the balloons, buoys, barometers, and sondes that supply the observations are scattered about wherever weathermen are physically and financially able to park or launch them. From that raw material, however, deductions and extrapolations can be made to help you arrive at your grid.

At time X, held within this grid, you now have a snapshot of the atmosphere worldwide—its varying temperature, pressure, motion, and humidity from sea level upward. When you then run the model—when you turn on the equations—they'll start telling you where everything in the grid is going to go to next.

Rising and falling, raining and shining, gusting and drifting, arid and sodden, the planet's assembled air masses proceed to grind and blend and flow, doing whatever the laws of physics intend them to do. If your data are sufficiently accurate, and your equations sufficiently competent, the net effect should be a plausible foretelling of reality. If you then want this numerical engine to forecast what a hurricane's going to do, you simply feed the storm into the machine with all the other data—or, to be more fair and precise, you rely on assorted groups of extravagantly intelligent people to figure out different ways of trying to do that.

To begin with, the initial data snapshots fed to the equations were crude; in absolute terms, they remain rough-focused today. In early models, for example, hurricanes were assumed to be perfectly circular, though even in the best models developed since, you can't possibly enter a true picture of everything that's going on everywhere at once. The computer isn't built that could handle it; if it were, everyone on earth would have to stop whatever they were doing to gather and load all the data. Even then, we'd probably miss something: for example, the Chinese butterfly fluttering from one flower to another, and thereby setting off the chain of events that results in Dennis moving north instead of west.

With this proviso, however, compared to rolling a marble about on a board, numerical models still take the analogy to a whole new level. The board's become a virtual 3-D weather map now; as for the marble (because it's interacting with what's going on around it), it's got fuzzy edges.

The main drawbacks to numerical models are twofold. First, compared to real weather, they have "coarse resolution"; that is, the grid points in all but the very best models are (give or take) 100 miles apart. So anything smaller than 100 miles across (like the core of most hurricanes) won't actually show up. To incorporate the hurricane, therefore, you have to factor it in mathematically; you have to enter it as a "bogus vortex."

The model most trusted at NHC is called GFDL after the Princeton outfit that devised it, the Geophysical Fluid Dynamics Laboratory. For hurricane forecasting, this model gets around the resolution issue with a "nested grid"; that is, within the global pattern overall, each box of atmosphere as you get closer to the storm is more tightly drawn and focused. The nearest box, picturing the storm's immediate vicinity, has grid points only some twenty miles apart.

To do something like this, however, you have to sacrifice one class of information in order to contain more data from another class that you think is more relevant—so what you put in and leave out of any given model depends on what you want it to do for you. In simple terms, therefore, to look at a hurricane in the Atlantic, you might decide that the Indian Ocean doesn't exist, or that all land is flat, or that all land is bone dry. Any such decision frees up iron to run equations on the thing you care about right now—namely, strong winds over hot water near Florida. So you may be more focused—but you might also be missing something.

The other drawback to numerical models is that they don't have any memory. Unlike statistical models, which have long, deep memories packed with every storm there ever was, numerical models think each hurricane's the first hurricane they've ever seen every time you feed them a new one.

Consequently, all numerical models can sometimes do something moderately or even wildly unrealistic. Given a glitch in the data or a dodgy dose of physics, in the real world a hurricane can be bearing down on a densely populated coastline, while in cyberspace a model can decide that it's ceased to exist.

This may help to explain why NHC's models all got Mitch wrong. Computer models, of necessity, are packed with assumptions; you haven't got perfect data from every place. One of the main methods of data collection, for example, is the humble upper-air network: the regular launching of weather balloons, which began in the thirties. The United States sends up two sets of balloons daily from all over its territory; too many other countries are too poor to do that, and Honduras doesn't send up any balloons at all. Between that and an instrument failure on a key satellite, it may simply be that the models in late October 1998 didn't know well enough what was really going on.

It's an ongoing concern that among wars, poverty, and the short-termism of governments busily paring down budgets in every way they can, the world's upper-air network is being steadily degraded. Even in America (perhaps believing that satellites have better vision than they really do) misguided congressional pennypinchers tried recently to cut U.S. balloon launches to one set a day; in other words, to halve the data flow. This cut was successfully resisted—but there are too many holes in the data map anyway.

For this reason among others, NHC uses a suite of a dozen models; to rely on one alone would be foolhardy gambling. These dozen models throw the forecasters a fan of tracks; the specialist on duty must then judge which models are reading the storm in hand most acutely.

NHC tries also to maintain a reasonable degree of consensual steadiness to the forecast track, rather than flip-flopping back and forth because one model or another can't make up its mind. If they did that (it's called "the windscreen wiper effect") they'd drive the emergency management people up the wall. Is it going here or there? Do I evacuate or not? Rather than pitching that kind of curve ball, working from a dozen models leads you not only to the most likely but also to the most consistent prediction.

Three of the twelve models are statistical, four are hurricane-specific versions of hugely sophisticated global models, and the remainder are somewhere in between. Eleven are American, one is English (the UKMET global model, which performed best of the lot in 1998), and to a certain extent, one of them's based not on what the weather's doing overall, but rather on what the hurricane's doing by itself.

This last is called BAM, standing for Beta and Advection Model. It comes in three versions, Shallow, Medium, and Deep, each looking (as the names imply) at the storm's behavior across different depths in the atmosphere. Based on work by an Australian named Greg Holland (among others), BAM takes account of a complicated spin-off of the Coriolis effect within and around the circulation of the hurricane called "beta drift."

In essence, the impulse to spin gets stronger as you move farther from the equator. Therefore, because the wind on the north side of the storm is a shade closer to the spinning axis of the earth, when it curves around the storm toward the south side (moving farther away from the earth's axis) it's moving to a place where it wants to spin less. Conversely, wind moving from the south side to a higher latitude at the north end of the storm wants to start spinning more. At neither end, however, can the wind adjust as much as it would like to its new location, because it's moving too fast around and within the storm itself to make that adjustment.

This means that as wind arrives at the north end of the hurricane, you get a knot of high pressure impacted within the overall circulation, like stacked traffic that can't go as fast as it wants to. At the southern end, meanwhile, you have another pile-up, only this time it's a knot of low pressure, because the wind here is moving quicker than it wants to.

These knots are called "beta gyres"; their presence means that instead of being truly symmetrical, the hurricane's a little egg-shaped, tugged toward the low at the bottom, compressed into the high at the top. These gyres are also pretty large; their effect can reach out several hundred miles from the core of the storm. Because of this they apply torque to the cyclone, so that even if there were no larger steering flow—if the hurricane was occurring in a weather void—it would still head off somewhere of its own accord anyway; in the Atlantic basin, it would travel northwest.

As you'd expect, it's fantastically difficult to separate this self-steering from the background flow. In a storm traveling at fifteen miles an hour across the Atlantic, it might account for between 10 to 20 percent of the hurricane's local motion, and that's why hurricane tracks tend to wobble—but the presence of the BAMs on NHC's roster illustrates how different models focus on different things. They have to, because the weather is too complicated for any one model to contain it all. So the forecasters look at the different models, they look at the satellite images, they look at the data coming in from ships and planes—and after that, it's a judgment call.

It's fair to point out that some meteorologists maintain an unfashionable lack of faith in the models—correctly so, in the sense that beyond the next few days, the farther ahead the models look, the more fallible they get. For hurricane forecasters, however, they're the best game in town. As one of them says, "Our focus is short term—and if you're standing in the path of a hurricane, the advent of the next Ice Age might not appear to be a high priority."

Tropical Storm Dennis loitered northeast of the Bahamas. At NHC that Wednesday afternoon Lixion Avila called the forecast on Dennis, while James Franklin handled Cindy and Emily. The forecast center, normally a quiet, orderly space conducive to a reflective, deliberate pace of work, now teemed with activity; the glass partitions giving onto the conference room were pulled back, and that space had filled with reporters and their equipment. The place hummed with bustle and urgent voices; meteorologists strode hurriedly from workstations in the Tropical Analysis and Forecast Branch, moving between emergency management officials in uniform blue shirts, with FEMA printed in yellow over their chest pockets.

On the side of the room facing the darkened space where the media readied their cameras and sound equipment amid a dense tangle of wires and cabling, NHC's PR man Frank Lepore prepared the desk from which director Jerry Jarrell would address them. The desk had a large screen showing an infrared satellite loop covering the whole Atlantic basin; the screen was topped with stickers saying Department of Commerce/NOAA/NWS. To reinforce the PR, Lepore put a white board with more NOAA stickers on it on the table behind Jarrell's head, propping it between computers by the TV screen.

Behind this impromptu front-of-house studio for the cameramen, Franklin and Avila whizzed back and forth through the crowd on roller chairs from desk to desk, keyboard to keyboard, pulling clipboards in and out of slots in the work surfaces, taking sheets of new data from passing hands. Behind them, looking down on the whole scene, three orange storm logos sat on a giant wall map; if and when these storms became hurricanes, the logos would turn red.

Near the center of the room, one desk had a bank of telephones running along the middle of it. At four o'clock, Avila on one side of the phones and Franklin on the other led a conference call, updating dozens of people and institutions along the Atlantic seaboard with the latest news and forecasts on the storms. Among many others listening in were National Weather Service staffs from Puerto Rico to New England, officials and meteorologists at the National Climate Prediction Center outside Washington, at the Kennedy Space Center on Cape Canaveral, and at the vast naval base in Norfolk, Virginia.

The call served as a final coordination of everyone's knowledge and readiness before the next advisories were issued at five o'clock. Talking slowly and clearly, first Avila and then Franklin ran through projected latitude and longitude fixes for each storm at regular intervals through the next seventy-two hours. When they were done, one of the FEMA group said quietly to Avila, "Thanks for keeping it away from my house, Lixion. I appreciate that."

Now Jarrell could talk to the media, briefing them for the five o'clock headlines. The main local networks were there in person, with others elsewhere taking sound and pictures through a pool system. Against a constant hum of voices from all quarters, Jarrell explained how NHC was hoping and forecasting that the trough of low pressure now moving east through the continent would bar Dennis's path and keep him away out to sea. "Unfortunately," he said, "the trough is moving, and Dennis isn't. If he doesn't start moving tonight, I will be very uncomfortable."

Nonetheless, there was no call to get unduly exercised just yet; once Dennis did get going, the best call remained that he'd go a lot more north than west. Storm watches for Florida were unlikely tomorrow; they might be appropriate on Friday, but there was a while to wait yet. "It may be," said Jarrell, "that Dennis is just waiting for the center to re-form, and then he'll move on."

The official forecast predicted a Category 2 hurricane off northern Florida, east of Jacksonville, by Saturday morning. "It'll be a hurricane tomorrow morning," said Jarrell, "maybe tonight. Maybe already."

Asked if it was unusual to have three systems on the move all at once, he said calmly that it wasn't unheard of. (There had, in fact, been four named storms simultaneously active in both 1995 and 1998.) What was unusual, he pointed out, was for these three to be so close together. "They interfere with each other. It's a problem for resources, because we need a lot of planes, and it's a problem for some of the models. Some of them don't know that all three storms are out there."

While he talked, reporters muttered urgently into cell phones, stepping cautiously through the mess of cables underfoot; cameramen set up their tripods for live reports on the imminent news shows. One station prerecorded a one-on-one with Jarrell; in a corner at the back of the room, a radio man shouted staccato microbursts of hyperbole into a microphone. "Chances are," he yelled, "that Dennis will be a *major* hurricane. . . ."

The forecast at this point contained no such suggestion.

TV reporters stood before their cameras, nervously patting their hair into place, checking their makeup or the folds of their jackets, rehearsing little spouts of verbiage under their breath. One said uncertainly to her studio, referring to the forecast center behind her (which had somewhat quieted now that the latest advisories were out), "It's not as busy as it would be if we had a hurricane warning. Er . . . I have got *some* people behind me, right?"

Radio Man shouted in his corner, "Say when? One two, one two. Dennis is building his power in the Atlantic. Dennis is building. Dennis."

The top of the hour passed and a tumble of reports skeltered out, an excitable jabber containing a lot more heat than light. Amid the hubbub, to one side of the room, the man who'd prerecorded his one-on-one with Jarrell now watched it air on a small monitor screen and had a sudden panic attack. In a loudly shrieked whisper he called for his soundman. "Joe! Joe! There's no line to my mike!"

He pressed his ear to the monitor in a lather of fear. The soundman scurried over to soothe his fevered soul, edging up the volume against someone else's piece to camera. It's all right, he reassured the reporter, it's all right, people can hear you. . . .

In a small room around the back of the forecast center, in an atmosphere more sober altogether, Max Mayfield and the Hurricane Liaison Team ran a video conference call for emergency management staff along the East Coast. "Well, folks," said the senior FEMA official, "we thought this would just be the regular briefing. But we think we're going to have to give you the whole wagon load."

Mayfield ran through the forecast possibilities. If you pasted the average track error around the path officially predicted for Dennis, the westward bounds of it just skirted the Florida coast. Mayfield said, "This is going to get a lot harder before it gets easier. It's certainly going to come close enough to give us a scare." On the other hand, as far as the risk inherent in Dennis staying stationary was concerned, "I don't think I'd pay too much attention to it."

Dennis was upgraded to a hurricane late that evening. In the small hours he started slowly picking up speed, moving west-northwest along the northern rim of the Bahamas—as the forecast had predicted.

I n the next six days, HRD flew eleven missions in and around Cindy, Dennis, and Emily out of Miami, Bermuda, and St. Croix in the U.S. Virgin Islands. It would have been twelve, if not for the banal fact that the Gulfstream jet got a flat tire one day and had to be grounded.

In other ways as well, where flying Bret had gone smoothly (apart from the lightning strikes), flying these storms had a fair set of wrinkles. One P-3 had to turn back from Dennis when the plane's hydraulics started leaking; another flight pattern had big holes punched in it when the Federal Aviation Authority barred entry to a substantial rectangle of airspace off Georgia and the Carolinas. The military was using it, and never mind where the hurricane was going—a situation that led to heated exchanges, including at one point the forthright assertion that certain parties were a bunch of MFSOBs. This did not, as Hugh Willoughby put it dryly, work wonders for interagency relations—but a degree of frustration, compounded by fatigue, was understandable in the circumstances.

One Miami-based TV news show added further to the list of unwelcome complications when, having been allocated one seat on a P-3 flight for a cameraman, they then demanded a second seat for their reporter pretty much as the plane was boarding and ready to leave. Hectic parlays ensued on cell phones, and more heated exchanges between AOC staff, the TV station, and people higher up the NOAA PR chain. To the dismay of the scientists, it finished with the man from the Discovery Channel getting bumped off the plane in favor of the news reporter.

HRD had thought that Discovery might address their work with at least a reasonable degree of seriousness—unlike the news crew, who further endeared themselves to all concerned by trying to do what Willoughby called "a Captain America thing" on Gerry McKim. This entailed chasing off to McKim's family at one point without prior notice, to ask if they got nervous when the man of the house was out flying. Not forewarned, McKim's family thought something bad had happened to him, leaving McKim "fit to be tied."

Unlike one set of their counterparts on a previous mission, this particular crew at least had the grace not to ask the pilot to throw the plane around in the air for them so they could make their report (and the reporter) look more heroic.

"I hate the TV news media," said Frank Marks bluntly. "It's so transient. Dan Rather," he snorted derisively, "standing on the beach with his hair flapping."

Happily, the reporter from Discovery got to fly the next day. Since they landed in Bermuda that evening, he also got to have a pleasant overnight, and then to fly Dennis a second time on the way back home—causing Marks contentedly to observe, "There is justice."

He finished content on the research front as well—because these missions into Dennis pulled off a piece of practical science that had Pete Black so happy he was virtually levitating. The advance had to do in part with that particular thorny issue of measuring a storm's wind speeds precisely; more generally, it had to do with quantifying the transfer of energy (in the form of heat) from sea to air, and hence the potential for a storm to intensify in any place where that heat transfer could increase.

The instruments employed to pursue these objectives weren't new; what was new was the combination in which they were used and the software that made sense of the data they collected. The instruments in question were two step-frequency microwave radiometers, one on each plane, plus a radar scatterometer on 42, and Ed Walsh's scanning altimeter on 43.

The former pair are "passive"; that is, they don't send out any pulse, they just read the natural "emissivity" of the ocean beneath them. All objects radiate a certain amount of energy across a range of frequencies; the emissivity is simply the rate at which that energy is being given out. So if the ocean is absolutely flat, with absolutely no wind, it'll still have a background emissivity that you can take as a mean; it varies with temperature and salinity, but you can factor those variables into the equation.

When the wind starts to blow, the ocean gets foamy; air bubbles are injected into the water by the breaking of the waves, and that changes the emissivity. The stronger the wind, the foamier the water, the bigger the change—so this change in emissivity can then be calculated as an indicator of the true wind speed.

There are, of course, many complex thickets of physics and mathematics to be hacked through before you finally get an answer. Another force involved is wind stress—the torque applied to the surface of the sea by the wind—and the sea's emissivity also varies according to that stress.

To calibrate the stress, you have first to account for the fact that waves in hurricanes behave very differently than waves in, for example, the giant winter storms that blow through the North Atlantic. In the latter, waves more readily reach their full potential height (in extreme cases, seventy to eighty feet, and occasionally worse) because the winds are blowing largely in one direction. In a hurricane, however, depending on its size, the winds have a more or less sharp radius of curvature; they don't blow consistently one way, but turn all around the compass instead. Excepting perhaps where they mass up in the eyewall, this means the waves don't often grow as tall.

Pursuing an accurate measure of wind speed, you need also to use the scanning altimeter to read these wave heights. Then you add in the scatterometer. This is an active radar sending down a pulse, and measuring "back scatter" from the waves as the pulse returns—that is, measuring all the tiny ripples and dimples excited over the surface of the waves by the wind. This gives you not only wind speed but wind direction as well—and if you then combine the readings from these different instruments, the result is a continuous record of surface winds below the aircraft. What's more, it's a record that can be relayed back to the forecasters very nearly in real time.

Combining the readings from the different instruments involves writing some seriously smart code. Back in the spring, Pete Black had come up with one key piece of it, an algorithm (in essence, a mathematical translating tool) that went a long way toward doing the trick—but having it work on the ground is a long way from having it work on the plane. Trying it in Bret, they got a lot of "software bumps"; only about 30 percent of the data was getting transmitted. Then they tried it in Dennis, and the error-checking routine started throwing gremlins at them.

While the ground crews turned the planes around, Black and several others went cyber-plumbing. Besides the error checking, something else was going haywire; Black thought it was interference from ground radar, because every twenty seconds they were getting a big spike shooting through the data. As the days went by, they ironed out the code; meanwhile, Black told the electronics engineers to neglect one of the six frequencies they were working on, where he thought the radar was cutting into their signals.

On the sixth day, on their last flight into Dennis, it worked; a record of what the wind really looked like was back in Miami within twenty minutes of the instruments scanning it. Frank Marks was in the air; ninety minutes into the mission, he got a radio patch through from Pete Black on the ground.

"Usually," Marks said, "when you're flying and they come through at you from the ground, it means something's wrong. In fact, this is probably the first time I've ever been called up from the ground and not been scolded for something I've forgotten to do. But this time, all I got was Pete yammering, *Go, go, go.* It was fantastic. He was just babbling away. I tell you"—Marks chuckled—"he was sensor dude *du jour* down there."

As he flew in the storm Marks had a wonderful image in his mind of his friend and colleague, ten feet up in the air, scampering around the media room at NHC trying to explain to baffled newshounds just exactly what it was that they'd managed to achieve. At the debriefing a few days later, Black would describe it (with more hesitant shyness than pride, the man seeming transparently free of the latter) as the highlight of his career—this from a character reputed in earlier, more cowboy-style days to have flown into hurricanes at insanely low altitudes, and to have a wealth of theories and data sets littered about unused on scrap paper and old napkins that most others could only dream of.

It was, Frank Marks said, "a new gold standard for surface wind measurement. Jerry Jarrell tells me he can retire now. This data's come in, and the front door at NHC's been fixed."

Nor does the story stop there. In this business, Pete Black said, "you get instant gratification, and you get delayed gratification." The wind measurements were the immediate payoff, material that you could get to the forecasters fast, and which could help to improve their output.

Then you go home. You add to that data the air temperatures gathered by the dropsondes and the sea temperatures from the AXBTs, and now you have all the parameters you need to measure the energy flux in the storm—the quantity of fuel being fed from the ocean into the air.

This was something they'd never had before; in the past they'd always inferred it, making mathematical assumptions to arrive at an informed guess. Now, however, they could seek to calculate what it really was—just exactly what transfer of heat was taking place, and what influence it had on the way Dennis behaved.

Working this out would be the delayed gratification. It was the next paper waiting to be written down the road, once the season was done—and the fact that HRD's budget didn't stretch to employing enough people to make sense of all the data they gathered was not, right now, going to dim their satisfaction.

All in all, said Marks, notwithstanding nails in jet tires, leaky hydraulics, fenced-off chunks of airspace and vexatious TV types, Dennis had been a good storm for them. As hurricanes go, he wasn't anything special to look at, or to fly in. Systems as spectacular as Bret make up less than 10 percent of what HRD gets to see, and a good thing too. If there were more systems like Bret, a lot more people would end up dead or homeless. On the contrary, once you set aside the satisfaction of the research, many storms weren't much more exciting to fly in than riding a bus with lousy suspension in dense fog.

If Dennis was aesthetically unremarkable, however, he was both logistically and scientifically rewarding. As Marks put it, "Short ferries, long flights, big data sets, and a new tool that works. And"—he grinned—

"Bermuda's gorgeous. There are worse places to have to set down in for the night, that's for sure."

In the mid-Atlantic, Cindy became the second Category 4 storm of 1999. She was substantially larger than Bret had been, and she threw the rope of her giant inflow around Emily; laced together by curling strands of cloud, the two storms came to look like an inverted treble clef. Finally Cindy dragged the smaller system in and swallowed her whole, before becoming a victim higher up the meteorological food chain herself. She rolled into the maw of a huge low pressure system over the North Atlantic, and that was the end of her.

Away to the south, Dennis crawled along the top of the Bahamas, washing high surf and heavy rain over Eleuthera and the Abacos. Fortunately for those thinly peopled strands of coral, swamp, and pink sand, Dennis remained a lopsided, ill-formed thing, with the worst of the wind field thrown out to the east; as he crept along the northern rim of the islands, he could only manage a clumsy sideswipe.

The models watched this ungainly storm, and scratched their mathematical heads. One model took Dennis to a landfall over Jacksonville, but the general if somewhat sloppy consensus was that if he made landfall at all, he'd do it somewhere in the Carolinas. Florida looked out of the woods; a high pressure system over Cuba was spinning wind eastward from the Gulf across the middle of the peninsula, and that had firmly barred the storm's way. As a result, in the satellite images Dennis looked like slow-motion film of a bullet hitting a wall, his leading edge punched flat, outflow blasting back and away to the east on either side of him.

The main fear now was the possibility that, as Dennis headed up the Florida coastline, fended off by that airflow, he'd run up the Gulf Stream and intensify. Thirty to fifty miles across, packed deep with hot water destined eventually to keep Great Britain from icing over like Labrador, the Gulf Stream is a rich potential source of hurricane fuel. Oceanographers started dropping smart buoys in Dennis's path, with auto-ballasting sequences that set them sinking down a hundred meters, rising to the surface and sinking again, measuring water temperatures all the while. At NHC, meanwhile, the forecasters watched this lumbering, lurching Category 1 storm and wondered if the zombie 'cane might suddenly gain new power.

Dennis stumbled past the Bahamas and kept on moving northwest the way they said he would. On Friday, watches were posted along the northern half of the Florida coast, from Sebastian Inlet to Fernandina Beach on the state line. At nine o'clock on Friday evening, in Blackbeard's Oyster Bar on Highway 1 at New Smyrna Beach—about dead center in the watch area— the news headlines came on, and the bar fell silent. The barmaid pressed up close to the screen, looking nervous to the point of tearful. When she turned away from the forecast, plainly not reassured, a friend leaned over the counter to pat her on the arm. "Don't worry," she told her, "it'll be like Bonnie last year. It'll go away."

Early Saturday morning, the eye was abeam of Miami; outer rainbands skimmed a whisker away from West Palm Beach. The Weather Channel became excited and, sponsored as they are by Home Depot, started to film people buying plywood. Reporters were posted on Daytona Beach, on Tybee Island off Savannah, on Folly Beach by Charleston, and on Wrightsville Beach up at Wilmington. For days to come, these unfortunates would be obliged to report hourly that the surf was up.

On Saturday afternoon, Dennis was clearly visible from the observation gantry at the Kennedy Space Center on Merritt Island. He was a striking bank of white and gray cloud out to sea; untroubled, tourists went about their holiday business in a sporadically gusty breeze from the north, the faint outer edge of the hurricane now idling up the coast. As NHC had forecast, Dennis was shading onto a course more and more due north; happily, he was also mostly to one side of the Gulf Stream, unable to pull enough heat from it to strengthen too much.

By Sunday morning, it seemed Dennis might soon turn fully northeast and miss the American coastline altogether. Storm warnings tracked his path along the shore, extending now to Surf City in North Carolina. In Charleston, a pair of TV crews stood around by their vans, wondering whether to bother pointing their cameras from the battery over a mildly choppy gray sea in the harbor. Up and down the coast, reporters tried to lean into unremarkable winds as if they were greatly fierce and newsworthy. Behind them people jogged or walked their dogs. One man nattered shirtless on his cell phone, pointing and waving at the camera, laughing.

On Sullivan's Island toward the end of Sunday afternoon, across the leaping arches of the new bridge dramatically spanning Cooper River, the last few surfers made the most of the waves. The water was as warm as a bath; a gray overcast spun impressively through the sky in a dense, hurrying, coiled flow of rotating cloud. That evening it rained, and the wind gusted to maybe twenty-five or thirty miles an hour; it blew flags out straight, or wrapped them around their poles, and it sent the rain skittering through the streets at steep angles to the ground. Downtown Charleston was empty; many locals had cleared out, and many vacationers had canceled their bookings.

Locals who'd stayed muttered darkly about television scaremongers. They'd been through Hugo ten years before, they said, and (to coin a phrase) Dennis was no Hugo. All the same, he was a big system, with a messy eye sometimes stretching eighty miles across, and somewhere in his heart he held winds touching 100 miles an hour; if he'd come ashore, they certainly would have noticed it.

Tiles would have parted from roofs, and parts of downtown most likely would have flooded; perhaps not deeply, but enough to give people a carpet of "pluff mud," the sticky marsh filth that stinks of dead fish and sewage and oyster shells. "You can understand people leaving," said one woman, re-signed to the loss of business.

But Dennis gave Charleston a miss anyway.

Picking up speed through the night, he zipped past to the northeast. Monday morning dawned bright and clear. Somewhere up the coast toward Wilmington, the Weather Channel's Jim Cantori melodramatically held up a wind meter; it showed winds of twenty-five, twenty-one, twenty-two miles an hour. He interviewed a man in a uniform who'd just driven seventy miles down the coast into town, and he asked him, "Where did you get into the really bad stuff?"

The man in the uniform told him that he hadn't really, not anywhere.

"Still the wind howls," cried some other idiot in an anorak on a beach.

Dennis accelerated along the coast—then, abruptly, he came to a dead halt. He sat off North Carolina's Outer Banks and threw big waves at them, declining slowly all the while. Highway 12 through the islands was closed, sporadically covered in tidal flooding or by drifts of sand sometimes five and six feet deep. Several small communities were cut off, and houses along the shore were damaged or, in a few cases, destroyed. If they could find a tactful way of saying it, hurricane researchers would regretfully shrug and tell you that if you build a house on the shores of the Outer Banks of North Carolina, then sooner or later you can most certainly expect this to happen to you.

What was happening to Dennis, meanwhile, was neither normal nor clear. For over four days he sat pretty much stationary, describing an aimless little loop 160 or so miles to the east of Cape Hatteras. He was trapped in an "omega block," so called because the isobars delineating the pressure systems around him looked like that Greek letter. It's a situation where the atmosphere finds an equilibrium, and nothing moves. The storm (no longer a hurricane) had two troughs of low pressure dug down on either side and a ball of high pressure above; all three were weak, all three produced nearly equivalent steering flows that canceled each other out, and the net result was a storm in neutral, going nowhere, kicking up surf.

Dennis wasn't really even a tropical storm anymore. He was breaking up at different levels and thinning out as an intrusion of dry air slid inside him off the land; he was turning into some kind of subtropical hybrid. He was, said HRD meteorologist John Kaplan, "the most bizarre system I've ever seen. Toward the end he was going at eighteen, nineteen miles an hour, then he just stopped on a dime, flat out. That's weird. And then he just sat there. . . ."

The models were baffled too. One took Dennis rapidly inland to the Kentucky-Tennessee line, another shipped him up to Lake Erie, others sent him back down the coast to Georgia, or away southeast across the ocean, while CLIPER had him taking off for Newfoundland like a scalded cat. Knowing the omega block had thrown the models off the scent, the forecasters ignored them and (again correctly) left Dennis where he was, the storm that wouldn't die.

Finally Dennis gave up and brought himself in about five in the afternoon of Saturday, September 4, after a life span nearly two weeks long in which he'd traveled barely seven hundred miles. During those two weeks he'd briefly scared a lot of people from the Bahamas to the Outer Banks, in a final fit of pique he'd dropped a tornado on Hampton, Virginia—overturning half a dozen cars, wrecking the roofs of several apartment buildings and a residential care home—and in the days leading up to and during the Labor Day weekend, he'd cost the North Carolina coastal tourist industry several million dollars.

Four people drowned in the surf, but aside from those individual tragedies and the scattered damage and economic loss, Dennis otherwise brought much-needed rain to a drought stricken East Coast. He was, in sum, not much of a storm by cyclonic standards, and he was by no means all a bad one. As a young meteorologist named Ryan Boyles at Carolina State in Raleigh would later put it, "Away from the Outer Banks, Dennis in this state was generally considered a welcome rain event—many counted it as a blessing—and the general attitude was, 'OK. Now we've had our storm for the year.' "

Likewise at HRD, with Dennis finally poised to teeter onshore on the eve of the holiday weekend, Friday's maps discussion closed with the happy words, "Maybe we can get a rest now."

The hurricane season tends to divide into bursts of activity, with lulls of two or three weeks in between, but the first half of September is the statistical peak and Hugh Willoughby doubted whether they could ease up just yet. He said, "I wouldn't be surprised if we get something off the next wave, or the next one after that. The normal cycle now would be to get something starting way out east."

Frank Marks suggested having a party over the weekend. It was, he said, "metameteorology. You plan a party, another storm blows up."

Sure enough, within forty-eight hours he was eyeing a tropical wave in the mid-Atlantic. Before long that wave would be Floyd—a storm as big, and very nearly as powerful, as Mitch had been on Guanaja the year before.

ZCZC MIATCPAT3 ALL
TTAA00 KNHC DDHHMM
BULLETIN
TROPICAL DEPRESSION EIGHT ADVISORY NUMBER 1
NATIONAL WEATHER SERVICE MIAMI FL
5 PM AST TUE SEP 07 1999

. . . TROPICAL DEPRESSION EIGHT FORMS IN THE CENTRAL TROPICAL ATLANTIC . . .

AT 5 PM AST . . . 2100Z . . . THE BROAD CENTER OF THE TROPICAL DEPRESSION WAS
LOCATED NEAR LATITUDE 14.6 NORTH . . . LONGITUDE 46.2 WEST OR ABOUT 980
MILES . . . 1575 KM . . . EAST OF THE LESSER ANTILLES.

THE DEPRESSION IS MOVING TOWARD THE WEST NEAR 14 MPH . . . 22 KM/HR . . .
AND THIS MOTION IS EXPECTED TO CONTINUE FOR THE NEXT 24 HOURS.

MAXIMUM SUSTAINED WINDS ARE NEAR 30 MPH . . . 45 KM/HR . . . WITH HIGHER
GUSTS. SOME STRENGTHENING IS FORECAST DURING THE NEXT 24 HOURS . . .

. . . THE NEXT ADVISORY WILL BE ISSUED BY THE NATIONAL HURRICANE CENTER AT
11 PM AST.

BEVEN

STRIKE PROBABILITIES ASSOCIATED WITH THIS ADVISORY NUMBER CAN BE FOUND
UNDER AFOS HEADER MIASPFAT3 AND WMO HEADER WTNT73 KNHC.

NNNN

6

FLOYD

The tropical wave moved westward at ten to twelve miles an hour, with others queueing up behind it. Moisture rose from the sea as vapor, climbing into the sun-baked sky, accreting around the tiny nuclei of Saharan dust particles into miniscule droplets. These merged with other droplets, condensed into clouds, released heat from the stilled water molecules to set the clouded air rising farther, faster, building thunderstorms—and Coriolis began, slowly at first, to set the whole body of disturbed air spinning.

The American people took their last summer holiday on Monday, September 6; not so the HRD scientists. They met early that morning and put AOC on alert for a deployment to Barbados the following day. Their goal was to catch genesis, that phantom moment when depression becomes storm—but the wave grew too fast for them.

By six-thirty on Tuesday morning, when Marks, Willoughby, Rob Rogers, Mike Black, and Pete Black met again at NHC, it was plain that genesis would have occurred long before they could get there. They were surprised that the forecaster then preparing to go off the night shift hadn't classified the wave as Tropical Depression 8 already; it had all the makings of a named storm within twenty-four hours.

The definition of a TD, the move from messy disturbance to organized depression, is a fuzzy call requiring intuition, a certain feel about things—but in essence, if the satellites show you thunderstorms and a closed circulation in mid-ocean, and you've got nothing else to go on, you're on the brink of making that call. The reasons for not making it, equally simplified, are twofold. First, if it's no immediate threat to anyone, there's a natural conservatism; you want to be sure it'll really build, and not prove to be a transient chimera. Second, if you leave it to the next forecaster, you save yourself some paperwork.

There were similarly banal factors in HRD's decision not to go to Barbados. The likelihood of being too late to study genesis was the main reason, but the other reason was money. They still had ninety-five plane hours left—but the federal financial year was coming to a close, and they couldn't afford the personal travel expenses. Containing a certain degree of frustration, Marks said, "We're short of time to get there, and we're short of a dollar."

In the end, he could live with not going. He played hurricanes the same way a gambler plays poker; he'd gone aggressive early, been rewarded with good material from Bret and Dennis, and now it was time to start hanging on to his cards. With five storms named and gone already, the remaining opportunities were unknown but finite. It was time to pick and choose what they flew—so compared to landfall, or Pete Black's air-sea interaction experiment, studying genesis wasn't a priority. Besides, it did look as though there'd be plenty of storms to choose from.

The nearest wave was an anemic cluster of clouds barely hinting at development, barely even detectable over the northern end of the Lesser Antilles. It looked likely to get sheared apart; on the other hand, some of the medium-range models were turning it into a storm once it got across into the Gulf of Mexico in a few days' time.

Behind that lay TD8, though not officially classified as such just yet; behind that again lay an odd, two-centered wave crossing the West African coast, looking uncannily like the dead wave that spawned Dennis and Emily. Behind that in turn, way back over Nigeria, a huge bolus of storms was blooming, probably the most spectacular disturbance the Sahel had set down on the ocean's doorstep so far.

These could be Floyd, Gert, Harvey, and Irene all in a row. At the National Centers for Environmental Prediction outside Washington, where most of the computer models are housed, they run ensembles—blended pottages of predictions, in which a model is given a range of different initial data and cooks up a range of possibilities accordingly. These are "What if?" forecasts; they try to capture the different ways a storm might develop, catering to the inherent unpredictability of the system overall.

To date, they'd been working well all season, correctly seeing storms several days before they actually evolved—and right now, they fancied all four of these waves to grow into storms. So you could believe this—or, as of Labor Day and the imminent peak of the hurricane season, you could simply take it as meaning that the atmosphere was primed, and anything could happen.

"A lot of this now," said Pete Black, "is serendipity. You might be answering questions at the end of the season that you didn't even think to ask at the start."

Frank Marks said, "We're in a mode now where basically, we wait for NHC to task us. Unless something gets into the Gulf and we can do air-sea over the warm eddy, or if it looks like a landfall—then we'll fly it. Or unless we get a Cat 5. Because then Pete will say"—here he mimed a man climbing up the walls, swinging from the bar across the partitioned cubicle's doorway—"*Goddamn, we got to fly that storm.*"

"If we get a *historic* storm," said Willoughby mildly, "of course we'll fly it."

Considering the state of the map, Pete Black said, "We may well get one. If one of these gets close, we've got a problem."

In colonial times, many storms were named after the saint's day on which they struck. During World War Two, more secularly minded meteorologists started routinely giving women's names to hurricanes—often the names of their girlfriends—as a convenient shorthand. This practice was formally adopted by the Weather Service in 1953, after a phonetic alphabet (Able, Baker, Charlie), used for two years beforehand, proved confusing, since these were also radio call signs.

In the seventies, it was decided that masculine names should share the responsibility for bad weather. From 1978 in the east Pacific and 1979 in the Atlantic, therefore, the names began to alternate between male and female. Ethnicity got the nod a little later; with the high likelihood that a storm's victims might speak Spanish or Creole rather than English, names like Henri, Jose, Pablo, and Paloma worked their way onto the lists.

The names are agreed on at international meetings of the World Meteorological Organization. At present, there are six lists for the Atlantic basin with names from A to W (missing are Q, U, X, Y, and Z) and these lists rotate down the years. When a storm wreaks significant havoc, that name is retired; there will never be another Andrew, another Camille, another Hugo or Mitch.

The sixth name on the list for 1999 was Floyd. Formally classified as TD8 in the five P.M. advisory that Tuesday afternoon, the wave became Tropical Storm Floyd twelve hours later, early in the morning of Wednesday, September 8. At that point, it was 800 miles east of the Windward Islands; the intensity forecast had it growing into a hurricane in thirty-six hours, with winds reaching 100 miles an hour in three days.

By then, the forecast track took Floyd to the north of the Lesser Antilles, past Anguilla and the Virgin Islands. After that, in theory, the storm would meet a trough of low pressure just as Dennis had done, and recurve away from the American seaboard; this, at least, was what the models said.

On Virginia Key, the maps discussions that week were led by a research associate from the Rosenstiel School across the road. He said, "I would not be so bold as to make that forecast just yet."

Wherever it went, Frank Marks told him, "it looks like you get to do a major hurricane this week."

The post-grad said dryly, "I can't tell you how thankful I am."

Outside, a spectacular thunderstorm drove sheets of rain past the building. Another one the morning before had left my street on Miami Beach a foot deep in water, a thin soup of downed leaves obliging people to wade down the road with their trousers rolled to the knee, their shoes in their hands. Now, some of those who'd come for maps from Rosenstiel were soaked to the skin. Marks grinned and said, "This is Florida. Didn't you look at the radar before you went out?"

Floyd looked like a giant apostrophe. By midnight that Wednesday, moving west-northwest at sixteen miles an hour, he was 500 miles east of the Leewards, with the barometric pressure in his heart steadily falling, and wind speeds rising to sixty miles an hour. Exhaust plumes of high cloud emptied mass out of the core of the system; bundled thunderstorms flared orange on the infrared, monster updrafts blooming over the ocean in the night.

In North Carolina, where soaking rains from Dennis had broken the East Coast's drought, entomologists were forecasting a plague of mosquitoes. Early Thursday morning, the Weather Channel faintly hinted that Floyd might also end up somewhere in the mid-Atlantic states—but that, said their forecaster, was way too far ahead to call with any certainty just yet.

In the small hours, 450 miles from the Leewards, Floyd was already big enough that the more northerly islands would surely feel the leading edge of him soon; from Guadeloupe north, there was going to be at least a minor impact. The forecast track still had the center skirting across the top of the Virgins and Puerto Rico; the uncertainty now concerned how much of the storm's movement had a northerly component, and how much of it was westward.

North was good; north meant recurving and staying away out to sea. West, on the other hand, meant the islands, and Florida beyond them. At HRD, the first hints of nervousness were creeping in; they were beginning to doubt the satellite images, detecting hints of a wobble to the west. Moreover, wherever this system was going, it was getting better organized; thunderstorms were wrapping all around a center growing steadily more distinct.

Intensity forecasts suggested winds of 80 miles an hour by Friday morning, over 90 by the evening, and 110 by Sunday. Around the monitor screens on Virginia Key, different voices debated the possibilities with mounting anxiety.

Were the initial data being fed to the models correct? Would the big, V-shaped trough of low pressure hanging off the North American continent dig down and fend this system away? Would the area of high wind shear over the islands inhibit its growth? Would it beat that shear, and erupt in intensity as the water beneath it grew hotter? Would it turn?

Would it come to Miami?

"We only have thirty-six hours, max, before it gets to the islands. They've got to go to advisories there soon."

"They'll have high cirrus outriders over them already. They'll be under advisories by tonight."

Frank Marks mulled his flying options. With two more waves behind Floyd looking threatening as well, NHC was getting jumpy; another multiactive burst would mean another scramble to keep enough planes in the air. The Gulfstream jet was already out there, monitoring the steering flows around Floyd; it looked as if the forecasters would start tasking the P-3s soon as well.

Trouble was, 42 had an engine problem and wouldn't be ready before the weekend. In theory, in seven days' time, it was then supposed to go to Austria for an alpine air chemistry experiment—but, said Marks, "if it's operationally necessary to keep it here, it won't go. If Jerry Jarrell wants it, it stays."

They'd know better what they were doing by tomorrow night, once the data had come in from a couple of days' surveillance flights; then the models would be better informed, and they and their masters could maybe see more clearly what Floyd planned to do. If this had happened last year, with the hours that NASA had brought HRD on a program of joint experiments, they could have flown Floyd day in and day out, the way they did Dennis—but for now, Marks and Willoughby could only count the hours and the last pennies in their straining budget, and wait.

"What concerns me," said John Kaplan, "is the current motion. It's going due west, or near enough. GFDL has it turning north of west by now, and it hasn't happened yet. If I lived in Puerto Rico, I'd be nervous."

Kaplan had a slightly shy, nervous demeanor at the best of times. The first storm he'd flown in had been his last; he was a motion sickness type, a hurricane called Emily had given a violent, grinding turmoil of a ride, and he'd been powerfully unwell. He'd decided there and then that he was better staying on the ground, or flying in the Gulfstream jet well away from the worst of it. You weren't much use on a plane in a storm, he said with an edgy grin, if you were dropping your breakfast.

Around him, other scientists debated what experiments they might fruit-fully do in Floyd; Kaplan watched, remembering Peter Dodge eating a burrito in the middle of Emily. He shook his head ruefully and said, "That was the most amazing thing to me. How can you do that?"

That Thursday evening, tropical storm watches were posted in Antigua, Barbuda, Anguilla, and the smaller islands just behind them. Overnight Floyd deepened and, as forecast, became a Category 1 hurricane; the motion was still west-northwest, he was now 215 miles off the Leewards, all the long-range models had him growing into a major hurricane, and they all had him closing on the American seaboard.

Through Friday morning, as the circulation at different depths in the atmosphere became aligned, an eye began forming on the satellite pictures. The storm slowed a shade as it grew, braking to about ten miles an hour; this only gave it more time and room to develop, and by the middle of the day, the note of tension at HRD's next meeting was markedly sharper.

"There's a disturbing trend in the models," said the post-grad leading the discussion. "They have a consensus turn back toward the west in forty-eight to seventy-two hours."

Packed into the small space before the monitor screens, twenty-five or thirty people gave a deep collective groan. Printouts showing the latest fan of track projections passed from hand to hand. If you drew a line through the middle of the swath of tropic ocean into which the computers were now sending this hurricane, that line ran along 25 North.

"And what city," inquired Hugh Willoughby quietly, "is on 25 North? Apart from Timbuktu?"

"So," said Frank Marks grimly, "there'll be cheap real estate in South Florida next week."

He told how one former director of NHC used to speak of a "magic box," a rectangle of ocean just northeast of the Leewards. He said, "Any storm that hits Miami, it goes through there. That's not to say that if it goes through there, it'll definitely come here. But if it does come here, it'll have gone through there first."

Floyd was headed straight for that area. "The forecast track," said the post-grad, "is a line plumb-dead on South Florida, and I think it will slowly intensify. I don't see any reason why it shouldn't."

"I do," said Stan Goldenberg.

Goldenberg is an excitable, fast-talking man with understandably good reason to be nervous about hurricanes; in 1992, Andrew blew his house to pieces with him inside it. He was with two other adults and six small children. At one point as the walls caved in, he'd ended up with the kitchen stove crushed across his back, trying to keep one of his three young sons' mouth and nose above the rainwater rising on the floor all about them.

Now he said, "Floyd might not intensify slowly. It might intensify *rapidly.*"

He and the others put the discussion leader on the spot; the post-grad plumped for a prediction that Floyd would still be offshore on Monday.

"OK," said Goldenberg, "your five-day forecast of intensity and landfall."

"And," Kaplan told him, "your whole career depends on it."

"Anywhere from Brownsville to Maine."

"And interests in Reykjavik," said Willoughby with a grin, "should monitor this storm?"

The post-grad noted that one medium-range model had Floyd making landfall between Jacksonville and Savannah. He said, "I'd say this'll be at least a major hurricane, that we have something to worry about in Florida, and that it'll be on us by Tuesday night or Wednesday morning."

From around the crowded space came several sharp exhalations of breath.

Frank Marks called MacDill. The P-3s had been tasked by NHC to fly surveillance the next day; the final decision point was 7:30 on Saturday morning, before the scientists who'd crew those missions caught commercial flights to Tampa. They planned at least one eyewall penetration in 43, to run step-frequency wind measurements and to get some dropsondes down into the worst of the storm; 42 would look at the steering flows.

Marks wouldn't be flying these missions; over the weekend it was Rosh Hashanah, the Jewish New Year, and unless a major storm was right on the beach, that holiday was sacred. Willoughby liked to joke that September contained three events—Jewish holidays, the end of the federal financial year, and the peak of the hurricane season. Of these three things, he said, the easiest to move would be the hurricanes.

Somehow, as Floyd bore down toward Florida in the busiest period of HRD's year, bureaucratic ritual dictated that Willoughby was obliged to conduct his staff's annual performance reviews. He was, therefore, rather glad that Marks wasn't flying; it meant he could forget the desk work and fly in Floyd himself. He'd been flying storms since 1969, when he'd gone into Typhoon Olga in the west Pacific as a twenty-four-year old ensign in the navy; I suspect that you could no more have kept him out of Floyd than you could have invited Fidel Castro to do a walkabout in Little Havana.

It was agreed that he'd lead the crew taking 43 into the eye; Mike Black would lead the team on 42.

"Right," said Willoughby, grinning with happy anticipation, "better get my burritos ready."

Mike Black laughed, and told him he was only allowed to use four dropsondes.

O ver lunch and hot sauces, they explained the meteorology. The main features determining where Floyd would go were a big ellipse of high pressure over Bermuda, and two troughs of low pressure—one hanging down over the islands in the storm's immediate path and the other farther back, dropping down from the Great Lakes toward the Gulf.

The troughs are valleys in the atmosphere, drooping wind flows draped down between heavier masses of high pressure; on their forward side the wind blows from southwest to northeast, and sometimes a succession of these can pass across the eastern seaboard, working as a kind of hurricane shield for the United States. Any storm approaching one of these will be vacuumed up and away to the northeast, as Dennis had been.

The first trough in Floyd's path was weak, and it was lifting out of the way. That left a hole for the storm to slip through toward Florida; it wouldn't be able to go north, because the Bermuda high behind the departing trough was a horizontal wall of heavy dry air, a ridge that the hurricane couldn't penetrate. In that case, Floyd would roll westward along the base of the ridge toward Florida—and, almost certainly, it would intensify as it did so.

The high pressure rotates clockwise, giving the storm an extra dose of spin as it rolls along beneath it; it's like a hand set down over the top of a snooker ball, rolling it away across the felt. Furthermore, the heavy air dropping down toward the ocean next door to the hurricane helps the storm to breathe; up high in the atmosphere, it allows more exhaust air to fly out and away over the top of it, thus increasing the inward pull at the base.

If the ridge of high pressure got in Floyd's way, two questions then followed. First, how big was the ridge? Did it stretch back far enough toward the east coast to keep Floyd pressed down all the way toward Florida? Or was it small enough to let the storm roll around up the back of it, and skirt north up the coast like Dennis? Second, there was the race between the looming hurricane and the next low trough slipping down over the continent before it—which of them would get to the east coast of Florida first?

"It's five days away," said Mike Black, "so we really don't know. Right now, Floyd could go anyplace from the Keys to the Carolinas. That's a big piece of real estate—and this has all the makings of the big hurricane of the year. Bret was strong but it was small, it fit nicely in that slot between Corpus and Brownsville. This is twice as big as Bret, or bigger, so the worst winds will extend way wider—and there's no slot like that, with just cows in it, anywhere up the East Coast, even if Floyd was small enough to fit into it in the first place."

He sighed and said, "It's amazing how things change. Yesterday we were talking about where it'll curve. Today we're talking about where it'll hit."

When they flew tomorrow they'd see how weak the first trough was and whether the ridge of high pressure was building in behind it. Then on Sunday, said Black, "that could start reminding me of Andrew. It's a matter of timing. When you go out there and you find the high's on top of the storm, and you realize it's making a beeline for Miami . . . there was just that sense of dread on the plane that day. But right now, there's a rule of thumb. If it gets north of 25, it'll miss us."

Marks agreed. He said, "I don't think it'll hit Miami. But until it gets north of 25, I won't rest easy on it."

Willoughby told everyone to prepare their homes over the weekend. He wanted that out of the way for the sake of their own safety, certainly, but also because, given the near-certainty that by Monday Miami would be under a hurricane watch, they'd then have to start barricading the lab. A watch meant clearing the basement, locking it up, getting storm shutters ready for the doors and the windows; a warning meant putting up the shutters, and closing all the computers down. They'd have to do all this, while still managing the logistics of two or three crews flying missions in and around the storm even as they prepared their families, their homes, and their workplace to go through it on the ground.

In among all that, said Willoughby, if the storm ran over Florida, "the scientific priority is Pete's experiment in the Gulf. We'll fly landfall, that goes without saying. But if it looks like it's going out west across the eddy, that's what we really want to do."

Where they might do it from remained uncertain; if the storm crossed the peninsula, MacDill would be closed. Tampa, he mused, "isn't immune to the possibility of an exit wound."

In short, from every point of view, this was a rerun of Dennis—but on a scale altogether more threatening. Rob Rogers, a recent recruit to HRD, grimaced and revealed that in the last few days he'd just finished buying a house.

"Oh well," someone told him, "at least you're insured."

F riday evening, Floyd was 400 miles east-northeast of San Juan, Puerto Rico. As feeder bands blew wind and rain across the islands, the Weather Channel got edgy: "We will encourage all of you along the eastern seaboard to keep an eye on this, and to get into preparedness mode. With each passing hour, it gets more impressive."

The winds around the eye started topping 100 miles an hour in the small hours of Saturday morning; at the same time, unnervingly, the storm track started shifting more west than north, and virtually all the models agreed on that. At 6:45 A.M. at the National Hurricane Center, an animated graphic derived from a medium-range model ran on a monitor screen by one of the forecasters' workstations; it showed Floyd barreling square into South Florida in four days' time.

The atmosphere, imaged as a mass of little flags on sticks showing wind speed and direction, bent and yielded around the hurricane like springs in a mattress. Floyd, and the two waves behind it, were red marbles with fuzzy, yellow-green surrounds, darting in speeded-up motion toward America. It was a cartoon of the near future, and it was a frightening one.

Willoughby reckoned that the huge eruption of thunderstorms that had blossomed over Nigeria and was now moving past the Cape Verde Islands over deep ocean was a tropical depression already; it would indeed be christened Gert very soon. The double-headed wave in midocean between Floyd and proto-Gert, he thought, would surely become Harvey not long afterward.

At the desk looking into the media room, hurricane specialist John Guiney, coming to the end of the night shift, did an interview for a TV news show; in the forecast center behind him, James Franklin came on duty.

While Guiney talked to the camera, Franklin sat muttering under his breath before the Storm Index Database Management Screen, with visible imagery showing the new cyclone developing off Africa on another screen to his left, and the animated marble that was Floyd running on a loop to his right, crashing into Florida over and over again.

Toward the back of the building, HRD used a narrow cubbyhole of an office to prepare for the day's flights. Both P-3s were going, as planned the day before. Frank Marks drew flight patterns, talking all the while on the speaker phone to colleagues at home and to AOC at MacDill. Willoughby loitered in the doorway, glad to be away from his desk, eager to be flying.

He'd have liked to get inside the eye of this hurricane more than just the once, but he wasn't complaining. He readily accepted that finding out what was happening around the storm to steer it—the "synoptic flow," the strengths and weaknesses of the high ridge and the low troughs—was more important to the forecasters right now than what was happening at the core of it.

"At this point," he said, "intensity isn't much of an issue, because everybody's expecting a major hurricane. At this point, everybody's just sweating the track forecast—because the odds are fifty-fifty to one in three that this'll be a landfall that goes down on the short list. You don't often see that kind of agreement in the models. Unless they're all wrong. They don't really go between the *I* and the *A* [in-house jargon for a direct hit on Miami] but just now it looks like Boca Raton, points north. So this is tense. But look"—he shrugged—"a lot can happen in four days. You can have three or four phases like this for each actual hit."

The flight patterns were settled; today's missions, said Marks, would be run by "the goyim crew," while he sought peace before the storm in temple, with his family.

"It's very much more likely and appropriate," mused Willoughby, "that hurricanes will strike on the Day of Atonement rather than the Feast of Passover."

Floyd was now 1,300 miles from Florida. A voice on my car radio as I drove home said, "Looks like this thing's got us in its sights. We don't have the option of sitting and doing nothing about this one."

In Miami Beach, my apartment was two blocks back from Ocean Drive. In 1926 the sustained winds there would have been at least 130 miles an hour, gusting a lot worse than that, and the sea would have come through my street five or six feet deep. On a barrier island, Miami Beach is one of the first places to be evacuated when any hurricane threatens South Florida; I went to bed wondering when I should pack my things. Should I still take the laundry down to Valetone a block away, on 14th and Washington? In four days time, would Valetone still be there?

This has all the hallmarks of a major hurricane. Floridians should prepare for a direct hit from a major hurricane."

Even when you know it's coming, even when you work on it every day—especially when you work on it every day—this is not what you want your television to tell you at six o'clock on a Sunday morning. Doubts and fears started nagging and pulsing in the back of my mind; I began wondering if it might not have been better to stick to writing about sport. It was fine to fly in a storm—I wanted badly to fly in this one—because I trusted the men in the cockpit, and I wanted to see what it was like, and I knew I'd be glad all my life to have had the privilege of those spectacular moments in the eye.

But to be on the ground before a growing beast like Floyd—that's something else. When you know all that it might do, when your mind's stacked with accounts through five centuries of the true horror that going through a hurricane involves, and then you see this one bearing down out of the ocean on you now—at this point, getting the story becomes utterly inconsequential. At this point you don't want the story to happen, because you don't want people to die, and you don't want the survivors to emerge in the aftermath to find that their city, in just a few appalling hours, has been thrown halfway back to the Stone Age.

The winds around Floyd's eye were now blowing at 110 miles an hour; hurricane force winds extended 70 miles from that center. At 385 miles east of Grand Turk, moving due west at 13 miles an hour, Floyd was on the brink of becoming a Category 3—and when you added the average margin of error to either side of the forecast track, all you could say was that probably, sometime late Tuesday, in about sixty hours' time, somewhere between Key West and the Florida-Georgia line this hurricane looked set to come ashore.

Stragglers from Miami Beach's many nightclubs idled home in the thinning darkness before dawn as I set off for the National Hurricane Center, and I wondered how many of these people were paying Floyd any mind. As with car wrecks or cancer, there are a lot of souls who think hurricanes only happen to other people—and very few souls, by contrast, who'd actively seek them out for a living.

Hugh Willoughby, being one of those few, had thoroughly enjoyed his ride on 43. In the cubbyhole at the back of the forecast center he said happily, "No bounces. Piece-of-cake flight. I hate to work nine hours for only one penetration, but I'm glad I did it. Really glad I did it. Of course, I could get fired for spending all this money—but if I join the list of NOAA people who've been fired for that, I'll be in distinguished company."

Flying now was a world apart from the early days; for a start, the instrumentation was so much better. He was particularly impressed with the software James Franklin had written for transmitting the data from the new dropsondes, but the design of the planes was superior all around.

"Especially back in the navy," he said, "I worked with so many things designed by people who were ergonomically challenged. You'd fly into a Cat 3 at night at seven hundred feet over the Philippine Sea, and you couldn't strap in because if you did, you couldn't reach all you needed to. You had racks of electronics and to work some of them you had to pull trays out, and the trays had sharp corners. One guy got bounced into one of those, he had *nasty* cuts, and we couldn't suture him, obviously. So we put on butterfly strips, made sure his eyes weren't dilated, and continued the mission. Men were men in those days. Or as my wife would say, men were idiots."

We watched the fuzzy marble on the model graphic; it was still crashing into Florida, then rolling right up the coast to spin away northeast from the Outer Banks, scouring the seaboard for the best part of a thousand miles like a pinball arcing clean around the top of the machine.

Another model had Floyd coming overland in South Florida, crossing into the Gulf of Mexico by Naples, then recurving so abruptly that it went straight back over the peninsula again, through Orlando and Cape Canaveral before returning to the Atlantic.

Willoughby considered the likely societal responses in Miami to a major landfall. "Firearms," he suggested, "are not an asset in a hurricane. People don't make rational decisions in rush hour traffic here—so what are they going to do in a Cat 4?"

He'd grown up in Arizona, where his father had been a mining engineer; he still had his father's pistol in the safe at home. He'd thought about getting it out during Andrew—"frontier Dad"—but compared to what happened to a lot of other people, his neighborhood wasn't too badly damaged. The second morning after the storm, the *Herald* landed on his doorstep and he realized that, at least where he lived, things wouldn't be too disorderly. Now he looked at Floyd, and pondered whether he should take the gun out and oil it.

"Where we'd be in trouble," said Pete Black, "is if the storm accelerates. If it gets here before the trough does. I still think it'll recurve just offshore. . . ."

I asked if he was a natural optimist; he gave a thin, dry smile.

Filling in for Frank Marks, Black was organizing the Gulfstream jet and one of the P-3s to fly synoptic flow missions for the forecasters again. He and Willoughby wanted to send the P-3 into the eye and do some research for themselves as well, but they couldn't afford it.

The relationship between NHC and HRD on these arrangements seemed mutually respectful and supportive, but with both agencies strapped for money, the odd grumble did arise. The scientists were happy to be tasked by the forecasters; it meant they got the plane hours, the aviation fuel, and the dropsondes on NHC's money instead of theirs.

On the other hand, they still had to pay their overtime and travel costs when they were working for the other agency. It was, Marks had told me, "a social contract. One that needs to be renegotiated."

Of these expenses Willoughby said simply, "I wish they'd pay us. But the way to put it is, if we weren't broke, I wouldn't raise it."

Their early morning decision point was looming—did they fly the other P-3 or not?

At the front of the house, Jerry Jarrell talked to the cameras. The eight o'clock advisory had just upgraded Floyd to a Category 3, still making for the general vicinity of South Florida. "We think it may turn," he said, "but it'll be a very close call. It will damage many homes in the area that it hits, and there's nothing to stop it getting stronger."

Willoughby and Black agonized, then decided to hold off flying on HRD's time and money until the hurricane was closer. Behind his habitually civil manner, the decision left Willoughby all but grinding his teeth. He sighed and said glumly, "I hate this. I was pumped to fly again."

It was all about when they could do the best science, within the constraints of a budget pared to the bone. Willoughby said of these daily decisions—whether to fly now or wait for a better opportunity—"I'm a wimp on it compared to Frank, and I calibrate that in. And Pete *always* wants to go. . . ."

With an ironic little grimace Black said, "I'm trying to show some judgment on it."

The decision was to wait. Floyd might be a Florida landfall, he might get into the Gulf and cross a warm eddy, he might recurve and start threatening a Carolina landfall instead—so, though they were champing at the bit, Black and Willoughby opted to hold off for a day.

"Of course," said Willoughby, "if the bottom drops out of this thing now—if the pressure plummets and it starts tearing toward Miami at twenty-five miles an hour like Andrew did—well, you can get me a plate, and you can feed me a whole flock of dead crows. But I think we'll fly tomorrow, and I think we'll be primo."

Jerry Jarrell hunched over the model forecast tracks with James Franklin and Lixion Avila. He was a wiry, aging man with a deeply lined face and a slow, drawling accent. He said, "You'd like to be able to tell people to forget about this thing. We could do that for a lot of people with Dennis, until it got to the Carolinas, but this one's much more serious."

The track they thought most likely was a common one—in the last few years Bertha, Fran, Bonnie, and lately Dennis had all done much the same, and Wilmington in North Carolina had been hit by pretty much everything that could reach it. The late nineties were looking like a replay of the fifties, storm after storm barreling up the coast through the Carolinas and New England—but to do that as those others had done before him, Floyd still had to turn.

If the next trough coming off the continent weakened like the first, Jarrell thought, the turn wouldn't happen, and Floyd would come to

Florida. "None of the models suggests it," he said cautiously, "but I'd contend that none of them suggested the earlier trough would weaken, either."

In the latest track fan, all three BAMs—shallow, medium, and deep—brought Floyd into the middle of the peninsula. Curtly, Avila dismissed them: "These are junk."

Jarrell picked out GFDL and the navy's NOGAPS tracks, the forecasts from the more sophisticated global models; these took Floyd farther north. He said, "There's some good names up there. Where's UKMET?"

Avila ran a finger along where the British global model, like the BAMs, had Floyd staying on a course west into mid-Florida. A dapper, brisk little man, he looked at me with a sharp grin and said, "That's just some English guy with a pipe and a cup of tea."

Their general feeling was that maybe, just maybe, we could begin to hope that Miami at least wouldn't be getting a visit from Floyd—but it was still way too early to be sure, and Hugh Willoughby was going home to get his storm shutters out. He would put them up that night, he said, or maybe first thing Monday.

As he left, James Franklin was writing the eleven o'clock advisory; apart from Floyd, he was also upgrading TD9 by the Cape Verdes to Tropical Storm Gert. In a couple of days' time, when Gert crossed 50 West in mid-ocean, the Air Force Reserve would need to start flying recon on it, in case it started threatening the islands. Right now, HRD had the Gulfstream jet at St. Croix in the U.S. Virgins for synoptic surveillance on Floyd; that afternoon, one of the P-3s was flying from there as well, recovering in Miami late that evening.

John Pavone, coordinating these missions for the forecast center, asked Pete Black, "Are you ready to put your finger in the dyke when the air force starts having problems? They haven't started screaming yet. . . ."

Black told him, "The next two weeks, John, that's our reason for being."

Floyd was now bigger than the entire state of Florida. In shape he looked like the classic heavy-duty sawblade, a rolling circle of cloud with a clear, perfect round eye.

"It's bursting in all directions," said James Franklin. "It's much more symmetric, and it's got tremendous outflow. I'm forecasting Category 4 in twenty-four hours."

The sea surface temperatures just ahead of the storm, just northeast of the Turks and Caicos, were a broiling 32°C. Franklin updated a pencil line of the official forecast track on a detailed chart through those humid waters; the line aimed straight for Cape Canaveral.

He expected landfall there, or a desperately near miss, about the middle of Wednesday morning. Admittedly, he said, "we're on the left side of the guidance—that is, most of the models keep it a little further off-shore—but we have a land bias generally. We'd rather keep people paying attention than not; once you lose that attention, it's hard to get it back. So if we see the model guidance start taking it away from land, we'll only adjust gradually."

The latest model runs weren't entirely trustworthy anyway—there were some glitches with the computers up in Washington—but GFDL had Floyd heading a touch farther north, passing close by Jacksonville, and NOGAPS had it farther out yet, just beginning to curve toward South Carolina. So would there be wind in Miami?

"No. It'll be breezy, and it'll be very, *very* hot."

They were now forecasting a turn to the north, but, said Franklin, "When you're forecasting a turn, particularly two days in advance, you're never comfortable until you see it."

That's because, within the average track error across a seventy-two-hour forecast, it remained the case that Floyd could hit anywhere in Florida. "Except Pensacola," he said, and turned away to get on with his work.

T his system is not going to go away. Be prepared. Start thinking about what you expect to do in the worst-case scenario."

Floyd continued to strengthen through Sunday afternoon, the winds rising to 120 miles an hour. At four o'clock he was 265 miles east-northeast of Grand Turk, still traveling due west at twelve miles an hour. Tropical storm warnings were raised in the Turks and Caicos and the southeast Bahamas, and a hurricane watch went into effect for the central Bahamas—meaning the former could expect a sideswipe from the bottom half of the storm within twenty-four hours, while within thirty-six hours the latter might be catching the worst of it.

"This is a dangerous hurricane. This is going to be a major problem for a lot of folks. If indeed it does make landfall as a major storm, this will do extensive damage."

The five P.M. advisory from NHC edged the wind speed up to 125 miles an hour; Floyd was now 800 miles from Miami. The hurricane watch in the central Bahamas was upgraded to a warning.

John Hope, the Weather Channel's veteran forecaster, said, "This is kind of a grim situation. This is a powerful hurricane, getting stronger. . . . You've got a day or two to get prepared. At the moment it's not quite as strong as Andrew was, not quite as strong as Hugo was in '89, but it's headed that way."

At landfall by Charleston, Hurricane Hugo killed twenty-six people, five of them children only eight years old or younger. Fifteen deaths were caused directly by the storm, those people either were crushed or drowned; two of the others had heart attacks, two were electrocuted, one died in a chain saw accident trying to clean up the mess afterward, and the others lost their lives in house fires lit by candles during the many days of power outages that follow any major landfall.

One victim was Cheryl Lee Christianson, forty-one years old. Her husband was a carpenter; Cheryl Lee made ball bearings for a firm producing heart-lung machines in Troy, New York. They'd left home the day before Hugo struck to attend their son's graduation from marine boot camp at Parris Island, Charleston; they arrived the afternoon before the storm to find the city evacuated.

They went to a relative's mobile home at St. Stephen in Berkeley County. Cheryl's husband said, "About eleven o'clock at night the trailer started rocking. The trailer lifted up off the foundation. The lights were off. There were a couple of candles and my nephew scurried over to blow them out. Just as he did the wind picked up again and completely demolished the trailer on top of us.

"My wife and I were still alive at this point. We saw what appeared to be light and we tried to get out, when the front wall collapsed on us. We crawled on our stomachs through the front of the trailer, and we made it to our car. We got inside our car.

"Another trailer was ripped off its steel frame. It smashed in the side of our car. We felt we were safer outside on the ground. We got out of the car and laid on the ground. We were there for a few moments. The wind blew some more, and it tore the bottom of the trailer off and blew it over the top of the car on my wife. . . . It crushed her immediately. . . . I tried reaching for her, and all I could do was touch her."

Floyd was growing into a storm like that one. Intensifying faster than Franklin had forecast, by six o'clock that evening the wind speeds around the eye had climbed to 140 miles an hour, and they were still increasing. This was now a Category 4 storm and a huge one, with winds of hurricane force spread across a core area 115 miles wide; the area of tropical storm force winds, of winds exceeding 40 miles an hour, was nearly 300 miles wide. Worse, it was accelerating, moving at 14 miles an hour along the bottom of that high pressure ridge—and still it was heading due west.

In my apartment I packed my suitcase. I had an ironic, somewhat querulous alarm that, having come to Florida to write a book about hurricanes, a hurricane would now reward my hubris by destroying all my notebooks and tapes—but if Floyd did indeed settle on Miami for a destination, there'd be bigger things to fret about than my paperwork.

I was staying on 14th and Drexel, in the Art Deco district of South Beach. Across the road, a giant banyan guarded the playground of Fienberg-Fisher Elementary; past the school, cafés and tourist stores lined Washington Avenue. They had great pork chops at the 11th Street Diner; they did sterling breakfasts at Puerto Sagua, the Cuban place on 7th and Collins. I tried to imagine winds of 140 miles an hour roaring down these pleasant pastel streets, the sea spilling in to fill the whole ground floor, block upon block reduced to rubble, foundations swept clean, bodies floating . . . but you can't imagine it. Only those who've been through it can ever truly know just how bad this can be—and I didn't want to join their number. My home and family back in Yorkshire, just then, seemed a whole planet away.

Across Washington on 14th stood the splendidly dingy Club Deuce. When I was done packing I went for a beer, and Melissa the barmaid asked me where Floyd was going. I said there was a fair chance we'd be under an evacuation order before the end of tomorrow.

She said, "They came around with the leaflets telling us to leave South Beach when Andrew was coming. I said I wasn't leaving. They said, Fine.

Get a pen with indelible ink, and write your name and your Social Security number on your forearm. Then we can identify the body when the storm's done with you. So I left."

Please, please, please, folks, take this seriously."
Early Monday morning, the winds in Floyd's heart were blowing at 155 miles per hour; he was on the brink of Category 5, with a distinct, immaculate eye nearly thirty miles across. The swath of endangered terrain around the latest forecast track was edging a shade north, with the tiniest tip of southwest Florida just slipping out of the projected danger zone—but this still depended on a turn that hadn't happened yet and which wouldn't happen, if it happened at all, for many hours yet.

Hurricane warnings were in force in the central Bahamas, with watches in the northwest of those islands; the latter watches were upgraded to warnings at five in the morning. Watches were also now in effect from midway down the Florida coast at Flagler Beach to Hallendale on the Dade-Broward county line. This, in theory, meant they figured Miami was out of the woods.

I listened to a woman calling a local radio station as I drove to NHC. "I'm confused," she said. "Am I under a watch? What's a tropical storm force wind? Should I put up shutters?"

I ground my teeth. How can you live in South Florida and not know this?

At seven o'clock at the forecast center, the metamedia show was back—a whirl of cell phones, cameras, cables, and wires; Jerry Jarrell doing interviews under portable lights from here to eternity; Radio Man shouting in the corner.

In their office Pete Black told Hugh Willoughby, "I hate you, you know that? You sit there being a faceless bureaucrat for weeks, then you get to fly the best storm we've had in years."

Willoughby grinned and said, "I don't like severe turbulence, you know that."

Black gestured toward the zoo in the media room, frowning. He said, "I don't like the turbulence in there, that's for sure."

"The only way to get any peace," Willoughby retorted, "is to go out and fly in the middle of a raging hurricane."

Somewhere amid the hubbub two forecasters came off the night shift, and two others came in to replace them. One of them would have to deal with Gert, which itself was probably a hurricane by now; if that and Floyd hadn't been about, the other system between them might well have gotten a name as well. It never did, though; Floyd loomed too near for them to worry about that.

Jack Beven was one of the forecasters going off duty. "This is the business end," he said, tight-lipped. "The only way I can put it is, it's going to get worse."

The model tracks had unclustered somewhat, adding to the difficulty of the forecast call. Only one of them still had the hurricane coming into Florida; the rest were all now calling for it to make a turn to the north. "I want to see the turn by this evening," said Beven. "If not, with a storm this big and powerful . . ."

He left the rest unspoken; it hardly needed to be said. For now, the official forecast track kept the storm just a hair's width offshore, turning north to pass Jacksonville in three days' time; if Florida didn't get it, however, someone else almost certainly would. UKMET, for example, now had Floyd going straight into Charleston. One of the forecasters asked if someone could fly synoptic flow off the Carolinas; if the storm ended going up that way, he said, "we need to know what's happening out there."

HRD juggled planes. The Gulfstream and 43 were in Miami, 42 was in Bermuda. I asked Willoughby if he regretted not flying the day before, seeing how fast the storm had deepened; he said, "I do, but not a lot. It'd have been a nice data set. But to rationalize it, what the storm's like at landfall will be determined today and tomorrow—and landfall's more important."

He said, "If we'd been fat on resources, we'd have gone."

Frank Marks was back after Rosh Hashanah; he looked around at his colleagues and said, "Any reasons why we shouldn't go today?"

Pete Black said firmly, "No."

With a filthy grin Marks asked Willoughby, "Have we got enough money to do this shit? Just rubbing it in, Hugh."

Later, over breakfast, Chris Landsea would say of the paucity of their budget, "I'm shocked by it, and I'm embarrassed by it."

John Pavone reported to the HRD team that the air force was taking a beating at 10,000 feet; Marks planned patterns for 43 and 42 at 12,000 and 14,000 feet, respectively. This was certainly no storm to be flown into low or lightly. If you believe in the relationship between barometric pressure and intensity (which not everyone does) then 922 millibars is the line a storm crosses to become a Category 5. Floyd had fallen from 935 the evening before to 917 now.

They said 905 would be historic. You get to 905, said Willoughby, "you're talking a category that you can't safely do in sign language if you're holding power tools."

Floyd was now as strong as Andrew, and three times the size.

At eleven o'clock that Monday morning, the hurricane watch was extended south to include Dade County, and the city of Miami therein.

At 12:30 on Virginia Key, Joe Cione led the maps discussion. Everyone was there—oceanographers, secretaries, admin, and support staff. This wasn't just meteorology now; this was about whether or not you still had a house on Wednesday evening.

Cione told them, "The nine-million, the ninety-million, maybe the ninety-billion dollar question is, where's it going to go? In the short term it's on a heading at 280 degrees, a shade north of west. Inside twenty-four hours, the official forecast expects a jog to the north, taking it up by Jacksonville and Savannah. . . ."

Tension hung thick in the air; several people were plainly bursting to be told one way or the other, somehow, anyhow, that Floyd wasn't coming where they lived. These people had been through Andrew; they'd seen the southern suburbs of their city pulverized, they'd heard their roofs pounding and thudding through the night, they'd felt their walls rock and shudder, and they didn't want it happening again.

Hectically nervous, one guy said, "I drew a line from last night's position and it was hitting Biscayne Bay and downtown Miami and I know you're not supposed to extrapolate like that but it was *very chilling*."

With many of HRD's people flying, it fell to younger members of the team to try to ease people's fears. Sam Houston was a trim, tanned, handsome figure with a head of tousled blond hair and a laconic manner; he was doing a thesis on wind field analysis at landfall.

"Operationally," he told the packed and fretful gathering, "we've got teams coming in from Texas Tech and Clemson to put the portable Doppler towers up. We're expecting either a landfall or a close approach by Melbourne and Cape Canaveral; at the farthest south, it'd be Jupiter Beach. The Keys are about the worst place to evacuate in the whole nation and they haven't put Monroe County under a watch, so they must be comfortable. Until they put a watch up in the Keys, I'm not real worried. If you see us putting Doppler towers up in the parking lot, *then* worry. But I live out on Key Biscayne, and I'm sleeping there tonight."

Joe Cione explained how the guidance was based on the race between Floyd and the low trough. On the satellite images he showed how the western side of the eyewall had eroded a little through the morning; the storm might be hitting a spot of higher shear, but the change was more likely due to the storm's own internal dynamics. He told how the eye had shrunk from thirty-five miles across to twenty; there was probably an eyewall replacement going on, the shrinking of the inner wall and the formation of a new, concentric outer ring. He said, "It's difficult to maintain this level of intensity for long. It's borderline Cat 4/5, but we'll see some fluctuations either way. It was 917 millibars this morning, it's up to 921 since. . . ."

Pete Black shrugged and said, "That's just noise."

Another voice asked anxiously, "You don't see substantial strengthening?"

Sim Aberson smiled and said quietly, "It can't strengthen much more than this."

Cione said, "Do whatever you do for a watch. At the moment, we're on the good side of the storm, the left side—we may get brushed by winds at seventy-five miles an hour, but I wouldn't panic just yet."

Putting up proper storm shutters (and taking them down again) is a tiresome business. "For a watch," said Pete Black, "you take out your shutters, and you count them."

Sim Aberson was working on the effectiveness and accuracy of the computer models; he knew how they worked as well as anyone there. He said, "I live at Dania Beach up in Broward, farther north than anyone—and I'm not putting my shutters up yet."

AOML's deputy director Judith Gray asked if we could expect tropical storm force winds, and if so, when. Calm and efficient, she announced, "If there's a warning tomorrow morning, the lab is closed. The mayor will say tomorrow if he's closing the schools. If we get a tropical storm warning, everyone's on administrative leave. Keep the computers on tonight; if we still have a problem, we'll shut them down tomorrow."

Sam Houston held up his hands. He said, "Look. I wouldn't have these guys drive all the way from Texas to put the towers up in the wrong place. I think Floyd will just brush us." Then he let loose a sly and wicked grin, adding, "So any preparation you do now may help for Gert."

Aberson told the gathering that the first model runs using the morning's new flight data would come in at 14:00, with another set soon afterward at 15:15. He proposed meetings in the conference room downstairs to run through both sets of new tracks as soon as they appeared. The maps discussion broke up and little huddles of people drifted away, talking fast in animated and fearful whispers.

The man who'd plotted Floyd's arriving directly into Biscayne Bay said he couldn't concentrate, he hadn't done a stroke of work all morning; he said the storm frightened him, and Miami frightened him too. "If this thing's still coming west tomorrow morning, this city will be chaos. The traffic will be chaos. People will be running red lights, they'll be behaving badly. . . ."

Rob Rogers stayed behind a moment, watching Floyd silently grinding into the Bahamas on the monitor screens. He said, "The forecast's for it to get really close, maybe a couple of hundred miles off the coast, then to make a sharp turn. So we're totally depending on the models. What if they're six hours off in the timing?"

In essence, what if Floyd made the turn as forecast, but waited to make it until it was sitting on top of Miami?

Rogers said ruefully, "I've lived in my house for thirty-six hours, and now I'm thinking of boarding it up."

Tracks for a dollar. Tracks for a dollar."

At two in the afternoon the conference room was packed. Aberson walked through the waiting crowd toward the lectern with a sheaf of printouts. A slim, slight figure with jet-black hair spilling down his back to his waist, he looked untroubled and confident. He said, "I know everybody is immediately interested in Gert. . . ."

The latest satellite fix on Floyd marked the eye of the storm at 24.3 North, 72.8 West—100 miles from San Salvador in the Bahamas, 500 from Miami. It was, he said, a little bit fast, but still within the guidance. He then reported that GFDL, the most trusted of the computer models, was now shifting the track a hint farther right, away from the Florida coast. "Now the problem with storms is, they like to slow down before they turn, just like you do when you're driving down the street—"

Some wag chipped in, "Not in Miami."

Aberson worked quietly to reassure the crowded room. True, he said, the BAMs all brought Floyd ashore, but none of the other models agreed with them—and when the BAMs went off on their own like that, they were always wrong.

The guy who couldn't work or concentrate twitched on the edge of his seat. "The last half hour," he blurted, "the track's been 265, it's been *south* of west."

Calmly Aberson told him, "That's a wobble. You have to look across six to twelve hours to see what's really happening."

Judith Gray updated them on matters practical. The Rosenstiel School across the road had closed, as had much of downtown. "People are driving home," she said, "and they're driving stupid."

"Stupider than normal?"

"Yes."

Back in his office, Aberson was as confident in private as he'd been at the lectern. He believed in the science, the science was in the models, and the models were his work; he'd done statistical schemes cutely dubbed POMP (Prediction of Model Performance) and on that evidence, he believed NHC's forecast of a turn to the north was a good one.

One hour later, he wasn't so sure.

Aberson strode out of the computer room with fifty Xeroxes of the next set of model runs at 15:12. He said simply, "I don't like the look of this."

He told the conference room, "I have good news and bad news. The good news is, we're not going to take a direct hit."

He put an acetate map on the overhead projector. As the image of the latest tracks came up on the screen a noise rose instantly around the room, part groan, part gasp, part scream.

The storm was accelerating, traveling at sixteen miles an hour now, still heading on 280 degrees, only the faintest shade north of west. The new fan of model projections took Floyd onshore into West Palm Beach, or at points north of there toward Cape Canaveral. If this was correct, said Aberson, Miami would definitely have tropical storm force winds, Fort Lauderdale would get at least a Category 1 impact, and where the eye came onshore the landfall would be catastrophic.

His previous sense of certainty was undone. All the models were "feeling the trough"—and with it still being over land, tracked by balloon launches all the way, the data on its forward motion were reliable. But if Floyd was speeding up, it would win the race.

Rumor of a mandatory evacuation being called at six that evening for Key Biscayne, Miami Beach, and the other barrier islands went whipping round the room. Sam Houston shrugged. "I'm not moving out. They can arrest me if they want. Where will all those people go?"

Pete Black appeared in the doorway. In a sudden silence filled with staring eyes he said, "If it's not north of 25 by eight in the morning, prepare for the worst."

Fear broke out in a quick hubbub of voices. Above the noise Judith Gray called out firmly, "Prepare your homes, prepare yourselves, and watch television."

Black was deeply anxious. He didn't spell it out in public, but he had three grounds for fearing that Floyd's turn to the north might happen too late. First, these big, intense storms often tended to move left of the guidance. Second, they made their own steering regardless of what was going on around them. And then third . . .

"It's only over a three-hour span, but even if it's a wobble the mean motion is still due west—and all the time we're mindful of how badly the models busted on Mitch. People thought maybe that was because it was moving slowly, and because it was so far south that we didn't have good data. But the thing is"—Black grimaced—"maybe the models just do a really crappy job on big intense storms."

Maintenance staff was putting up storm shutters as I left the building. Metal clanged against tiles and window frames, echoing around the dim space of the atrium. My chest was so constricted with dread that it ached.

Hammers, saws, and power drills banged and whined along Washington Avenue as the stores and restaurants boarded up—not all of them, by any means, but enough to make a persistent, nerve-jangling soundtrack. Radios yammered on the sidewalk as people toiled to protect their businesses; in the blazing, sticky sunshine, the words *"un huracán significativa"* drifted on the air.

Lines of cars were beginning to build along the road outside every gas station. Governor Jeb Bush declared a state of emergency; all road tolls were lifted, to ease the flow of the spreading evacuations. I went to the bank, and realized I'd forgotten my PIN number. Floyd was 450 miles away, and I had twenty-seven dollars. I felt like a complete idiot.

A young German couple in my apartment building wanted to know what to do. If an evacuation was ordered, should they go?

I told them they should, absolutely. It wasn't forecast to come here but it might, and if it did, Miami Beach was no place to be. In a direct hit from a Category 4/5 hurricane there'd be winds beyond imagining, and a huge surge of seawater raging down the street.

In the circumstances, it was hard to tell them to stay calm. They didn't have a car. I said if an evacuation was called, they should take one of the emergency buses off the beach and never mind where it took them. One night in a little discomfort wasn't too bad a price to pay for that extra degree of safety—and if an evacuation wasn't called, fine, stay. Floyd wasn't going to be here tonight, and there was no need to panic. Just get up early, look at the Weather Channel—and if it hadn't crossed north of 25, get out.

The woman wailed, "I never thought of such a thing. I never imagined such a thing. What about my stuff?"

I asked if it was insured; she said it wasn't. I looked at her. Who goes on holiday in Miami during hurricane season without insurance? Who goes to Miami without insurance, period?

I told her she should take what she could carry and forget about the rest. I do realize that one's wardrobe is a matter of high import to a lot of people in Miami Beach—this being a place where Rollerblading is an art form and the principal places of industry are the gym and the tattoo parlor—but as she fretted on about her stuff, eventually I had to tell her, look, your stuff won't be of much use to you if you're dead.

O n the campus at FIU that evening, there was no need anymore to get a permit for the faculty staff's parking lot; they'd evacuated the university. Inside the forecast center at 18:45, Max Mayfield was in the media hot seat. Hurricane watches had been upgraded to warnings from Florida City at the head of the Keys all the way up the state's east coast to the Georgia line. Mayfield told the cameras that right now, their biggest immediate worry was for West Palm Beach.

Amid the scrum in the conference room, a Hispanic soundman called home and got his answering machine. He left a message for Ernie telling him to bring in the plants, "like you did last time. You have Michael's beeper number? Tell him to come back home."

The cameras were tiered in two lines; three in front on short tripods trained on Mayfield, four more behind them on taller stands with lights for reporters going live.

There was now, said Mayfield, a mandatory evacuation order in effect for all barrier islands and beaches.

The seven o'clock news point was imminent; reporters discussed with their crews whether this event was big enough to interrupt the Dolphins game on Monday Night Football. Sure, Floyd was big, but surely he wasn't *that* big. . . .

Floyd, said Mayfield to anyone who was listening, was three times the size of Andrew, and stronger than either that storm or Hugo. "We're confident that it will turn north, but the timing of the turn is uncertain. If the core goes just a *little* left of the forecast track, it could cross onto the east Florida coast. You need to make preparations."

When it came to it, much of the reporting out of NHC was as sound and responsible as was merited by the severity of the situation. The local NBC man in particular was a model of good sense, urging people to get ready right now; if they left it until morning and found themselves waking up to tropical storm force winds, it'd be too late to start putting up shutters or plywood then. You try walking about carrying window-sized sheets of board and metal in fifty mile per hour winds. . . .

On the other hand, some of the reporting was little short of hysterical. There was the woman who merely howled at her camera, *"We are talking mass destruction!"*—which was certainly true enough, but a little advice on how to get prepared for it might have helped.

Lixion Avila stepped briskly through the foyer. He'd been on duty twelve hours, and it was time to go home. As we stepped outside he said, "Not here. Not Miami. It's going to turn. At Great Abaco in the Bahamas, it's going to turn." He gave me the faintest dry hint of a weary grin and said, "Following that damn British model right along the line."

Billy Wagner, the spry little Cajun in charge of emergency management for Monroe County, joined us. "It's going to turn all right," he said. "It's just going to do it so damn late, and it's so big. Look. We're in the circulation already."

In the darkening evening the wind was gusting, shaking the branches of the trees, waving the palm fronds to and fro, tugging at my shirt, stuttering fitfully out of the northwest in the front edge of the storm. Overhead, clumps of purple-gray cumulus rolled around through the sky in ranked and ordered lines.

On Highway 836, heading back to the beach past the airport, the out-bound lane was dotted with people towing their boats away to the west. At the coast, a steady stream of traffic rolled along the causeways out of Miami Beach; yellow school buses commandeered for the evacuation rumbled past among the cars. The cruise liners normally moored along the docks were all gone; for some reason I found that more unnerving than any other one thing. The huge, gleaming pleasure palaces lining the quayside by the causeway were an integral element of the cityscape; now they'd all fled, and the view was like a mouth without teeth.

On the front door of my apartment building, I found a piece of paper taped to the glass. It said simply, "Dade County has issued a manda-tory evacuation. This is not optional."

There was a message on the phone system too, a short message, very much to the point. Left by a hurried and nervous voice, all it said was, "You have to leave. Thank you."

I knew the face behind the voice. I imagined him in the office, working his way through three different buildings' worth of apartments and hotel rooms, leaving that message over and over and all the while thinking, I want to leave too, *I want to leave now. . . .*

My building was empty. The hallway was dimly lit, muffled, airless; the sense of abandonment was palpable. My car sat alone in the road outside. I went for a walk; there were still people about, but not many, and the hammers and drills banged and whined. Knots of people waited at bus stops to be taken away; hotel guests sat on front steps in nervous groups looking this way and that, whatever bags and cases they could carry clutched in their hands or kept close by their feet.

A lot of places were closed, but not the Deuce; the Deuce was packed to the rafters, thick with smoke and loud talk and Counting Crows on the jukebox. At the bar, the people I'd got to know there said Floyd wasn't coming to Miami. I told them the only thing I knew—if it wasn't north of 25 in the morning, they should leave—but I'm not sure how many of them would have.

I went to bed early, but sleep was impossible to find. The silence of the empty building was deafening. I lay there mulling my options. There was no reason to leave the beach right now; on the other hand, in case Floyd didn't turn, I'd set the alarm clock painfully early to avoid a panicked final stampede off the island in the morning. If Floyd didn't turn, the roads would be anarchy congealed—and I couldn't afford to be stuck in that because I couldn't afford to miss HRD's dawn meeting at the forecast center. I couldn't afford to miss that, because I wanted more than anything to fly in this hurricane.

Apart from anything else, it felt right then like a NOAA P-3 would be just about the safest place to be.

As of the eight P.M. advisory that Monday evening Floyd was at 24.4 North, 74.1 west, 35 miles northeast of the island of San Salvador, 400 miles from Miami, and still moving due west. At ten-thirty, I acknowledged that I was no more likely to sleep than I was to grow a third arm; I got up, threw my suitcase in the trunk of the car, and drove back on empty roads to NHC.

Hugh Willoughby reported that their last pass through the eye that evening had been beautiful; he'd watched a crescent moon rising on a bed of stars across the cloud-rimmed hole in the still, black heart of the hurricane. They'd been thrown around by one updraft rocketing skyward in the eyewall at nearly forty miles an hour, but they'd had no bad bumps otherwise; just the odd instrument problem.

About this time, Mike Black was landing at St. Croix in the other P-3; as soon as he could find a phone he rang John Guiney, the forecaster working the night shift. Were they still standing by the turn? Would his family be OK? Would he still have a house when he got back?

Guiney said they were indeed standing by the forecast, and that they still believed Floyd would turn. Black would say later, "He really reassured me"—and as calamity loomed ever closer, Guiney and his colleagues stayed stalwart through the night.

A Swiss post-grad from Rosenstiel kindly offered me a foam mattress in his spare room; once he'd finished banging boards against the windows, I got to bed about one o'clock. Another refugee from the beach, an Irish research student seconded from the insurance industry (getting a taste of what their pay-out might look like up close and personal), was sleeping on the sofa.

We had four hours' sleep; the alarm went off at five o'clock. In the new advisory Floyd was 275 miles away, moving west-northwest at fourteen miles an hour. The map fix was 25.1 North, 75.9 West; by one-tenth of a degree, at least as far as Miami was concerned, the storm had crossed the magic line. It would be no consolation to the island of Eleuthera, over which the west side of the eyewall was now arriving, but Floyd was beginning to turn.

Outside, it was eerily calm; the roads remained all but empty. At NHC Willoughby said, "It's pretty much following the forecast track. The socially responsible person in me worries that an awful lot of people up the coast might still be impacted even if the track does verify—but the truth is, these forecasters have done a brilliant job."

The only criticism might be that they'd raised the warning in Dade County six hours later than they did for points north of there. The answer to that is that they never believed Floyd would come to Miami, but as the track continued westward, and with the turn expected so late, extending the warning south into Dade was merely taking out prudent insurance. It was, in Willoughby's phrase, "a hedge against an improbable event," and as a result a lot of people were no longer in the most vulnerable places, or engaged in vulnerable activities, and everyone's children had stayed home, and people with special needs had started moving into shelters in good time.

You need to do these things in good time, because a hurricane might not give you much time. You need to do them because, though the forecasters got this one right, any one of them will tell you that next time they might perfectly well not—which is why, at NHC that morning of Tuesday, September 14, they were putting up the building's storm shutters anyway.

The lab on Virginia Key was closed. Deprived of his computers, Sim Aberson drew the day's flight patterns with a pencil, otherwise known as a Universal Graphic Output Device.

The base at MacDill was shut down as well (the air force having zero tolerance of any threat to their assets), so 42 was at Tampa International on a mandatory down day for maintenance checks. 43 was going into Floyd as the storm turned north across Great Abaco; the Gulfstream jet would examine the synoptic flow out in front of it, in case the hurricane now started heading for the Carolinas.

The latest update from Lixion Avila took the core of the storm perilously close to Melbourne by mid-Wednesday, halfway up the Florida coast. At this point, the plan for Wednesday therefore involved 43 flying that potential landfall, with 42 on standby to follow on in the evening if Floyd remained offshore. The Gulfstream, meanwhile, would spend Wednesday over the ocean looking at Gert, which itself now contained winds of 105 miles an hour.

In HRD's cubicle, Frank Marks's voice crackled over the speaker phone from his motel room in Tampa. Running through the mission plans, he told AOC's program manager Jim McFadden, "I don't want to push the crews too hard."

McFadden said, "If they squawk, I'll tell you. Hell, you're nearer to them. If they squawk, you'll hear it first."

Pete Black arrived, and reported to Marks that the weather in Miami was balmy. "There's a north wind about ten knots, a little stronger on the beach. It's a typical South Florida morning—except everybody's got shutters on their houses."

It was worse in Broward, the next county north, with gale force winds beginning to arrive in Fort Lauderdale. Up at Dania Beach, Sim Aberson had boarded up the night before; coming off the night shift, John Guiney was heading home to try to do the same now.

On the line from Tampa, Marks checked that everyone's wives were getting reassuring, informative news on which scientists were flying, and where and when they'd be landing. It's worth noting that flying in hurricanes isn't an activity in which women are well represented. I met only one female meteorologist who flew a storm during three months in Miami, a visiting Australian, and though this is something that Hugh Willoughby would like to see change, it may be hard to change it too fast. At the bottom line, I suspect, women are smart, and men like roller coasters.

New model guidance came in. The consensus trend on Floyd was a path still staying close offshore, but sliding a little to the right, and accelerating toward the Carolinas. HRD rejigged their plans, starting to think about flying a landfall up there during Wednesday night. Both P-3s were due fifteen-hour inspections; Pete Black worried that they might have no planes available just when they were needed most as Floyd neared Savannah, more likely Charleston, maybe Wilmington. It was, he said, "one of the more complex situations in some years. Two storms, both big, one huge and threatening landfall."

In the Bahamas, Floyd was giving Eleuthera a shorter version of what Guanaja had gone through ten months before. Up the coast, meanwhile, two million people were starting to evacuate the shoreline; the main highways out of Jacksonville and Savannah would very soon be clogged solid. Airlines stopped flying; at Cape Canaveral, the space shuttles were locked down tight. Across the state, theme parks were closing—including Disney World, for the first time in its twenty-eight-year history—and hotel staffs were pitching all the patio furniture into their swimming pools to keep it from blowing away.

At the front desk at NHC, senior hurricane specialist Miles Lawrence briefed the media. He said it was gratifying that the forecast had turned out correct, at least for southeast Florida, "but it's too early to forget the whole thing. There could still be winds near hurricane force at Palm Beach. If the exact track's correct the strongest winds will stay offshore, but it only takes a fifty-mile shift for the coast to start getting the eyewall—so I don't think today's the day to be planning any outside activity. Floyd's still getting closer, and people should be ready in case the unexpected happens. This is just a good day to stay home."

I didn't have that option; I had a plane to catch. Each P-3 has twenty-one seats and now one of them had fallen free for me.

During my five-hour drive to Tampa, Floyd began draping his rainbands across the southern half of the state; stretches of Interstate 75 caught downpours so heavy that the sky turned a purplish black in the middle of the day and visibility fell to near zero through water running an inch deep on the windshield. Lightning burst and flared across the countryside.

That evening, Floyd's winds were reported to have fallen from 155 to 140 miles an hour. This, said Max Mayfield, "is the difference between being run over by a freight train, and being run over by a semi tractor-trailer. Neither prospect is good."

B y Wednesday morning, the biggest evacuation in the history of the United States was in progress. Close to 1.5 million people in Florida, at least 300,000 in Georgia, and another 800,000 in South Carolina were leaving their homes. On the mid-Florida coast, the refulgently named Jeanene Fwart of Indialantic told the *Tampa Tribune,* "A lot of the diehards stayed until Tuesday morning. Then even the diehards freaked out."

Hastily gathering whatever they could pack and carry—pets, sleeping bags, coolers of food—all along the seaboard people fled inland. Most traveled light; a few packed rental trucks with all the household goods the vehicle would take. Steve Carter from Satellite Beach was one of the latter. He said, "I couldn't get it all, but better something than nothing."

Shannon Bellinger from Melbourne just took a carton of cigarettes and a six-pack of Coke. He said, "I've lived here all my life, and this is the worst one I've seen. You'd have to be crazy to stay."

From the Atlantic shoreline they made for Tampa and Tallahassee, Macon and Atlanta, Charlotte and Augusta; in all too many places, highways and interstates duly seized up, with traffic wedged motionless for hours.

Interstate 4 into Tampa was bumper-to-bumper clear across the peninsula from east coast to west; behind the crawling traffic the Space Coast lay deserted, the homes and businesses shuttered and boarded, the residents all gone.

Farther north, the roads out of Savannah ground to a dead halt. Some people were snared in gridlock for ten, even fourteen hours—not a good place to be in baking humidity with no toilets and no toilet paper, but still a good deal better than the coast in a Category 4/5 landfall. Charleston emptied too; after Hugo, they don't need a second invitation to run from a major storm there. Mayor Joseph Riley Jr. said, "I love seeing people on the streets of my city, but when a hurricane comes, what I want to see is a ghost town. And that's about what we have."

As the flight grew in volume and disorder, recriminations started flying even before Floyd had come ashore. Heading inland from Charleston, Interstate 26 was converted into a one-way road—but not soon enough for Mayor Riley, who told South Carolina Governor Jim Hodges bluntly, "What you're doing is running the risk of killing my people."

Meanwhile, preparations for evacuation on a similar scale were under way in North Carolina; for the fifth time in four years, the forecast track now pointed toward that state. In Raleigh, the state capital, they were still mostly worrying about how to manage a major wind event and a major storm surge on the coast; the fact that it had already started raining, at this point, seemed less of an immediate concern.

In New Zealand, President Clinton cut short his visit to the gathering of ASEAN leaders. Georgia had already joined Florida in declaring a state of emergency; South Carolina was asking Washington for permission to do the same. One of the lessons learned in Andrew seven years before was that it was no good waiting until after the event to call it an emergency; relief materials needed to be flowing on their way to any likely affected area well ahead of time, otherwise thousands of people could be left squatting in sodden, swamp-humid wreckage without power or food or water for days.

FEMA had blankets, cots, generators, mobile kitchens, food, water, 250,000 pounds of ice, and 18,000 rolls of plastic sheeting ready to move. Asked how much it would cost, the agency's director, James Lee Witt, said simply, "We'll look at that later."

. . .

Floyd was enormous. The eye was 110 miles offshore from Cape Canaveral, and the entire state of Florida had disappeared beneath the system's circulation; it filled all of the giant bight from Miami to Cape Hatteras. Hurricane force winds extended over an area 250 miles in diameter around the eye; there were tornado outbreaks in Georgia, and tropical storm warnings now extended all the way up to Delaware, 1,000 miles north of Miami.

In Frank Marks's room at the Tahiti Inn on South Dale Mabry in Tampa, Mike Black urged that they should fly both planes. He said, "This is potentially the biggest landfall event since Camille. This is an unprecedented event."

Marks spoke quietly, protecting a throat dry and sore with exhaustion. He said wryly, "There's no such thing as an unprecedented event."

"OK," said Black. "But scientifically, I don't care about politically, I want both planes."

The storm was accelerating. More often than not, if they bypass Florida and start bearing down on the mid-Atlantic states and New England beyond them, hurricanes get picked up by the jet stream; they start ripping north or northeast at thirty, forty, even fifty miles an hour. The present motion suggested a strike on Wilmington about midday Thursday; the HRD team reckoned it'd get there a good bit quicker than that.

It was eight in the morning on Wednesday. Between their own work and their missions for NHC, they'd been flying Floyd for five days; they lived on a handful of hours' sleep each night between late set-downs in Tampa, Miami, Bermuda, or St. Croix, and dawn starts to get planning on the next day's research. Over Great Abaco in 43 the day before, the data systems had started crashing; they'd limped home keeping the instruments just about running. Now AOC's electronics engineers would have to go crawling through the wiring, hacking through the software to try to fix it in the six hours that remained before takeoff.

Half a dozen people were in Marks's room, leaning against the walls, slumped in chairs, sitting on the edge of the bed. Ed Walsh said his altimeter had seen fifty-foot waves off Melbourne from 8,000 feet. There was a buoy out there whose all-time record wave was fifty-two feet; any way you looked at it, Floyd was at the top of the range.

Pete Black came on the speaker phone from NHC in Miami. He said, "Jim McFadden wants to know, do we fly?"

Marks told him, "If 43 can fly and we can get something, we fly. But if the main data system's not working, if the BTs aren't working, if the radar's not working, what's the point?"

"I agree," said Pete. "So fix it and take off later."

"OK, but the planes are at Tampa International, they're not at MacDill. It's harder for the maintenance crew, they've got to run back and forth. . . ."

"Ay ay ay."

"Caramba," said Peter Dodge.

Frank told Pete, "I'm just throwing you curve balls here."

"No, that's a slider."

"How's your swing these days?"

Pete chuckled. "Getting pretty weak."

They reckoned if Floyd went on picking up speed, this was going to turn into a landfall mission; they talked about pushing back 43's takeoff to 15:00, leaving 42 on standby for departure at midnight. That'd leave a two-hour gap without a plane in the storm; on the other hand, they could juggle their timings to catch landfall with some finesse here, because Floyd was so close that forty-five minutes after takeoff you were right in the thick of it.

Frank asked, "How about we move 42 up to 23:00? It's Sam Houston's call, but I'd do it. Better to move it up, then delay later if we have to. If it starts recurving, we might need to delay."

"No," said Mike Black. "It's going to hit Morehead City at least."

Hugh Willoughby cut in from Miami to report that Sam Houston was planning around a landfall about two o'clock Thursday morning—in which case, 42's night flight would have to leave earlier, not later.

They settled on 43 flying at 15:00 to do landfall if it happened that fast, and air-sea interaction if it didn't. "If the data system's back up," said Frank, "we'll go. Scientifically, we want to go."

Hugh asked, "No matter where the storm is?"

"It's going to be interacting with the Gulf Stream, and approaching an earlier landfall than forecast, or both. According to Sam, it could be nearing landfall by the end of 43's flight."

It was hard to call. They'd watched the eye re-forming the day before; the storm was getting into some wind shear, and adjusting to that new factor.

Compared to the earlier days, said Frank, this was now one big, really *sloppy* hurricane.

He called out to Miami, "Is Pete Black calm?"

Pete told him, "I want to be like Mike."

Frank laughed. "We all want to be like Mike."

Sam Houston reported a problem at exit 26 on Interstate 16 in Georgia. He had a truck there with fuel for the portable Doppler team from Texas Tech, and the state troopers weren't letting it through toward Savannah; he needed someone to get on to the state police and clear that up. Frank asked Pete Black, "What if the Texas guys don't get diesel?"

"Then we don't get data. And that's bad."

Across the room, Mike Black worked on new flight patterns for landfall with Peter Dodge. He called out to his namesake for a track forecast; without hesitation Pete called back, "My best guess for five P.M. is 31 North, 79 West."

That would be 225 miles from Wilmington—suggesting a landfall in that city at two or three in the morning. On the Internet, Frank found a NOAA buoy reporting fifty-four-foot waves.

In the words of the latest advisory, "All preparations to protect life and property should be rushed to completion in the hurricane warning area."

Another voice from Miami called out, "Frank? Today is the tenth anniversary of September 15, 1989, Hugo. *Be careful.*"

Frank answered, "We know. We were just talking about it with NPR yesterday. They said, 'Don't you guys ever get scared out there?' " He laughed; it was something they'd talk about a lot that day, with each other, and with AOC men like Gerry McKim, who'd kept their plane in the air in Hugo's eyewall ten years ago to this day.

When I asked Frank about it later he said, "I had mixed emotions. It's not often I get scared about what we do, but whenever I think about that flight I remember how scared you can be. The mention of the anniversary certainly jogged my mental state. I thought about how people might view what we do, and what it would be like if they could see it the way we do—kind of a cross between great fun and scientific curiosity. There is an exhilarating aspect to flying into the eyewall that never seems to get old, and I suppose that's why I still do it. I think none of us really wants to grow up."

The handrail along the ceiling of the center aisle in 42 still has the dent in it where the life raft flew loose and crashed up into the top of the cabin. The date, September 15, 1989, is marked against the dent with a little tag of red Dymotape. Loving their planes the way they do, the AOC maintenance guys wanted to take the dent out, but the men who'd survived Hugo said they should leave it. It was, said Hugh Willoughby, "a badge of honor."

Several of those present had not only experienced the Hugo flight in mid-ocean, but had also been present on the ground in Charleston when that storm made landfall. Over breakfast, one of them described the experience.

They'd been late getting there, because some of their equipment was delayed in the baggage handling system. It got rerouted to Atlanta when it was meant to be flying into Jacksonville, holding them up six hours before it came back; by the time they got on the road, the storm was on the brink of coming in.

"The drive from Jacksonville to Charleston was pretty hairy. The power was down, there were no lights, the rain was so bad you could barely see the road. We got to the airport as the eyewall was arriving; we plugged the computers into the radar and went to work. Then the eye came over. We stepped outside, and the smell of pine hit you like a smack in the face.

"In the morning we saw why. It was like waking up in a different place. The building where we'd worked and slept was well protected and even in the eyewall we were thinking, OK, OK, it's not so bad. Then we went outside, and Jesus . . . every pine tree in sight, *every one,* was snapped off ten feet up the trunk. It was like a whole new horizon."

Mike Black said they'd thought they could see the destruction of the forests on the radar; there were so many pine needles blowing everywhere that they'd acted as scatterers in the radar beam.

He laughed; in those earlier days, they'd done some crazy things. Before they'd set off for Charleston he'd called Bob Burpee, then HRD's director, and Burpee had recommended that it was too late, that they better not go. Black told him, "No, no, it's OK. It's just a light drizzle."

He remembered one hellish deployment, spending five days through a Labor Day weekend hopscotching back and forth along the Gulf coast trying to catch landfall on the ground in Elena. They paid $24 a head for motel rooms in Apalachicola in the Florida panhandle; the power went, the room flooded, "and still they charged us for it. I suppose at least the bed was dry."

Today would be his fifth flight in five days. He shrugged and said simply, "It's excitement, but it's also duty. We have to understand these monsters."

As we spoke, millions were fleeing from Floyd. Thinking of those people, one of the other guys said, "I think people always find something to give them hope. They dredge up a memory of a storm that they can say looked like this one, and it recurved and went away, or it came in and they got through it OK. I think it's in the nature of human beings to find some cause for hope."

In North Carolina's state capital, Raleigh, that morning, as he had been for several days already, meteorologist Ryan Boyles was in and out of the emergency management center in the basement of the governor's Department of Administration on Jones Street. They had generators, satellite feeds, a briefing room for Governor Jim Hunt to speak to the media—and they were trying to figure out what was coming their way.

"Two days out from the hit," Boyles said later, "the scary part was the winds. We weren't real worried about the rain. It looked a lot like Hugo and that started us getting nervous, because the forecast track had it coming right through the Triangle [the booming metro zone comprising Raleigh, Durham, and Chapel Hill] and the Triangle's never experienced hurricane force winds, at least not in modern times. Fran was bad two years ago and that only gusted up to seventy here inland, so we knew if Floyd was worse, there was nothing we could do to get ready for that. People would just *not* be prepared. The area's so full of new people; they've come in from the west and the north, and they don't know what it was like here in the fifties with a storm like Hazel.

"So Fran would have just been like a foretaste, and Fran was *horrible*. There was no power for a week, people were picking trees out of their houses—and that was the concern, the wind. It was still a Cat 4, and we were mobilizing for that—but meantime, from Monday evening it's started raining. Not heavy yet, not what was coming—but it's started, and any moisture from Dennis that had run off or evaporated was getting replenished. We weren't worried about imminent flooding, but we knew there'd be some. It's tough to call how bad flooding will be but we just thought, those places that always flood in heavy rains will flood now. We weren't worried about the wider basins—and then by Wednesday, we were thinking maybe by the time it gets here, it won't be that bad anyway."

He shook his head ruefully and said, "Right."

Because all the time as the storm approached, all through Tuesday and Wednesday, it went on raining and raining.

C hris Landsea looked at Floyd on the TV screen in Frank Marks's motel room. He said, "It's getting sheared big time. It's dying. It's going to be a mess."

Frank thought maybe, maybe not. There had been storms that moved so fast that maybe wind shear didn't hinder them; the Long Island hurricane of 1938 had raced up the coast at nearly sixty miles an hour, far faster than any forecast system could cope with at the time, and at landfall—mostly in the storm surge—it killed some 600 people. Even in 1987, Emily traveled so fast toward Bermuda, turning from a tropical storm into a hurricane on the way, that the island only got a couple of hours' warning.

The latest fix set Floyd 260 miles south of Myrtle Beach, with the worst winds falling to 125 miles an hour—which still made it a powerful Category 3, lifting and pushing a huge mass of seawater forward beneath it, raising tornado watches all along the coast of the Carolinas, and dropping torrential rains as far north as Pennsylvania.

So would it stay that strong, or was it beginning to die now? Would it get sheared apart? Or would the heat in the Gulf Stream boot it back up?

"We don't know," said Frank. "And that's why we're flying."

While the beaches were evacuating, he'd spent Monday evening putting shutters up on his house and helping two of his neighbors do the same. Then one of the P-3s had come into Miami to drop off Willoughby's crew, and

Marks had boarded about nine o'clock to take a cargo of AXBTs on to Tampa. He said there hadn't been much time to say good-bye to his wife.

The printer wired to his laptop chuntered and whined, turning out maps of coastal radar coverage off the net; sheets of the latest storm data spilled from the fax, spreading across the floor around his desk. The flight pattern they were working up had short legs in the core to study the cyclone's evolution, with longer legs in front and back of it to see how it was interacting with the ocean. They'd do passes along the beach as well, and put Ed Walsh's altimeter to work on the waves.

The room emptied as the rest of the team went to make ready to fly, or to rest up if they were working the night mission on 42. Frank eased up and said thoughtfully, "NPR asked me yesterday, Is this still fun? Good question. Doing this, getting out in the plane, executing a plan—yes, that's fun. It's all the logistical details that are wearing. Who's where, who isn't, who's getting where and how, multiple planes, multiple personalities . . . but to do this job, you've got to be willing to take lumps to permit growth.

"It's like being a teacher. You've got to know who you can push, and you've got to let people fix their mistakes. Mike Black's a great example, he's real quick on his feet. And Pete, he sees a storm, he's like a bloodhound getting a scent, he can't turn it off. But we do give each other a lot of grief about it. We kid hard; we can be cruel. Look at how well Chris took all the ribbing about the dead wave. He was pretty gracious about that."

Peter Dodge came in, looking pleased with himself; he'd been to Office Depot and rounded up a treasure trove of clipboards, pencils, smoke-colored plastic triangles, and maps of North Carolina. Mike Black followed him in to examine the booty. He grinned and asked, "Did they have any lead scientist project forms?"

The crew for 43 gathered at 13:00 at Tampa International, the three-strong HRD element—Marks, Black, and Landsea—toting a weighty supply of savory bagels. In the plush reception area of a firm called Raytheon Aircraft Services, they sat on settees and wicker-backed chairs with Gerry McKim, Phil Kenul, and navigator Dave Rathbun to run through the flight pattern. A local TV news crew hovered over their shoulders as they worked.

Outside, Lear jets and Cherokees dotted the tarmac. The wind was gusting at twenty, twenty-five miles an hour, tugging at flags, snapping at the palm trees; puffs of cloud scurried fast in arced bands overhead. We'd be taking off straight into the outer edge of Floyd's circulation—assuming we took off at all. AOC's engineers were still working on the data system; Phil Kenul reckoned they'd fix it and we'd fly, and one of the engineers would come along to troubleshoot.

Frank said, "We're going in at eight thousand feet. If we can't do that, we'll go to twelve."

Rathbun raised an eyebrow. "Eight thousand feet? Wow."

McKim said briskly, "We'll do eight thousand."

Kenul chipped in contentedly, "We'd *love* to do eight thousand."

"It's just," said Rathbun, "we haven't been under ten thousand all season. . . ."

The flight pattern was changing again, as Floyd continued to accelerate; 120-mile legs would likely turn into 150 miles, when you added in the motion of the storm as you flew them. They'd have to make a guesstimate of where the center would be when they got to it, then constantly update that mark, and file it with Air Traffic Control on the hoof as we took off. At least, Kenul said, grinning, "no one else but the air force is crazy enough to be out there. The only idiots out there will be us."

The eye of the hurricane was sixty miles across. On a TV on the wall, the Weather Channel reported a tornado warning now in effect for Bear Creek, South Carolina. To one side, Jim McFadden and Peter Dodge worked over preliminary plans for 42's flight later that night. Over in the foyer, a two-man CNN crew and a reporter from *Newsweek* stood around with a NOAA PR woman. "Hey, Jim," she shouted across the room, "they want pictures of the plane."

McFadden nodded OK. As they moved toward the glass doors to get out on the standing area, McKim looked up and barked at them, "Don't get on the plane. Don't *touch* the plane."

He'd been in Floyd twice already. So far, he said, "it's been a very smooth, well-behaved storm. The big, well-organized ones often are."

Dave Rathbun wasn't so sure it would be that way today. Floyd looked to be weakening—and whether intensifying or disintegrating, when a storm's changing gear it's often more turbulent than one that's rolling along in a steady state. If this unraveling structure was approaching landfall now, the wind field starting to shake with friction against the ground, it would more than likely be bumpy.

The year before, working at 5,000 feet, they'd flown Earl making landfall over Apalachicola; the coastline there has a stubby little promontory jutting south into the Gulf. Earl's center was southwest of the jut, so the winds were coming onshore from the southeast, on the right-hand side of the promontory. Flying east to west and trying to follow the shoreline, to jog down and up around the curve of it, at first on the eastern side of the leg they were fine; they were coming in through smooth winds off the sea.

On the western side of the promontory, however, where Earl's winds were turning around the top of the storm to go back offshore from the northeast, those winds had been rocking and grinding against the land below for twenty-five, maybe fifty miles. On top of that, sometimes you can't necessarily tell from the radar what's weather and what's terrain—so what you think is the ground might actually turn out to be cumulus stuffed with friction-bucked, thunder-packed updrafts.

Rathbun said, "We got our asses kicked. It was bouncing us up and down like a basketball. We tried it for ten minutes, then I had to call up to flight and tell them I couldn't see what was wind or ground, and we pulled out. So if Ed Walsh wants to run along the coast today, OK, we'll do our best, but he'll have to live with what he gets. You try and give these guys what you can, but there's a limit. Most times you break it off, but sometimes you just go a bit further—and then, unintentionally, you can put the airplane in jeopardy. 'Cause when you get to where you can't tell the difference between the weather and the land, it's time to go do something else."

We boarded 43 at 15:20. I was parked at the Cloud Physics Station, and briefed by Frank Marks on how to read and record the AXBT data. When he'd pulled up the right channels and screens he said, "It's easy. You listen. You press a button. You write."

"Yeah"—Mike Black grinned—"but you've got to watch the data scroll too. But you can do that. There's an HRD directive that you've *got* to do it."

"But you've got to multiply by 1.5," said Frank. "There's a fraction in there. . . ."

"And then," said Mike, plainly keen to burst out laughing, "you've got to run the algorithm. . . ."

My job was to take the temperature of the sea. This involved listening on the headset for each BT drop, then waiting a couple of minutes until the instrument hit the water. As soon it was down, temperature readings started popping up on the screen; the idea was to catch the peak reading, note it, time in seconds how long it lasted at or near that peak, multiply that number of seconds by 1.5, and then we'd know how deep the water stayed hot.

I fiddled edgily with assorted buttons and dials, and wondered about the likelihood of my being able to multiply any number whatsoever by 1.5 in the middle of a major hurricane. I felt light-headed with anticipation, stacked with adrenaline; it never once occurred to me that I might die doing this. I figured Gerry McKim hadn't flown 230 missions into hurricanes just to mess it up today.

As we made ready, Mike at the workstation behind me asked idly, "Where are we going today then?"

Frank told him, "MacDill."

"Hell"—Mike grinned—"nine hours is an awful long time to spend going five miles down the road."

Flight director Barry Damiano came down the aisle. He said, "Six penetrations today. You got any idea on this one?"

Mike shook his head. "It's such a hard one to call. A lot of rain, for sure. It'll be messy, probably not much of an eye—but it's going right up the Gulf Stream, so who knows?"

We started to taxi at 15:41. Around the plane came the clink-clunk sound of heavy metal buckles snapping closed on canvas harnesses. Mike leaned forward to offer me a pair of compasses. He said, "An abacus is also available."

Voices from cockpit and control tower crackled in the headset. "NOAA 43, ready for takeoff, three-six right."

"NOAA 43, cleared for takeoff."

I wondered if I should have eaten that second onion bagel with the jalapeno sauce.

McKim didn't pause at the head of the runway; as he turned the plane the engines roared, and we leapt smoothly forward. We were in the air at 15:48, my headset a buzz of many calm voices swapping headings and wind speeds.

"NOAA 43, Tampa departure, five hundred, climbing three thousand."

"NOAA 43, have a good day."

McKim flicked off the seat belt light four minutes later. "Everybody be real careful walking around. If you're up, hold on, and if you're down, stay down."

Tampa below us was bright and sunny, the sky flecked with hurrying clusters of white cloud. Ten minutes after takeoff McKim said, "OK, we're about thirty minutes out of this storm. Everybody make sure your gear is all secured and out of the way. We don't have much time before we get there."

We were at 5,000 feet, climbing into a brilliant blue sky. The ceiling above was decked with high, banded white plumes drawing closer together as we advanced, while below us a flat bed of fat, fluffy overcast was also thickening fast. We were in a truly strange place, a thin wedge of clear air between what was going into the storm at the base, and what had been shot up and out from the top of it. The broken shield above was Floyd's exhaust, an anvil of ice crystals slowly falling at about one meter per second; underneath lay puffy cumulus that wanted to rise but couldn't, suppressed by the dry, subsiding air dropping out and away from the hurricane. It was a sliver of turquoise clarity, with pale, thin bands of clear sky to either side narrowing and fading into the gray wall fast approaching ahead. It was like flying into a fissure in the sky, toward a vast cavern of darkness.

Half an hour after takeoff we vanished into cloud, and the plane started gently to twitch and bump. Behind me, Landsea and Black had Floyd's eye ahead on their radar screen, a ragged doughnut of flickering, jolting blue and orange.

Jacksonville ATC picked us up. "NOAA 43, maintain seven thousand."

"How far do your radars reach out at seven thousand?"

"A hundred, a hundred twenty miles."

"OK, you'll probably lose us on the east side of the storm."

Word came of a tornado warning area up by Wilmington. From the cock-pit: "I really don't think there's anything going on in there, but . . . take a look at our tracks, see if we're going there."

"There's an area they won't clear us into."

"You're kidding me."

"Hey, Phil. Does he know what we're doing out here?"

"Yes he does."

"Do we go in there no respect?"

"Do we go in there no regard?"

"I *know* nobody's in there today. There's a warning in there, nobody's playing in there today."

"You'd have to be *crazy* to go in there. You'd have to be an *idiot* to go in there. And that's right where we're going."

JAX ATC said it was OK by him if we went in there, but there was some bureaucrat up the line trying to block it. The cockpit dubbed him Giantkiller.

"Can we ignore him?"

"ATC says if we can't get hold of him, go in anyway."

Mike Black's first sonde found surface winds at sixty-five miles an hour. "Frank? First sonde looks good."

"Five minutes to sonde in the eyewall. Mike, are you doing doubles in the eyewall?"

The instruments thudded and hissed from their launch chutes. The first BT went away, and sent back no signal.

"Step frequency's saying ninety-two miles an hour at the surface."

"OK, we're thirty miles out, let's get the aircraft ready to penetrate. Clear up your space."

The plane was beginning to rock a shade harder.

"Data system locked up."

"I'm working on it."

"We got the outside of the eyewall coming up. Pretty quick."

"Don't worry about it. I'll get it working."

"Frank, we going to do an eyewall drop?"

"Mike, we won't be able to initialize it. . . . OK, there you go."

"Nice timing."

Terry Lynch, the electronics engineer, had fixed the system right on the cusp of the wall, squirreling through the software as the plane bucked softly, persistently in the heart of the storm. Rain streamed thick around the curve of my bubble window; BT data shimmered in white columns on the black ground of my screen. The sea was 28.1°C, 27.8, 28.7. I followed the colored line of the temperature curve on the other screen, tried multiplying 55 by one and a half, and became considerably confused.

"Air force is at thirty-six and closing."

"Yeah, remember they're dropping on us today."

Sudden daylight shone as we popped into the eye through blurred veils of blue cloud; abruptly, the step frequency readings on the surface wind speed fell to nine miles an hour. Floyd's eye was a huge space, vaster than Bret's had been and messier, with loosed clumps and strands of cloud strewn aimless and random at different levels within it—but still, curving all around the horizon, the eyewall loomed up toward blue swathes of gleaming sky, and between broken drifts of gray vapor the sea boiled and heaved beneath us. Ed Walsh called out that he had waves on his altimeter near fifty feet down there.

A few minutes of peace, a dropsonde idling down, finding tranquillity all the way—then, as suddenly as we'd entered it, we lurched out again into the northeast quadrant of the wall. The wind readings leapt and so did the plane, jolting up and sideways; I could see nothing through my window but dark water. I watched it race around the bubble enthralled, almost numb with a rapt absorption in the sheer scale of this storm.

The step frequency read ninety-five miles an hour at the surface; Floyd was huge, certainly, but it was also beginning mercifully to look as if he was weakening, falling apart, the wind field easing and broadening. Fifty miles out from the eye the cloud got gappy, breaking to show torn flecks of sea and sky. While the plane softly hummed and juddered, scientists and cockpit alike congratulated Barry Damiano on his targeting; he'd taken us dead center to the middle of the eye.

"Planning," said Damiano modestly, carrying on with his work. "Flight? When we hit the beach it's basically ten miles north to ten miles south of Charleston. I don't think we'll be in anybody's hairspace, but just to let you know."

"Ed, you there?"

"I'm here. I'm running."

We'd passed through the eye from southwest to northeast, continued to a point south of Cape Fear in the vanguard of the hurricane, then turned due west, aiming to hit land midway up the South Carolina shoreline. As we turned along each leg of the star pattern outlined across our maps, Marks and his colleagues were trying to gauge the strength of the storm at ground level, its relationship with the ocean, and with the wind shear now breaking it apart; the more you understood these things, the better you'd be able to call the likely direction and future behavior not just of this storm, but of the eight, ten, twelve, or fourteen that will follow it every year, ripping through this part of the world as surely and inexorably as the sun rises in the morning.

Meanwhile, if it was a relief to those in Floyd's path that the winds were now at least somewhat diminished from their worst, it was small relief only. Already, as differential windflows at high altitude blew the top of the storm far ahead of the lower core, the shape of it was changing from a perfect, spiraled circle to an elongated plume, and all along that plume the rain was falling without pause or mercy. Across east North Carolina, rivers like the Tar and the Neuse, filled to the brim by Dennis less than two weeks before, began breaching their banks. Over the wide, flat basins of the coastal plain, the floodwaters slowly, steadily spread far and ever deeper.

We were 117 miles from the eye, closing on Charleston through the front of the storm. In a pause between instrument drops Mike Black said mildly, "So, Floyd's basically a big Mixmaster at this point, yes? Cat 2."

"At *least* a 2," Chris Landsea cautioned, "but we don't know yet. We haven't been in every part of the storm."

In the back of the plane, Ed Walsh watched his altimeter scan the ocean ten times a second, picking out each individual wave. He was seeing crests thirty feet tall all the time, with forty-five feet not uncommon; beneath the eyewall, he found cliffs of water sixty feet high. In a big hurricane over open seas, he explained pensively, where the curvature of the wind is less acute, it's got more fetch to it; blowing longer and straighter it can kick up bigger waves, even if the storm's actual wind speed isn't so high.

"The way I look at this job," said Walsh, "it's like going to the zoo. There's a wild beast down there, and we're on the other side of the moat. I sure wouldn't like to be down there in a ship."

Early that morning the 150-foot ocean tug *Gulf Majesty*, towing a 700-foot barge out of Jacksonville, had been swallowed up and lost in this turmoil, pitching eight men out into the towering seas. At eight o'clock they'd told the coast guard their tug was foundering; five of them made it on board a fifteen-man life raft, then a huge blast of wind and water ripped it away off the deck. The rope holding the raft to the drowning tug snapped; the three men left behind had no chance of reaching it.

They jumped into the water, with nothing to hang on to between them but a broken broomstick. One of them had an emergency radio beacon—but they were 350 miles from port, out of range of any land-based rescue helicopter.

By good fortune, the aircraft carrier USS *Kennedy* had also left Jacksonville—trying, ironically, to keep out of Floyd's path—so it was now only 150 miles away. Alerted by the coast guard, the carrier turned toward the lost tug and launched two helicopters.

Following the homing beacon at five hundred feet, one of these helicopters found the three men in the water when they let off a smoke canister. The chopper dropped to sixty feet and Shad Hernandez, twenty-three years old, started lowering himself down on the rescue cable. He reported later that the tops of the waves were at eye level almost as soon as he started descending.

Incredibly, Hernandez had all three men back in the helicopter inside fifteen minutes; they'd been in the ocean three hours. Meanwhile, the other five men in the life raft were being thrown about like rag dolls on a roller coaster. Ship's engineer Mark Davis told the *Miami Herald* that the waves were so powerful, "they'd actually fold the raft in half. We'd meet in the center and all the water would pile up on us. Then everybody would start bailing."

About an hour after Hernandez plucked the first three men from the sea, the *Kennedy's* second helicopter rescued the other five men from the life raft. Mark Davis said simply, "These navy guys are awesome."

Two minutes to drop."
    "This is not a combo."

"I know," Damiano told Frank, "I got your little diagram here."

"I'm sorry, Barry. Not trying to second-guess you."

"I'd prefer little orange circles next time, though."

"Sorry. All I had was yellow. Ah . . . looks like we got a big rainband here."

"Everybody just use caution," McKim advised, "while we go through these little things here."

We were twenty-three miles from the beach. "Hopefully," said Frank, "the turn's before all that red stuff."

On the radar, angry blooms of convection boiled skyward in the rainband. The plane lurched, bucked, heaved. "Hey," called McKim, "we're in a storm environment, folks, you know what that means. Hang on."

"We got magenta on the nose," warned Frank, "you know what *that* means."

"Rolling air," said McKim. "Tell me, if this doesn't go landfall, are we flying tomorrow?"

"No."

We'd been in the storm ninety minutes; we were closing on Isle of Palms just outside Charleston.

"Ed, we on the beach?"

"I can't see, we got *lots* of rain here. . . . OK, I got it. We're right on the beach. You got a visual up there?"

McKim told him, "Sure. I got a bedsheet over my head. Like a big gray flannel bedsheet."

We ran along the coast in a streaming, whirling morass of vapor and rain, Ed calling little jogs left to keep us from drifting inland. From a dropsonde, Mike and Chris got surface winds at seventy-five miles an hour just offshore—Category 1 hurricane force winds, when we were well over a hundred miles from the center of the storm.

Damiano cut in, "That's twenty miles, OK, left to one-three-five."

We turned back south of east for a second run at the eye. Through my window, the props on the port wing were blurred discs carving through a semiradiant liquid murk; water hurtled past them over the wing. It was, as a matter of fact, an impressive visualization of the avionic principle of lift.

"Flight, I can't tell from the belly what's up ahead. How's it look?"

No answer came back. We were seventy-six miles from the eye.

"Er, Barry . . . are you looking at the radar? I'm on channel 13, there's a mess of blue inside those green swirls. I don't like it."

Frank said calmly, "I'm going to radar. Barry, can you make minimal adjustments on this run?"

"I'll try."

"Barry, just want to confirm, you want one-three-five on this track?"

"BT away."

I got 26.5°C, then a weird-looking graph with big spikes in it. It was supposed to run along flattish at the top of the temperature range in the surface water while you timed it for depth, then to drop away more or less sharply as the water started cooling eighty or ninety meters down. It wasn't supposed to look like the Alps. I wondered if it was the CNN guys in the back using the airphone again without asking first. Three times they did that; three times the signal from an instrument drop got screwed.

"OK everybody, seat belts on."

It was sixty-two miles to the eye; the plane was starting to buck and jolt livelier again. The gray slop of air-water thickened outside. Forty-four miles . . .

"Want a BT here, just a BT only."

Thirty-eight miles . . .

"Stand by to drop, three, two, one, launch."

28.4°C, twenty seconds, that made thirty meters deep. Not deep at all— but it could be in here that the storm had been over this water long enough to churn it and cool it, suck out all the heat, set the colder, deeper water upwelling.

"BT-sonde combo coming up next, BT and sonde in the eyewall."

My screen snapped blank on Channel 12, then flickered back up.

"Hey, Frank. This BT's stuck on 27. You think it's on the bottom?"

"Could be. We're on that Charleston Bump, you know, that shallow water?"

Ed Walsh confirmed, "Looks like a real crossfield wind pattern here."

The cockpit asked, "What's that?"

"Looks like a patchwork quilt. One wave'll come at right angles to another."

"That was for Phil. He's never been on a boat before."

"We in the eyewall yet?"

"Just coming."

"We got a north-south asymmetry in the eyewall, guys. . . ."

Pulled and stretched by the wind shear, the eye was growing egg-shaped. We burst out into the light, the ocean glowing a deep blue-green beneath, raked and hazed with traceries of white spray. Drifts of infilling cloud roamed the empty clear space. A dropsonde falling behind us in the eyewall found surface winds at ninety-nine miles an hour, with the step frequency calling ninety-eight.

Mike Black remembered that he'd come aboard with 296 eyewall penetrations; two more now made 298, with another two to go to make his third century. Scientists and flight crew totted up reasons for drinking beer when we got back on the ground. NOAA 43 drove once more out of blue-white light into the eyewall, on the southeast side of the hurricane. Dropsondes called both flight level and surface winds at 102 miles an hour.

Floyd looked as if he was down to Category 2—but he'd been the third major storm of the season already (meaning Category 3 or worse) and even as we were flying, 500 miles east of the northern Leewards Hurricane Gert was now also a large and ferocious Category 4, with winds in excess of 140 miles an hour.

In the seat behind me, Chris Landsea had good cause therefore to feel both satisfied and disturbed that the long-term forecast for 1999 was working out all too well.

L andsea did his post-grad studies at Colorado State, under the tutelage of Professor Bill Gray. Now in his seventies, Gray had made crucial advances some fifteen years before in understanding what signals in the larger climatic pattern tend to be associated with increases (or decreases) in hurricane activity.

Many of these signals remain poorly understood; when I told Landsea that I was confused about the Quasi-Biennial Oscillation, he laughed and assured me that everyone else was too. It seems, however, that every twelve to eighteen months there's a shift in the direction of the winds in the stratosphere, ten miles and higher above the surface of the Atlantic. They switch from easterly to westerly and back again—and when they're flowing from the west (probably because this diminishes the overall levels of wind shear across the ocean, giving storms a more capacious loft to build in) you get 50 to 75 percent more major hurricanes.

Better known is the link between hurricanes and West African rainfall. In the desert and semidesert regions of the Sahel, rainfall patterns appear to follow a multidecadal pattern; in meteorological parlance, there's "a large year-to-year persistence." In other words, if it's wet this year, next year will more likely than not be wet as well, just as dry years tend to be followed by more dry years in their turn.

As the news footage made only too plain, the Sahel was afflicted by a string of droughts in the seventies, eighties, and early nineties. As the famine appeals swung into action, however, there was a significant downturn in major hurricane activity on the other side of the Atlantic. In the forties, fifties, and sixties, by contrast, wetter times in West Africa had coincided with more cyclones spinning up across the water.

At first, the scientists thought there might be some causal link—that more African rain somehow kick-started more storms—but it's now believed that both are symptoms of another, larger feature. It's thought instead that both cycles (of African rain and of major hurricane activity) are caused by a sequence of rises and falls in the surface temperature of the Atlantic Ocean. If the Atlantic is warmer—and it only takes an average increase between one-half and one and one-half degrees centigrade massively to jack up the energy levels available in such a large body of water—then the Sahel gets rain and the hurricanes get large. Thus in 1999, the Niger River was in catastrophic flood, even as the warmer seas had spawned Bret, Cindy, Floyd, and Gert so far.

Another factor is El Niño, the Christ Child. More properly known as ENSO, the El Niño Southern Oscillation, this is a vast, tongue-shaped upwelling of warm water in the equatorial east Pacific. It has many well-documented and unwelcome effects, from choking forest fires in Southeast Asia to the decimation of the Peruvian fishing industry; the 1997 El Niño event is calculated by NOAA to have caused 22,000 deaths worldwide, and cost $33 billion in flood and drought-related damage.

One of El Niño's happier outcomes, however, is a stronger flow of westerly low-level winds from the heated Pacific across Central America into the

Caribbean. This raises the wind shear in the Atlantic cyclone basin and chokes off a healthy proportion of that region's hurricane activity.

In 1999, there was no El Niño. The opposite, colder system, La Niña, was in place instead—weakening, probably—but if Pacific conditions are either neutral or in La Niña mode, there'll be less wind shear in the Atlantic, and more storms.

Using these and other indicators, and working on a mix of statistical analysis and inspired intuition, in 1984 Bill Gray started producing long-term forecasts for each hurricane season; his forecast for 1999 was thus his sixteenth such effort. Given the fallibility inherent in our efforts to say what the weather will be doing tomorrow, never mind during the next twelve months, Gray's a brave man to stick his neck out and forecast how many hurricanes the coming season will produce. Over the previous fifteen years, however, eight of his forecasts had been statistically accurate, four had been so-so, and only three had been busts—a record any football manager would happily settle for.

The average Atlantic season generates nine or ten named tropical storms, of which six become hurricanes, with two of those growing to Category 3 or worse. In December 1998, however, Gray and his team (of which Landsea continues a key member) announced a forecast warning that 1999 would see fourteen named systems, nine of which would be hurricanes, with no less than four of them becoming major, intense tropical cyclones ranked at Category 3 or worse.

As Gray then updated his forecast in April, June, and at the beginning of August, on each occasion these ominous numbers stayed the same—the first time this had happened in sixteen years. So would the forecast verify? Did it, in the language of the trade, have "skill"?

On September 15, 1999, only halfway through the peak period of the season, we'd got to the "G" storm already, the seventh named system of the year—and four of those seven had been monsters, with two of the monsters making a U.S. landfall. So now, as we left Floyd's eye for the second time, and that storm bore down on the North Carolina coast, Barry Damiano asked Chris Landsea thoughtfully, "How many Cat 3s did we expect this year?"

"Four. So we got 'em."

"But we're still way off the total, yes?"

"Oh yes. I'm afraid you can expect more."

What was even scarier, he continued, was that all four big storms in '99 so far—Bret, Cindy, now Floyd and Gert—had developed into Category 4 storms. There had been four Category 4 hurricanes in the course of a single season in only four previous years on the record—in 1906, 1926, 1961, and 1964—so clearly the Atlantic basin just now was in an impressively alarming mood.

Worse yet, Stan Goldenberg at HRD had done work on the climatology strongly suggesting that in years when August and September were busy, more often than not the Caribbean would then spawn another huge storm in October—a storm like Mitch. And from an American point of view the trouble with that was, most storms like Mitch that start up in the southwest Caribbean don't go to Honduras. They go to the Gulf coast of the United States.

"You folks in Tampa," said Landsea, "you better look out next month."

"Global climate change," came a voice from the cockpit. "We're doomed, man."

It was 18:53; the evening began to grow dark. We were 118 miles southeast of the eye, turning to run north along the storm's eastern edge.

Floyd was falling apart. We had time for a break, and got coffee in the galley; Frank Marks drew hodographs to show how wind shear works, vector images of the wind blowing in different directions at different altitudes.

The movement of a hurricane is determined by the sum total of all the fluid pressures it feels from the atmosphere around it; if the wind shear is low, all the arrows in the hodograph point pretty much the same way. That's the direction the hurricane will move in, and as it moves, unhindered by conflicting windflows, the core can grow and get well organized; there's no tilt, and you get a bad storm with a clear eye.

In higher shear like that which Floyd was now feeling, the arrows in the hodograph spread out instead into a fan; the wind rolls around the compass as you rise up through the atmosphere. When this shear starts pushing at the storm, the vortex in the middle starts leaning—so Floyd was being stretched out, with the top dragging the bottom along in its wake. Also, more of the exhaust air was now blowing away ahead of the storm than behind it; it was like a man pushed in the back of the shoulders when he's running and losing his balance, falling flat out forward.

If this meant that the wind damage would be less than first feared, however, it also meant that the rain event in front of the storm was already well under way.

"Because it *was* a Cat 4," Frank said grimly, "the storm surge will still be huge. Plus you've got a lot of hills sloping up behind a low-lying coast. The hills bring down the rain—and between the rain and the tide there's going to be major, major flooding."

Floyd was so large, indeed, that while the back end of the wind was still gusting in Tampa, it was already raining in New York.

The scientists batted vectors and step frequencies about on their headsets. Phil Kenul said contentedly, "It's at this kind of moment that I'm glad I drank a lot of beer in college."

"I'm still at the point," said Dave Rathbun, "where I look out the window and say, 'Hey, that cloud looks like a dog.' "

We were heading due west, from the eastern side of the storm into the eye. Mike Black called surface winds at ninety-two miles an hour and climbing.

"You might want to hold on here, I see some cells coming."

"Is that the eyewall?"

"We're *in* the eyewall."

"I got a hundred miles an hour at the surface."

"I got a hundred thirty up here."

The plane was beginning to rock and slide again. It wasn't extreme; there were just periods when it went on and on and on. Too high on the thrill of the ride, and too busy besides, I didn't really notice it a lot of the time—but as the hours go by, you start to realize that the pummeling is seeping in through every inch of your body.

For all that, as we approached the eye for the third time, the voices in my headset stayed calm as ever.

"I think we'll see a hundred fifteen in this east side of the eye."

"We got a cell just north of us."

"Looks like it could still be Cat 3."

"On this track, the highest winds will be at Cape Lookout."

"When?"

"Five hours, maybe six."

The third penetration came with the late embers of dusk, and it was astoundingly lovely. The eye was sixty, maybe seventy miles across, a huge space of pastel and darkening blues, with a haze-fogged crescent moon in the azure sky above, soft-focused, tinged a creamy yellow. That this thing could be so spectacularly beautiful, and yet do such fearful harm . . .

"OK, everybody, strap in."

A great mass of convection was flaring in the northwest side of the wall, trailing orange streamers on the radar right through where we were heading.

"Gerry, you want to go in there?"

"Are we going into turbulence mode?"

"I think we'll get vertical incidents here."

They tried to figure out what it was—rain, shear, thunderstorm?

"Two minutes to the drop."

The plane shuddered in the grip of the wall.

"Here we go, folks, everybody strapped in and *hold on.*"

The storm wrenched us from side to side, metal rattling and clanging in the galley and the instrument racks.

"So," said Mike, "finally this thing's got a little kick to it."

"Stand by to drop, three, two, one, launch."

"They're out."

28.3, 28.5, 40 seconds, multiply by 1.5 . . .

"Well, that turbulence sensor's accurate. That was a combo, right, Barry?"

"Yes it was."

"When we get into some clear air here, I need somebody to check out my displays. I'm just blind here."

Floods of water poured past the window; outside all was black, jet black, nothing visible barring one of the plane's lights flicking faint sprays of red shimmer on the wing. JAX got in touch to help us out, keeping other ATCs off our back—people wondering who we were, and what we thought we were doing out in this.

"Thanks very much, sir," said McKim, "I appreciate it. We're busy out here."

"I'm trying to get a reading on the step frequency. . . ."

"There's a little peak here, Mike. . . ."

"I got it."

"Sonde away."

"That wasn't a bad leg through the eye back there, Barry."

"Yeah, I know. Dave owes me a soda."

"The surface winds went down to just about zero back there."

"Bull's-eye."

Getting out through the wall the plane jolted and stumbled from side to side for ten minutes, then McKim snapped off the seat belt sign. I went back to the galley for a few more chews on my unfeasibly large Holey Cow Einstein's Beef & Cheddar Cheese with Salad Onion & Garlic Bagel, leaned to get a Coke from the cooler—and realized that one of the engineers was fast asleep on a fold-down hammock above the table. He had a rope and canvas sling to hold him in, the only thing sticking out from his blanket were his work boots, and at 8,000 feet in the middle of Hurricane Floyd he was sleeping like a baby.

One hundred forty-nine miles from the eye, we made turning point 10 on the Georgia coastline at 20:08, and started heading southwest through the back of the storm to the farthest point south in the pattern.

"Belly radar?"

"Nothing but sea clutter."

It looked as if much of the rear quadrant had broken apart in the shear. Phil Kenul went past my workstation, grinning. "They got you doing science?"

I had to admit that I'd missed a few things. He smiled and said, "Just like us up there, then."

We were able to relax a little while; at the end of the leg, we turned north for another run at the eye. Someone announced that this wasn't a radar run, we were going to hunt for the center.

"Barry's got to find a wind speed of zero, right?"

"Hey, he did it last time. He can't improve on that."

"He can *match* it."

"He can get zero all the way down," said Mike. "Well, we can give him 0.1 somewhere."

The eye was elliptical now, dark and crumbling. There were a few bumps through the south side of the wall, a sonde took wind readings on the surface at 80 miles an hour, the red light outside my window flashed eerie off the spinning flare of the props in the sheeting rain, and all the while Damiano quietly called headings into the heart, three-fifty, three-thirty . . .

"Dead center."

Stars wheeled above us in the blackness.

"Looks like it's tracking direct for Wilmington. Landfall by three in the morning at the latest."

"We should have known. That poor place is just a 'cane magnet."

We hit the north eyewall and were thrown up, down, sideways in a long series of giant, heaving lurches.

"Barry, you see that?"

"Yeah. The magenta's northwest of us."

Everything was shaking, shuddering, like a giant hand kept pressing down on the nose of the plane, dragging us hard by spine and jaw along the ridges of a washboard. Eventually it eased and Mike said, "Well, that cell should rotate around to the northeast just in time to meet up with us again the next time we go in there." He sounded almost gratified that his 300th visit into the eye of a hurricane had turned out so lively.

Word came of a new air force plane coming in above us. The cockpit talked to JAX ATC; they asked who was onboard up here. McKim told him, then said, "We've all stayed in Jacksonville on past missions. How are you doing there?"

"Half the pier's disappeared. The beach took a pounding, the St. Augustine marina got beat up pretty bad. But overall we got off lightly. . . ."

We headed north out of the eye for another run down the coast. There was a period of general mirth at someone's image of Weather Channel reporter Jim Cantori standing on the beach there, what remains of his hair flapping in the wind, and a dropsonde whistling to earth right beside him.

"Catch that, Jim."

"Ed, you on headset?"

Silence.

"Someone tell Ed to get on headset."

Many voices shouted in unison, *"Ed! Get on headset!"*

"Hey, cool," mused Mike. "Stereo."

Ed Walsh came on from the back, and apologized. "Just retrieved my headset from the *Newsweek* guy."

We were ten miles from the beach, juddering and lurching as we banked to line up for the run southwest along the shore. It was 21:35. Someone asked Ed where he was based anyway, and he told them, "Boulder. I went there for a year's sabbatical. Seventeen years ago. I'm probably the subject of personnel seminars."

"I guess we're over the beach, right?"

It was getting rocky again; we were going sideways, abeam at this point of what ought, at least in theory, to be the worst winds in the northeast quadrant.

"This is what it was like in Fran. All night."

"This is why we don't like to go over land, right?"

"Talk, Ed."

"I'm still over water."

The headset hissed and crackled, the plane slipped and jumped. . . .

"I just got wiped out by rain. Are we still over water?"

"Step frequency says we are."

"Ed, how's your system?"

"Looks like we're still over water."

"Just barely."

We slithered and jerked on the wind. Frank called out, "We should break out of this band shortly."

"I've got rain at the moment. Step frequency?"

"Looks like we're right by the beach."

The cockpit told JAX we'd be running southwest for ninety miles, "and thanks for your help. We appreciate it."

"Don't worry about it. Hey, you guys are doing all the work. I'm just sitting here keeping out of the rain."

Ed pleaded, "How long to the end of the rainband?"

"What you seeing down there?"

"Nothing. Just rain."

"Should lighten up in fifteen miles or so."

"Hey, Mike," said Frank, "I just remembered: three hundred. Let me be the first to congratulate you."

"I'd get up and shake the man's hand, but I'd probably get thrown halfway back to the galley if I did."

"Track two-oh-five."

"Ed, what you got?"

"Still rain. It's wiping me out."

Mike told him, "It's the one thing we can't do, Ed. We can't control the weather."

"But a rainband," said Walsh, part frustrated, part resigned, "lying right along the coast . . ."

"Well, you'll get that with hurricanes sometimes. Rain." Mike paused, then he said, "OK. This one is a wet one."

The plane shifted five degrees left, ten right, trying to shadow the coast. Dave Rathbun chanted minute details of the geography below us, but it was fiendishly difficult; the shore was a ragged jumble of inlets and islands. McKim called out to double-check that everybody was strapped in as the rainband got worse, ten more minutes of shake and shudder notably worse than anything Bret had ever offered, a persistent thumping and banging, the wind kicking and beating at the plane until all the noise of metal rattling seemed internalized in your ears, and you felt the turbulence gnawing inward at your bones.

"Forty-three more miles."

"I've got good signal level . . . yes. I can see the waves."

"It should get better here, Ed."

"Hey, Frank. Could we go to point ten instead of fourteen, give Ed a few more miles?"

"No. The way the storm's moving, we'd be too far southwest of it."

"We got some bays coming up."

"We could drop a sonde here, the wind's coming offshore."

"We're half a mile inland. We'll come offshore at Folly Beach."

"I'll correct a little more left."

"Kiowa Island juts out here, you'll still be over land."

"Here comes the water. It's good . . . whoah, no. We're back over land."

"That's not land I see on the nose radar."

"What you got, Ed?"

"Water."

"Barry, how's that belly radar looking?"

"OK, Dave."

"Frank, would you concur?"

"There's nothing there. Just a couple of rain showers. I think it's time we turned back to the eye."

E d, for the majority of that run we were at most half a mile off, a mile, not more."

"OK, but a lot of the time I couldn't see much."

Trying to read how the storm surge worked against the beach, but badly thrown by the rainband, Ed's data probably wasn't too hot. He didn't complain; he said it was a learning exercise, and he thanked all concerned for their efforts. We had a few minutes between coast and eyewall where we could get up and stretch a bit; in the break, Walsh and the HRD men mulled over how they might do these coastal runs better.

Out of their discussion came the idea of trying to sawtooth back and forth across the shore. You wouldn't get a steady run, but unless the coast was a dead straight line (and what coast is?) you never would anyway. Whereas if you crisscrossed left and right, the altimeter should at least get a series of swipes, like a sequence of stop-frame images.

At 22:08, six hours and twenty minutes after takeoff out of Tampa, they started modifying the flight pattern to give Walsh another shot at a coastal run. As they hastily redesigned, Frank Marks judged the flight was going well. Most of the sondes and BTs had worked, the data system hadn't collapsed, they'd sent wind speeds in the front of the storm to NHC in real time, and tracking down the coast (if somewhat uncomfortable) was good for all of them, not just for Walsh.

"We got the offshore winds," Frank said, "and we've mapped the whole storm. So now we're rolling our own. It's an impromptu landfall." He grinned and said, "We'll start 42's mission for them."

Mike chipped in, "We couldn't go a whole mission and not change the flight plan. We'd never do that."

Floyd was moving fast just a shade east of north, stumbling clumsy and ragged along a line still bearing straight down on Wilmington at nineteen miles an hour; the eye would likely be there about two in the morning. Mike Black shook his head and said sadly, "Wrightsville Beach to Morehead City—a storm surge like this, they're going to take an absolute beating."

Track oh-sixty."

"How far to the eyewall?"

"Twenty miles."

The new air force plane was coming in on top of us; Damiano pulled us out of their way so they could drop sondes for NHC.

"Track oh-forty. They got responsibilities."

"Good call, Barry."

Scallop-shaped discs of convection built in the north side of the wall, flaming up on the radar.

"We'll be hitting some updrafts here, guys."

"OK, folks, time to rock and roll again. Let's see what happens this time."

We crossed through the tail end of a gaggle of thunderstorms. In the red flashing light outside, the rain streaming across the wing and the engines looked like a ghost river, slick and shining, laden with bursts of racing mist.

Despite rejigging the track in rough air to make way for the air force plane 2,000 feet above us, Damiano still took us exactly to the center once more. We turned and beat out of the eye through a sprawl of yellow-red mess on the belly radar, driving northwest now for Morehead City, aiming to get Ed Walsh a second long run down the beach.

This time McKim and Kenul shaded the plane back and forth across the coast, nudging left, banking a hint right. As we slipped and swung one way then the other Ed called out, "Oh, I see it, I see it, that's good. It's right in the middle of the swath. Maybe just a hair left."

Mike asked, "Can we drop sondes here?"

Frank told him, "No. We'll let Peter Dodge and Sam Houston do that now. Let's let Ed keep on practicing."

At 23:30 we went by Wilmington, evacuated and now flooding beneath us. Barry Damiano shook his head and said, "You feel for those people, you really do. Often we'll be called in after a hurricane to do a damage survey, and we'll fly along the beach at two hundred feet to see what it's done. So we know what they're going through. We know what they lose."

Our day was nearly done; 42 had taken off already to fly the landfall and was now 360 miles southwest of us, coming out to take over where we left off. We turned away from the beach, and started south for the sixth and final pass through the eye. McKim put on the seat belt sign; we headed through a curled spiral of rain toward the wall.

McKim asked, "Are we going straight through to the south side?"

"No," Frank told him, "there's nothing there."

"As soon as I get a fix on the center," said Damiano, "it's southwest and home."

We jolted into the middle of a fierce red blob on the radar. In the soaking midnight blackness it was unsettling not being able to see any hint of what was throwing you about out there but these bilious, shimmering signatures on the radar screen. The plane bucked up and down; there was a weird sensation of abrupt braking, leaving your stomach parted from the rest of your body a yard in front of you. Instruments fell away into the eyewall. . . .

"*Nice* last pass."

"I got the rattling eyeballs on this one."

My last BT had been giving 25.8°C or thereabouts for 120 seconds now. The hot water here could not possibly be 600 feet deep. Er, Frank . . .

"Write it down," said Mike. "It doesn't make sense."

Chris suggested, "Maybe it's floating."

"Or"—Frank laughed—"maybe the mixed layer depth is infinity."

"Go to one-seventy."

"Frank, Chris—I think that's all we need for drops?"

"I agree. Let's just take a look at the south side to make sure."

"Go to one-eighty."

"The sondes in the north wall just now got ninety-two miles an hour. But we actually got some of our strongest winds earlier on down the south side. What d'you think? One more for the record?"

The question hung in the air—as did the plane, easing through the peace of the eye. The spraying rains ceased, the blackness calmed, and we drew breath to hunt the empty center one last time.

"Nice going in the dark, Barry."

"OK, mark it there. No, hold on. . . ."

"Look at that. Zero knots. There's zero. Mark it."

Still Mike Black was hungry for one last set of numbers, a dog with a bone he couldn't bear to let go. He asked again, "Have we got a sonde ready?"

"I think we'll hold off, Mike. Let 42 do something."

"Dave, give me that center please."

The last mark on Floyd by 43 placed the hurricane sixty miles due east of Charleston.

"Jacksonville, this is NOAA 43, we're finished with our work here. We'll have a flight request. . . ."

Our guardian offered us a direct path to MacDill. McKim answered, "We'd *love* direct to MacDill. Thanks."

He climbed to 14,000 feet to get out and away fast and light. As we rose he said, "Hey, Dave. Nice job on that beach stuff. I don't know how you do that."

"Yeah," said Ed, "thanks. It worked out real well."

McKim turned off the seat belt sign. "Good job by everybody tonight. It was a fun flight."

Normally Frank Marks whiles away any idle time on a research mission doing origami. In Floyd there hadn't been any idle time, and no deftly folded little birds or animals came into being during nine hours and twenty minutes in the air—because they'd mapped this hurricane in more ways, and more thoroughly, than any storm they'd ever studied.

After the five days they'd flown in it already, this mission and 42 following on behind it gave them sixteen hours' continuous observation of Floyd approaching and making landfall. They had Doppler coverage from the plane meshed with ground-based radar to give composite 3-D maps of the wind field. From the dropsondes they had the vertical structure of the winds, and from the BTs they had the heat content of the ocean below. They had the surface wind field all along the coast from north of Wilmington to south of Savannah; material that would help determine reliable ground truth and assist those who'd engage in the grim business of the damage surveys.

The suite of instruments harvesting this data had been tested in Bret, it had worked for the first time in Dennis, and now they'd deployed it in the biggest storm to threaten the Atlantic seaboard of the United States since Hugo in 1989. Ten years earlier to the day, far out over the Atlantic, Frank Marks, Gerry McKim, and the rest of their crew had nearly died in that storm. This time, they'd achieved rather more—and it had all gone back to NHC in real time.

Work like this (and the work of many other scientists and engineers on satellites, on climatology, on computer modeling) has resulted in much improved forecasts for tropical storms. NHC's work on Floyd showed how accurately a storm's track can now be called—at least when the devil's playing a tune that the specialists recognize.

In consequence, many American lives have been saved. It used to be that most hurricane victims in the United States drowned in the storm surge on the coast, as 9,000 did in Galveston a century ago, and though a major disaster of that type remains a distinctly possible event (it only takes one busted forecast, one botched evacuation), the merciful fact is that it hasn't happened for several decades. The last three-figure death toll on the beach in an American landfall came with Camille in 1969—and even in that storm more people died from freshwater flooding inland than were lost on the Mississippi shore.

Indeed, freshwater flooding is now the gravest threat routinely posed by hurricanes to an otherwise well-protected, well-warned society. This has been statistically proven by Ed Rappaport at NHC, and it was tragically borne out by Floyd. Rappaport calculates that in the three decades since Camille, 589 Americans have been killed by tropical cyclones; of these, 347 (59 percent) were drowned in freshwater.

Overall death tolls vary from one source to another, depending on whether people count all deaths (including post-landfall chain-saw accidents, heart attacks, house fires, electrocutions, and car wrecks) or just those caused directly by flooding and wind impacts. With that proviso, Rappaport's NHC figures give an average American mortality since 1969 of just under twenty people a year—so the loss of seventy-five Americans in 1999 makes that hurricane season four times worse than the recent mean. Of those seventy-five, moreover, fifty-six were drowned in freshwater; all but two of them were killed by Floyd, the great majority in North Carolina.

That's because, of the three principal elements in a hurricane forecast—track, intensity, and rainfall—the flooding caused by the latter remains impossibly difficult to predict, and desperately difficult to avoid once it's happening in your street. You can say that it's going to rain a lot—but you can no more say precisely how much or where than you can win the lottery every time you buy a ticket. The rule of thumb used by the forecasters indicates just how crude a game this is; they simply divide 100 by the speed of the storm's motion in miles per hour, and then guesstimate that that's how many inches of rain you're going to get.

By that measure, North Carolina should have gotten five to six inches. Instead, what Wilmington got was over nineteen inches—during one twenty-four-hour period over a foot of water fell upon that city, and numbers like that were repeated all over the state and beyond.

An average tropical cyclone drops about 2,300 cubic meters of rain every second. To get that volume of water in perspective, consider the St. Lawrence River, the mighty waterway draining into the North Atlantic from the Great Lakes past Quebec. That river's average discharge of freshwater into salt is 6,900 cubic meters per second—so just a regular, midsized hurricane can launch a flow of water from the heavens equivalent to that of the St. Lawrence River *every three seconds*.

Like, Mitch, however, Floyd was no ordinary hurricane; Floyd was way bigger than that. From its inception as a tropical depression 980 miles east of the Leewards eight days before landfall, Floyd had sucked moisture from the Atlantic like an enormous sponge. Now, strung out into a long ellipse as the wind shear dragged it apart, it spent three long days and nights spilling its way across North Carolina, and onward from there through New

England. Floyd may have given Florida a last-minute reprieve, but as the *Miami Herald* aptly observed on Thursday morning after this hurricane had finally made landfall, "The time for mercy was over."

Floyd accelerated to thirty-five miles an hour, breaking up but still thrusting a huge fan of rain out ahead of the disintegrating eye. On Thursday evening, the remnant center passed close by Atlantic City; by Friday morning the storm was over Maine, heading out past the Canadian Maritimes to die in the North Atlantic. Otherwise, said one of the Weather Channel's presenters, somewhat ill-advisedly, Friday was going to be "a very pretty day . . . a good day to clean up after Hurricane Floyd."

The rain had begun to ease in eastern North Carolina through Thursday afternoon. In Raleigh, said Ryan Boyles, where everybody had been so nervous during the days before landfall, "people went back to work the next day saying, 'What a wimpy storm.' And then the pictures started coming in."

Across the northeastern United States on that pretty Friday, water was massing in lakes, gathering in swollen tributaries in the hills, spilling down inexorably into widening rivers, breaking out across towns and farmland in a creeping, unstoppable disaster. Lake Placid in New York was evacuated when a dam failed; half the little town of Bound Brook, New Jersey, disappeared under water, swamped by a river called the Raritan, which is normally no more than an unremarkable stream. Fires broke out downtown and couldn't be extinguished as firemen struggled to reach them in small boats.

From Virginia to Connecticut, nearly a million people had no power; many were expected to stay that way for days. Six hundred thousand more had no power in the eastern and coastal counties of North Carolina, where eighty-eight roads were already under water, including long stretches of two interstates. Much of Interstate 95 through that portion of the state was impassable; all the people who'd evacuated the flat terrain reaching seventy-five miles from the highway to the sea were told not to try going home, because there wasn't much chance that they'd make it.

Water moccasins swam in inundated streets. As the Tar slowly rose through Tarboro and Princeville and Greenville, 1,500 people were stranded on the roofs of their houses, in trees or on the flat tops of shopping malls. Thirty-five helicopter crews toiled to pluck them to safety one by one, while others were rescued in boats and on jet skis—but as surely as the water climbed so did the death toll, and the water would keep on rising for days.

By Monday, along a three-mile stretch of the Tar in Greenville, only the roofs of two-story buildings still showed above the flood. Grocery stores ran out of food; there was no clean drinking water. Still spreading, the inland tide was streaked with fuel from ruptured gas tanks, with human waste from submerged sewage treatment plants, and with millions of gallons of hog waste bursting out from breached holding lagoons on the state's huge, industrial-scale farms. Amid the filth, said one volunteer, "I can't tell you how many dead we have. They're still finding bodies floating."

Some of the bodies were the newly dead; others were human remains sprung by the water from low-lying cemeteries. Unknown thousands of animals were dead too; the carcasses of pigs, chickens, and turkeys drifted bloated though the drowning countryside. Great tracts of the eastern third of the state—across an area of some 18,000 square miles, an area home to over two million people—were reduced to insanitary swamp. On satellite pictures, small rivers that the space-borne cameras would never normally even detect were spread out into long, basin-brimming lakes, all too plainly visible.

Nearly 300 roads were now closed in twenty-three counties, and 30,000 homes were flooded; only mosquitoes and blowflies thrived. It was too early to quantify the agricultural loss, though it would certainly be several billions of dollars; the shrimp harvest was wrecked too, wiped out by the huge runoff of polluted freshwater into the sea.

Even two weeks after Floyd made landfall, around the basins of the Tar and the Neuse water still lay in wide, shallow ponds on the country roads. Vast acreages of cotton and tobacco lay ruined, mile after mile of crops leaning buckled, gray, silt-smeared, and dead. It was estimated that one in six of the farmers thus affected would lose their livelihoods for good.

In Tarboro, many streets were still closed; those that were open were still carpeted with broken vegetation and streaks of drying mud. Camouflaged HumVees chugged throatily in a mess of snarled traffic; ruined furniture stood in piles amid broken trees in disarrayed front gardens. A local newspaper gave poignant advice on how to restore flood-damaged family photograph albums.

As people struggled to clean up, throwing out mounting piles of wrecked furniture and sodden house insulation, a new problem arose; like everything else, the refuse collection service was crippled. For over a week, neither staff nor vehicles could move; those few that managed to get about had trouble tipping rubbish into landfills that had become saturated mud pits.

Obviously, the physical disorder and material loss mattered little beside the freight of human grief. Near Clayton in Johnston County, just southeast of Raleigh, Swift Creek flowed 500 feet out from its normal course. Paul Wesley Mobley, thirty-one years old, drove into the flood one evening on Cornwallis Road. The surging current snatched up the car and sank it in fifteen feet of water; Mobley and his daughter Emily, five years old, were drowned. It took thirty-six hours to find the bodies. "It's really a sad thing," said Emily's head teacher, "she was just a little sparkle."

For all those who survived, this was a disaster lingering on for weeks and months, and whose impact will continue long into the years ahead. The Tar crested forty-three feet above sea level—the river rose *twenty-four feet* over flood stage—and because the ground in eastern North Carolina lies low, and the river basins running through it are wide, these floods drained away as slowly as they'd risen. Cruelly, dragging out the suffering, nature brought more rain to at least some affected parts of the state every day for two weeks after Floyd had passed through. In consequence, some rivers didn't crest until a week after the hurricane; there were homes and communities that stayed flooded through all that time, and then a week or more longer.

At Carolina State, Ryan Boyles produced color graphics for the State Climate Office showing the rainfall distribution in Dennis and Floyd. For Dennis he mapped out the rain in different colors, with each new color representing one more inch over a forty-eight-hour period. For Floyd, however, he had to make each color represent two inches, and above fourteen inches he had to give up and stick anything worse than that in a single band. He said, "My software ran out of levels to demark it with. I ran out of colors. It was"—he sighed—"an amazing event."

In total, parts of nine different states were declared federal disaster areas—and for the people who had to endure it, the flooding produced by

Floyd was without any doubt a hideous calamity. It will, therefore, seem exceptionally harsh to say that, relatively speaking, the United States was lucky with this storm. But the truth is, it was.

First, Florida escaped a catastrophic strike by barely 100 miles—a strike whose toll in lives is unknowable, but whose economic impact would certainly have run to at least several tens of billions. Second, though the flooding was immense and horrific, for the most part it was slow; unless you were desperately unfortunate, you could get out of the way. And third, the United States is well warned, well protected, and well staffed with heroes in the military and in the emergency services—men like Shad Hernandez of the USS *Kennedy,* and so many others whose deeds go unsung.

Above all, however, the United States is wealthy, and the United States is large—and none of these factors applies in Honduras. Honduras is mountainous, compact, deforested, and destitute. In consequence, Floyd wrought havoc in several dozen counties—but Mitch destroyed an entire nation.

7

LA TORMENTA

Mitch hit Guanaja on Monday, 26 October 1998. It was a big enough system that while the hub of the winds tore that island to pieces, the southern half of it reached out across the whole of Honduras—and, like Floyd, Mitch was a storm laden with biblical quantities of water. As it spread overland, that water started falling—on fragile, deforested earth that was sodden with two weeks of unusually heavy autumn downpours already. As of that Monday Mitch started dropping a foot, in some places two feet, of rain on Honduras every day.

Still the forecasts said the storm would move away to the northwest; still it continued to defy them as, late on Thursday, it started nudging southeast from Guanaja. By then the winds had diminished so much that, technically, Mitch had stopped even being a hurricane; with the Bay Island seas sucked clean of fuel where the storm had stalled for three days, sometime that Thursday afternoon it reverted in status to a tropical storm. That's why the second hit on Guanaja was so much less harsh than they'd feared, as the eye passed away from the island—but for mainland Honduras, this would be no consolation at all.

Mitch made landfall between the coastal towns of Trujillo and Santa Rosa de Aguán; the latter lay at the mouth of the Aguán River, and it was utterly devastated. It got hit twice, by the storm surge coming in off the sea before it and by the river flooding down from behind. In a town of 6,000 people, over eighty houses were either swept out to sea or pulped beneath the river; two schools, the bus station, the library, and many farms and businesses were reduced to mud-caked rubble.

At the front of the town, a wide stretch of coastline reaching 200 yards inland simply vanished. Behind it, the Aguán spilled out for miles on either side of its course, inundating the valley across a distance running sixty miles back from the sea. Roads and bridges were smashed; when the flood receded, the river had shifted its course by a quarter of a mile and grown fourfold in size. Santa Rosa was cut off for months; the only way you could get there was by canoe.

At least forty people died. One woman, a thirty-two-year-old schoolteacher named Isabela Arriola from the nearby village of Barra de Aguán, sought refuge on the roof of a neighbor's house about a mile from the sea. It wasn't far enough away; with her husband and their three children, Arriola was swept into the water. They clung to the side of a small boat for a while, but her husband and two of the children were washed away; Arriola's youngest son was pulled from her arms by the power of the waves not long afterward.

In a feat of endurance as much tragic as epic, Arriola somehow fashioned a makeshift raft out of tree roots, branches, and a piece of wooden board. Surviving on a few pineapples, oranges, and the milk from a coconut that she saw floating past her, she was adrift in the sea for six days. When she was picked up by a helicopter from the British naval vessel HMS *Sheffield*, she was fifty miles out from the shore.

Not for nothing is the Spanish word for storm *la tormenta*—and what had happened to Arriola's town and her family was now starting to happen across the entire length and breadth of Honduras.

At the other end of the country, in the far south by the border with Nicaragua, Rafael Galindo lived in the little town of Concepción de María. Tucked into the crook of the mountains over a bend in the Tiscagua River, it was home to some 3,000 people and the center of a *municipio* covering 400 square miles of remote and awkward terrain.

When you left the main road, it took an hour to get there along narrow, winding dirt tracks cut across rivers and high hillsides, ducking through a steep-sided jumble of sharp ridges and peaks. One hundred forty villages and hamlets dotted the jagged countryside around the town, with a handful of families here, 200 souls there. They grew maize and beans, and a little citrus fruit; among these people, Rafael was a figure of some stature.

Thirty-one years old, married, with three sons aged five, six, and seven, he wore a short-sleeved check shirt, dusty white jeans, and pointed cowboy boots. His parents had a *deposito*, a little general store at the top of the town; Rafael himself was a dairyman, with eleven cows and a loan from the bank. Beyond that, he'd been involved with the occasional small aid project that had found its way to this faraway, disregarded patch of land—not that Honduras, before Mitch, had ever attracted too much in the way of aid.

That October, it had rained in Concepción de María every day for two weeks—then, on Monday, October 26, it started raining around the clock. For day after day it rained continuously, twenty-four hours a day, pounding on the roofs and the earth until your ears hurt with the endless noise of it. Water came in through the doors, it leaked in through the ceiling, it flowed down the streets and washed down the hillsides—until, on Thursday evening, the mountains could bear the weight of it no more, and the landslides began.

You could hear them, you could see them, you could smell them. As entire sections of mountainside began to fall away around the town, through the remorseless hammering of the rain you could hear one terrible roar after another, a grinding thunder of tumbling earth filled with the percussive crashing together of huge rocks. You could see them because, although the power supply was down in the pitch-black night and the sky was full of water, the rocks clashing as they fell sent out cascades of sparks; the slopes about the town flared with momentary bursts of violent ignition. And you could smell them; beneath each collapse the air would fill with a pungent mix of roots, mulched vegetation, torn earth, and the sulfurous tang of colliding boulders. The smell hung off the water spilling down the slopes; each time people smelled it coming again, you could hear their cries rise up in the darkness.

In the soaking, roaring, spark-studded night, Concepción de María became a scene from the Book of Revelation. Gullies that had never before harbored runoff streams wider than a yard now filled with masses of water, mud, stone, and smashed trees ten or twenty yards across, rolling and crashing down onto the town.

A quarter of a mile from Rafael's house, one landslide spilled over the house of a woman and her five children, burying it entirely; afterward they would find one little girl's body at the base of the slide, but for the others, they could only put crosses into the rough piles of earth and rock where the house had once stood. Another landslide blocked the swollen river; the Tiscagua backed up behind this sudden, instant dam until, when it burst through, it became a giant wave of debris-clogged water that tore whole trees from the earth in its path, rising twenty-five yards above its normal course.

It ripped two houses off the slopes just downstream, taking seventeen people to their deaths. The wave had a dreadful, deep sound to it, a noise Rafael couldn't begin to explain. Trees breaking, boulders smashing together, the water roaring—it was like nothing he'd ever seen or heard. In the reverberating, rain-drenched darkness, there were moments now when he thought everything would be lost, that everything would disappear, and that no one could hope to survive.

The first landslides started about seven o'clock; a second wave began two hours later. In that second onslaught, one collapse swept across the street twenty yards from Rafael's house. Water by then was spilling constantly through his house; there was no way to stop it. He seized his children by the hand and ran with his wife into the night. It was hard to orient yourself in the noise and the blackness; he was looking for an area that he thought might be safer, and he found a place between two landslides where other people were also gathering. As they ran there, one of his boys cried out to him, "Daddy, I don't want to die." There was nothing he could do but grip his son's hand tighter, and pray.

The mayor of Concepción de María was a small, nervous man of thirty-seven named Miguel Angel Aplicano, a poor farmer descended from a long line of poor farmers; for his job in the town hall, he earned $142 a month. The town hall stood opposite Concepción's whitewashed little church on a faintly cobbled dirt square; the mayor's office was a bare, dusty room filled with rickety slatted benches arranged before his desk for public meetings. The Honduran flag drooped off a short pole behind his chair; a fan turned slowly beneath the uneven ceiling.

The mayor lived just outside the town; on the day before the landslides started, as the rivers rose he had to abandon his family, and wade chest-deep through a swelling stream to get to the town hall. The phones were out; he kept in contact with village leaders around the *municipio* by radio. He told them to get everyone away from the rivers; in his own town he went with the police to bring people away from the banks of the Tiscagua, and give them shelter in the town hall.

During Thursday night, reports of landslides and of their accompanying death and destruction came in on the radio from all around the countryside. By morning, there were over a thousand people affected that they knew about—from a local population of 30,000—and they were beginning to hear also of children and the elderly falling ill, soaked and unsheltered as so many now were.

The shops were running out of food; there was no coffee or sugar, no matches or candles. The mayor went about trying to encourage people, telling them to keep their faith in the Lord—but as time went on, and more and more reports came in of people missing, of crops and property damaged or destroyed, so he became steadily more desperate.

Friday night was the saddest, the longest, the most difficult night of his life. By then they'd set up six different shelters in Concepción, and they tried to support them all with what little food and warmth they could muster—but by Saturday morning, many had passed three days and three nights without eating or sleeping. Always the mayor told the people that God wouldn't abandon them—but when they told him of whole families lost, or of finding dead children in the branches of trees, he found the mounting weight of the tragedy stifling his soul.

The worst thing was having to bear it alone; for days Concepción was cut off from the rest of the world. The city of Choluteca was thirty-five miles away; finally the mayor walked there on Tuesday, November 3, through a landscape scarred and gouged by rockfalls on every hillside. Along the way five bridges were gone, and though the worst of the flooding had receded, he still had to wade through each river. He thought if he could only get to Choluteca to tell them what had happened, then help would surely follow—

but when he arrived about five in the afternoon and saw what had happened there, he realized that Concepción's troubles were but flotsam drifting on a whole ocean of grief.

The Choluteca River runs along the north side of the town. Normally little more than a shallow stream, it had swollen on Friday, October 30, into a mud-laden giant flowing at 11,000 cubic meters a second. In this mountainous terrain the rise was neither slow nor steady; it was abrupt, a sequence of surging waves washing through the streets of the riverside barrios, rolling cars and pickups over and over until they were crumpled like so much scrap paper. Each wave was higher than the last; as the darkness settled that evening, the water was climbing to the roofs.

Hundreds of yards from the normal course of the river, Paola Sanchez lived in a house of daub and wattle in Barrio Pedro Diaz. The water reached there about six in the evening, coming so quickly that she had no time to get anything from the house before she ran. Her mother, her brother, her two sisters, and their families lived in shacks like hers all about her; they all lost everything. Their ducks and chickens, what little furniture they had, everything was gone in minutes. The water rose so fast it seemed to be welling from the very earth all about them. It was red with dirt, sometimes it was black; they had fruit trees ten and twenty feet tall around their houses, but the water came so fast and strong that it tore all but a handful of the biggest trees clean from the ground.

The men tried to stay with the houses. Santo Agripino Sanchez, Paola's brother, climbed onto his roof; so did two of his brothers-in-law. These two were swept away; their bodies were never found. By about ten that evening, the water was up to the roof that Santo was clinging to, and the house was giving way beneath it. The roof tipped and floated away, and he too was spilled into the water. It was as much liquid mud as water, a thick, stinking syrup filled with debris. He wanted to cling to the branches of a tree, but the force of the flood was too great, it was knocking them all down; he could find nothing to get hold of.

It was pouring rain all the time. He was swept downstream through the night with tree trunks all about him, seeing and smelling the carcasses of drowned cows floating past; he saw entire steel containers bobbing and wheeling through the eddying waves. His vision was fogged with silt and spray; logs crashed into him, knocking him half-conscious. He swallowed water, coughing and choking. He fought with all his spirit to keep his head up; he prayed to God to help him stay alive.

Away to the north, near San Pedro Sula in the Ulua Valley, La Lima is the headquarters of United Fruit's Chiquita banana operation. A town of 45,000 people, it stands on the banks of the Chamelecón in a wide, fertile plain rimmed with striking green mountains. Juan Ramón had moved there from Tela on the coast twenty-six years earlier; he'd worked for a while at Chiquita's American Club, then opened a little bar called El Monje a couple of hundred yards from the riverbank.

It had a tiled counter open to the sidewalk, set five yards back from the road, with stools anchored in the dirt in front of it. The serving area was a step down behind the counter; behind it, a few tables stood in a small open yard by a culvert. There was a toothless picket fence, a neon Bacardi sign, and a fridge packed with $350 in stock, a giant value to any but the wealthiest Honduran.

That Friday night, while Santo Agripino Sanchez struggled to keep his head above the bloated waters of the Choluteca, Juan Ramón watched helplessly as the Chamelecón poured through the doors of his little business. It had been raining for five days continually, never stopping day and night; the power had failed, and in the darkness now the river rose remorselessly out of its normal course. It spread through all the town and across the banana plantations all about it; it spilled a yard deep into El Monje's serving area, climbing to fill the fridge and wreck Juan's stock, overtopping the bar, leaving nothing that he'd worked to build untouched.

Around him the town was emptying. People fled to the main highway, the only raised piece of ground left above the floods; hundreds of others struggled to make their way to San Pedro's airport, only to be marooned there as the runways disappeared beneath ten feet of water. Juan Ramón didn't know it, but by morning he was in the middle of a lake twelve miles wide, stretching forty miles north to Puerto Cortés on the sea.

What losses he'd suffered, however, were as nothing compared to the sounds he heard around La Lima that night. Out of the smothered blackness of the town he heard the barking everywhere of terrified dogs, and the screams of desperate people crying out for help. "Oh my God," he heard them call, "oh my God, help me please, my children, my children. . . ."

As their voices rose in loss and terror through the night, Mitch ground across the tormented land with a slow and malevolent thoroughness. The storm tracked more or less directly southwest from the coast, passing right through the heart of Honduras. Before it left, it poured down its rains for six solid days. In satellite images of that period, Honduras simply vanishes beneath it.

Mitch was inland by Friday morning, passing over the mountains south of Trujillo; by Friday evening it was nearing Tegucigalpa, the capital city 120 miles south of the coast. The waters had started rising there already, but the first sign a lot of people had that things were turning very wrong was not the sight of the water but the sound of gunfire.

Winding into Tegucigalpa from the northeast, the Chiquito joins the Choluteca River in Barrio La Hoya, just south of the city center. Normally a trickle of a thing tucked away in a giant ditch, it was now so high that it started chewing away at one wing of the city prison. As the building crumbled and prisoners began to escape, a chaotic chase ensued and the guards started shooting. A secretary named Ofelia Barahona lived nearby, and it was the gunfire that really scared her that Friday morning, not the rain or the river. Like everyone else in the city, she simply didn't believe that the water could or would rise any farther.

She'd taken the day off sick, but at nine her mother pulled her from her bed to look at the Chiquito. From her living room she could see that the water was high; for safety's sake she packed some of her belongings, supposing something bad might happen, but not really thinking it possible. The worst thought she had was, if there was a flood, she wouldn't be able to park her car in the garage. So she moved the car out—then, she went to lunch with her boyfriend. While they were eating, her sister called on the cell phone to tell her the water was getting into the house; Ofelia thought there was no way that could be right, but sure enough, when she got back home about one-thirty, the river was coming in through the door. Then, suddenly, in less than ten minutes, it had risen to her chest.

She tried to save a few things, then realized that she had to get out; if she'd have stayed, she'd have drowned. The flow was too strong—it tore their heavy front door clean off its hinges—and looking back, she knew she was lucky. If it had happened at night, rising so abruptly like that, it would surely have pinned her in her bedroom, and she'd never have made it away.

If it was bad along the Chiquito, along the main course of the Choluteca it was unimaginable. As darkness fell that Friday evening, a shallow dribble of a river normally not more than a few yards wide was growing rapidly into a muscled, raging mass of dirt-brown, debris-choked water flowing at 8,000 cubic meters a second. That much water weighs 6,000 tons—6,000 tons of scouring impact *every second*—and what could stand before a mass and volume this great?

The river overtopped the bridges between Tegucigalpa and its twin city of Comayaguela on the west bank before the end of the afternoon; by Saturday morning all but the two oldest and most solid bridges were gone. The river swept away houses, shops, and businesses in district after district; the first few streets on the Comayaguela shore in the city center were reduced to a mud-choked war zone, the buildings roofless, gutted, and smashed.

In the south of the city, flooding started near the airport in Las Brisas and San José del Pedrega about four in the afternoon. These were poor and middle-class districts, but the wealthy weren't safe; fancy car dealerships in Colonia El Prado were soon flooded too, sending dozens of shiny Alfa Romeos and Toyota pickups swirling about in the surging waves. Later, cars from the city would be found washed all the way to the Gulf of Fonseca on the Pacific, the best part of a hundred miles downriver—but not all the cars in the floodwater were new off the forecourts.

Victor Leonardo Ruiz had been planning a Hallowe'en party at the Koko Loko, his family's restaurant on Boulevard Los Proceres; as the disaster unfolded and the party was canceled, he closed the restaurant and made his way south to Colonia Loarque by the airport. His father-in-law had a glazier's business there, with a warehouse full of windows and frames. Looking down from the warehouse, Victor saw cars beneath the water with their headlights on; he heard people desperately hitting their horns as they drowned.

There was nothing he could do but stare at the rising water in fear and dismay. It was full of dead people and animals, shattered trees, the broken contents of houses and shops; sometimes he caught the sharper stench of fuel and chemicals borne in the tide from riverside factories. Then, about four in the morning, the water came in a wave two meters higher yet, ripping clean through his father-in-law's business. A lake above the city called Laguna del Pescado had breached, and as it added its waters to the swollen Choluteca everything in the warehouse was lost in a moment, everything in a business that had taken thirty years to build.

As Victor watched, he knew there was nothing he or anyone on earth could do to stop it. Like Ofelia Barahona as the water had burst into her house the afternoon before, at that moment he knew he was utterly helpless before this indifferent and almighty force of nature.

Landslides all through the night only added to the misery. On the worst land around the city, many thousands of people lived in rudimentary shacks of wood and tin; they had no possible defense. One impoverished shanty-town, Colonia Soto, stood on a hill not far from the center; the whole face of the hill collapsed, and an entire neighborhood was lost in a rumbling avalanche of mud and stone.

How could ordinary people understand or be prepared for a disaster of this magnitude, when the engineers, the hydrologists, the meteorologists themselves had all been caught so wrong-footed? Marc Dawson was a Canadian engineering consultant working at SOPTRAVI, the Ministry of Public Works, Transport, and Housing. He was a burly, ruddy-faced man who'd been in Honduras for two years. On the afternoon of Thursday, October 29, he was at a meeting with the World Bank official who administered the country's infrastructural loan program; on TV in their conference room, they saw a forecast saying Mitch would most likely head out to sea from the Bay Islands toward Belize. They made plans to travel north and inspect the damage there on Saturday—then Mitch came south.

SOPTRAVI's headquarters were close by the Choluteca in Barrio La Bolsa, on the west bank in Comayaguela, and Dawson's office had a view looking down on it. That Friday morning while he prepared to go north, people were starting to come in and stare at the river. At first he was busy on the phone and didn't catch on—but normally you couldn't see the actual water from there, you could only see the wide gully it ran through. So then he looked, and he realized how high it had got. He went outside, and as he watched he saw one of the bridges starting to shake. It was about two in the afternoon; he went to the personnel manager and said maybe she should think about letting people get home.

Secretaries and clerical staff were sent on their way; engineers and drivers stayed. By five o'clock, there was water in the street outside the ministry compound. Dawson left his government Honda in the car park and loaded everyone he could fit into his own Isuzu Trooper. He drove a dozen people across into Tegucigalpa over the Puente Juan Ramón Molina (like so many others, that bridge would wash away during the night); then he rounded up a friend and they tried to go back for the Honda. By now, however, there was no way to cross the river at all; any bridges still standing were overtopped by the foaming brown waves of the flood.

During the night the ground floor of SOPTRAVI and all their warehouses filled with water. They lost all their contracts, all their personnel files, all their records as to who had a license to drive a taxi or a bus. Upriver, hard by one end of the Puente Mallol, the same thing was happening to the Education Ministry; that building was destroyed, and with it the records of an entire nation's schooling system. Honduras wouldn't go back to school for three months; for most of that time, the country's schools were pretty much filled with the homeless and displaced anyway.

D awn broke on Saturday to find Santo Agripino Sanchez still afloat in a turbulent mass of racing brown water. The power of the flood was intense, barbaric, ripping toward the sea with its cargo of corpses and carcasses, smashed buildings and vegetation. He was in the water until late in the afternoon, when finally it tipped him onto a small island of high ground near a little place called Sedeno. The flood had washed him nearly all the way to the sea.

He lay on the wet ground, exhausted, hungry, surrounded by water on all sides. He was stranded there for three days before a motor launch came by and took him part of the way up the river to San Lorenzo, twenty miles from Choluteca. From there he walked and hitched lifts back home to Barrio Pedro Diaz, where his family had gone five days without news of him. They were overjoyed to see him, of course—but he found that everything had been destroyed where he lived.

Before, they'd not been able to see the river. There'd been a whole barrio between them and the bank—but it had been entirely swept away. Now,
from where their houses once stood, there stretched a desert of rucked and
hummocked dirt, dunes of sand and silt strewn with broken lumber and
pieces of trees. A huge tree lay on its side, its roots a tangled silhouette
against the hot and empty sky. Dust blew in clouds down the street. In the
middle distance, the river now flowed through an ash-gray plain strewn with
chunks of smashed bridge. It was a completely new landscape; the flood had
dumped an entire beach on the edge of the city.

Behind and around them, fourteen barrios had been inundated. Choluteca had a population of 90,000, and 20,000 of them had been forced from
their homes. If they found anything left standing when they returned (buildings of wood and adobe were mostly altogether gone), they found their
ground floors and all the streets outside filled with three feet of sodden mud.

In some places it was worse; in some places the mud was ten feet deep.
Near where the Sanchez family had lived, there had been a football pitch in a
little park; now the goalposts were buried two-thirds of the way up to the
crossbar.

Santo was a short, stocky man of forty who scraped a living selling bread
from a basket on the handlebars of a little blue bicycle. In time, the munici-
pality would allocate him a plot of land elsewhere, but he didn't earn enough
money to build on it. He and his family instead had to start rebuilding hovels
of salvaged lumber amid the jumbled mounds of dirt where their homes had
stood before; many people had nothing better to build shelter with than flattened cardboard packing cases.

Santo's sister Paola had nowhere to wash her family's clothes. Her old
washtub, a small tank of rough brick and cement, had stood a yard proud
above the ground before the waters came; now it was buried, the edges covered with solidified mud. They'd had little enough as it was, but now they had
nothing. Paola stood begrimed with dirt, barefoot in a ragged green dress,
her shins and calves bruised and livid with swollen veins. She looked across
the wastes of wrecked earth and mourned her two sisters' lost husbands, and
wondered how the rest of them would go on. They could only wait for the
next rains in the spring, she thought, and see what the river did then.

As for Santo, he was glad to be alive—but he felt as if he could never
trust in anything again.

. . .

On Saturday afternoon, as the river tipped Santo Sanchez onto the sodden island that saved his life, back in the capital Marc Dawson made his way to SOPTRAVI's headquarters in Barrio La Bolsa. He found the building waist deep in mud. He tried to climb through a window into the conference room, but it was jammed shut; the water had piled all the furniture against it. His assistant scaled a storm drain to the third floor; it took three days to get in on the ground.

They laid planks across the mud, rescued everything they could, and moved to offices out by the airport; apart from the destruction, their compound was uninhabitable simply because it stank. There had been a coffee warehouse just upstream; now one and a half million sacks of coffee lay soaked and rotting all about, and the smell was so bad that people were throwing up in the street.

Compounding their difficulties, many of SOPTRAVI's best people weren't in the capital anyway. They'd gone north, expecting the worst problems to happen up there; now, with roads and bridges cut or washed away all over the country, they couldn't get back. One team that went to San Pedro Sula planning to stay for two days found themselves stuck there for eleven, wearing the same damp clothes all the while. Worse by far, however, they were working in the shadow of El Cajón.

Forty miles upstream from San Pedro, El Cajón is an enormous hydro-electric plant at the junction of the Humuya and Sulaco rivers. Before Mitch, a long summer's drought had left water levels in the lake behind it disturbingly low; one engineer had joked to his colleagues that if they wanted electricity in the coming winter, they'd need five hurricanes to pass by and fill the lake.

It was a body of water over sixty miles long, held back by a curtain wall 300 yards high. Now Mitch filled it to the brim in just five days—and if El Cajón failed, the calamities already wrought on Honduras would pale into insignificance. If El Cajón failed, San Pedro Sula and everything else in the Ulua Valley would be washed halfway to New Orleans, and hundreds of thousands of people with it.

For days the engineers lived in constant fear. Unable to get south, they watched helplessly on television as a great trench of destruction was gouged through the heart of the capital, and of course they feared for their friends and families back home—but their cell phones still worked, so at least they could speak to them. The specter of the dam, on the other hand, overshadowed all else.

El Cajón didn't fail; pretty much everything else did. Roads and bridges, power and water supplies, schools and hospitals—an entire nation lay in ruins. One engineer in San Pedro called home and learned that his mother had lost her house. He was trapped, he couldn't go to help her—and if the engineers couldn't move, who could?

Back in the capital on Sunday afternoon, Marc Dawson quit trying to get into the ministry HQ and headed into town to his girlfriend's restaurant. The place was packed with fifty or more people because they cooked with gas, so in a city without power, they had precious hot food. Then the news came through on the radio that the city's mayor had died—César Castellanos, El Gordito, The Little Fat Man—and for many people it was the final straw. All around him Dawson saw them running, screaming, banging their heads against the wall—because El Gordito had been hugely popular. Widely touted to become the country's next president in 2002, he'd started doing things for a poor and tattered city that had really seemed to make a difference—cleaning up the streets, bucking up the public transport system—and everyone had thought that if anyone could get them through this, El Gordito could.

Now he was dead, killed in a helicopter crash as he tried to survey the damage. The day he died was his fifty-first birthday; he left a wife and four sons. It was, thought Dawson, bad news upon bad news upon bad news.

The next day, amid reports of El Gordito's death, and of ruin and desolation from one end of the country to the other, *La Tribuna* ran a powerful drawing where normally they'd have had a cartoon. It showed a haggard man standing amid the debris, shaking his clenched fists at the sky as he cried out, *"Todavía no estamos vencidos!"*

We're not beaten yet.

It was a proud and an optimistic statement. It was also, unfortunately, a debatable one.

I n the first days of November 1998, the immediate aftermath of Hurricane Mitch was devastation and deprivation throughout Central America.

Guatemala and El Salvador had both suffered considerable damage, with several hundred dead; Nicaragua was worse, with much of the northern half of that country in particular swept by floods and landslides as Honduras had been.

In one appalling calamity, the crater of the Casita volcano near the border filled with water and collapsed, sending waves of sodden earth the height of multistory buildings down the broken mountainside, obliterating all the villages on the lower slopes in their path. It was, said one survivor, "a terrible, towering wall that just fell out of the clouds." In that one location at least 2,000 lost their lives, perhaps twice as many; no one will ever know for sure, as the bodies lie deep beneath new plains of mud many square miles in extent.

Nicaragua's defense minister, Pedro Joaquín Chamorro, reported seeing a pig nibbling at the corpse of a child. He said, "It's hard to believe it unless you've seen it with your own eyes."

For all the suffering of its neighbors, however, Honduras was hit the hardest; virtually nowhere was spared. In Comayaguela, in the shattered business district along the west bank of the Choluteca, amid the banks of dried mud that now filled all the roofless buildings many feet deep, five months after Mitch I saw the severed leg of a cow jutting from the dessicated filth. Strips of blackened flesh still hung from it, flapping on the dusty wind— and the storm had left grim sights like this in every corner of the country.

The authorities were utterly overwhelmed. As one government official put it, "Normally if you have something go wrong you go to COPECO, the emergency committee; they have maps all over the wall, one part of the country's affected, and the other parts send help. But what can you do if everywhere's affected? How can you plan for that, when your whole country's knocked down?"

Literally, physically, Honduras after Mitch would never be the same nation again. Rivers had shifted their courses, hills and mountains had been recontoured, settlements had vanished or moved, and roads and bridges were being rebuilt in new places; the country would require an entirely new map to be drawn.

Honduras had been wretchedly poor to begin with. Behind the thinnest veil of democracy, it was still run by a corrupt and feckless oligarchy; while this handful of *caudillos* drove too fast on their nation's rutted streets in glossy four-wheel drives with smoked glass windows, large numbers of a disregarded population struggled to get by on a dollar a day. And yet, by a dismal turn of irony, before Mitch things had actually seemed to be looking up.

San Pedro Sula in the north, the country's industrial mainstay, was the fastest growing city in Central America. *Maquilas*, the factories using cheap labor to make goods for export, were doing good business. Tourist revenue from the Bay Islands and the Mayan complex at Copán was rising; Roatán, the largest of the islands, had a new airport capable of handling international flights direct.

Cyber cafés were beginning to appear. A Holiday Inn was going up in San Pedro, and investors were putting money into other new hotels in Tegucigalpa; a somewhat wistful billboard on one building site showed a gleaming structure by a perfect new road, a road magically unsullied by rust-bucket traffic, with not a withered street person in sight. These developments may not, indeed, have meant too much to the average Honduran in the street—it almost certainly wouldn't have meant too much to the small farmer or the landless peasant—but Honduras in 1998 had been scheduled for a healthy rise in GDP of 6 percent.

Now, in the first days of November, any hope all this might have represented was gone, washed away as surely as the nation's infrastructure had been. Nearly a hundred of the principal bridges were damaged or destroyed; half had completely vanished. All the towns on the north coast were cut off; so was the capital, with the main highway severed in several places both north and south.

The best part of a million people were displaced from their homes—one in six of the population—and unknown thousands were dead or missing. Corpses both human and animal lay rotting in the streets. People returned to the wrecks of their houses to find limbs protruding from the ubiquitous mud. Power, water, and sewerage systems had collapsed; food and fuel were short, and rationing was imposed.

A curfew was set nationwide from eight in the evening to six in the morning; amid outbreaks of looting, civil liberties were suspended, and to all intents and purposes the country went under martial law. In Tegucigalpa armed men guarded every supermarket, with a limit set on the number of people allowed in any store at one time. Lines formed for everything, everywhere. The gasoline shortage in particular sparked mounting frustration, with lines of cars stretching miles back from any garage that had gas; no one could get about, and the capital teetered on the brink of major civil disorder.

Amid all this, the threat of epidemic disease loomed high; by some miraculous combination of luck and frantic hard work it was largely averted, but many who didn't get cholera or dysentery suffered from fungal infections on their feet instead, from spending so much time wading through the festering water.

Across much of the country, travel was only possible by boat or helicopter; it was a desperate struggle to get news out, or aid in. Wrong-footed by Mitch's unpredictable course, the world's media had gone to Belize or the Yucatan, and getting from there to where the disaster had actually happened wasn't easy. Nor was bringing in emergency supplies and assistance—where was it going to land?

Honduras had four airports claiming international status. One was on the holiday island of Roatán, which had escaped the worst of the storm and was largely irrelevant, one was at La Ceiba on the coast, which was completely cut off, one was outside San Pedro Sula and had been totally inundated—and to get an idea of how much traffic Toncontín airport in the capital could handle, one need only reflect on the fact that it has a grand total of three departure gates. If the American military hadn't had a substantial installation at Soto Cano Air Base, the immediate aid system would have bottlenecked completely.

In the principal Atlantic port of Puerto Cortés, meanwhile, hundreds of containers stuffed with supplies started backing up on the docks. At one point, only one out of seven container cranes was working; no one knew who some of the containers were addressed to anyway. Local journalist Gustavo Palencia reported in despair, "Honduras is chaos. The infrastructure is gone."

Bishop Leopold Frade announced simply, "Honduras doesn't exist anymore."

There were power cuts throughout the country; bloated bodies blocked the pumps and ducts of the hydroelectric plant at Morazán. Dr. Manuel Carrasco Villela, acting head of Tegucigalpa's main hospital, broke down in tears before the press. "Forgive me," he said. "It's been seven days of this, and it's going to get worse."

A report to London from the British embassy on November 2 said simply, "The scale of the disaster is unmeasurable"—a statement that would turn out to be quite literally true. We will never know how many died; horror, chaos, and incompetence combined to make the quality of the information coming into the central government, and being relayed onward by it to the world, pretty much entirely unreliable.

Officially, the final death toll in Honduras was 5,672, although Arturo Corrales, one of those in charge of collating the government's numbers, frankly admitted that he'd arrived at this figure by taking the best estimates of dead and missing available to him, adding them together, halving them, and settling on the number thus arrived at with the statistical equivalent of a helpless shrug.

It took at least two months before the international community could even begin to get a grip on the true impacts of Mitch; nongovernmental aid agencies said in March and April, four and five months after Mitch, that they still didn't have genuinely trustworthy information even then. And how do you help a country when you don't know what's really happened to it? In the short term, you can fix the bridges and the water supplies, with string and chewing gum if need be—but what then? How many were unemployed, how many hungry? Nobody knew. One UN aid worker told me she'd been in the country three months, "and I can't figure out if I've achieved anything constructive at all. But then, I can't figure out if anyone else has, either."

The challenge was monumental. Whatever the precise figures, much of the year's main harvest had certainly been ruined. Called the *postrera*, it's normally gathered in the closing months of the year, bringing in the maize and beans and sorghum that form the bedrock of the Honduran diet—but now Mitch had consumed it instead.

In the Ulua and Aguán valleys on the north coast, meanwhile, great swathes of the banana plantations lay buried in mud and silt three feet deep. It would take the best part of two years to get them back in production; in the interim, thousands of workers were laid off and faced destitution. Other export products like beef, coffee, watermelon, and shrimp were badly hit too; overall, an already fragile economy had been thrown twenty years backward.

Between lost crops and soaring unemployment, it was estimated by the World Health Organization in early 1999 that 810,000 people were in what it coyly termed "a food deficit situation." In short, one in seven were going hungry—but as the situation in Kosovo deteriorated and the eyes of the world moved on, aid workers began reporting that food promised to their distribution networks by the UN's World Food Program was failing to materialize.

Unsurprisingly, crime went through the roof. The number of Hondurans picked up at the Mexican and American frontiers attempting illegal entry multiplied fourfold. Men begged in the street to raise money for the journey, clutching tattered photocopies of the Mexican rail freight system, dreaming of Laredo and El Paso. An entire nation teetered on the brink of a collective nervous breakdown. In Barrio La Hoya, Ofelia Barahona spent six weeks cleaning waist-deep mud from her house; as it became clear to her that she wouldn't be able to get back into it before Christmas, she broke down and wept.

Traumatized children feared any sudden sound, and eyed the sky with terror any time it rained. The niece of an American expat collected classroom supplies worth $500 at her high school in the United States and sent it all down to her uncle; he took it to the school in the village where he lived outside the capital, and the children all drew cards to send back by way of thanks. Their pictures showed landslides, ruined buildings, cadavers floating in flooded rivers.

In Concepción de María, Rafael Galindo said, "Honduras is a country where men don't cry. But after Mitch, men cried like women."

Fear and superstition abounded. In Tegucigalpa, after the myth-invested Laguna del Pescado breached its banks and drained into the Choluteca, it was often and earnestly reported that mermaids and giant serpents had been seen swimming in the flood through the city.

To the north in La Lima, the mud dried and turned to dust, and blew so thickly down the streets that the shotgun-toting guards outside the bank wore face masks.

When I asked someone about the ruined state of the place he said, "First we had water. Then we had mud. Now we have dust and stones."

ZCZC MIATCDAT3 ALL
TTAA00 KNHC DDHHMM
TROPICAL STORM IRENE DISCUSSION NUMBER 1
NATIONAL WEATHER SERVICE MIAMI FL
11 AM EDT WED OCT 13 1999

SATELLITE IMAGES AND RAOB OBSERVATIONS FROM GRAND CAYMAN INDICATE
THAT THE AREA OF LOW PRESSURE IN THE WESTERN CARIBBEAN HAS BECOME
MUCH BETTER ORGANIZED AND IS NOW TROPICAL STORM IRENE. A
RECONNAISSANCE PLANE WILL PROVIDE BETTER INFORMATION ON THE LOCATION
AND THE INTENSITY OF IRENE LATER TODAY . . . CONVENTIONAL TOOLS INDICATE
THAT IRENE COULD REACH HURRICANE STATUS IN ABOUT 36 HOURS.

INITIAL MOTION IS UNCERTAIN . . . IRENE COULD TURN TOWARD THE NORTH-
NORTHEAST AND ACCELERATE. THIS IS IN AGREEMENT WITH THE GFDL AND UK
MODELS AND CLIMATOLOGY. WATCHES AND WARNINGS HAVE BEEN ISSUED
ACCORDINGLY FOR CUBA AND THE CAYMAN ISLANDS.

ALL INTERESTS IN FLORIDA . . . ESPECIALLY SOUTH FLORIDA AND THE KEYS SHOULD
CLOSELY MONITOR THE PROGRESS OF DEVELOPING STORM IRENE.

AVILA

NNNN

8

THE TROPICAL
UPDATE

Past Valetone on Washington, opposite the Club Deuce on 14th, a painted sign in the doorway of Tattoos By Lou proclaimed wryly, "Another Day in Paradise."

Beyond the Deuce lies Collins Avenue, a street splashed far north and south in pastel neon. With the dismal exception of the Amoco gas station, all shines yellow, red, purple, green, flickering solicitations for the Clifton and Beach Plaza Hotels, the Café des Arts, the Sushi Rock Sobe. One more block east, and you reach Ocean Drive—not quite so shiny and bar-packed this far north from the News Café on 7th Street, but plainly meaning in late 1999 to become so, as work proceeded on the gutted and boarded shell of the Winterhaven Hotel.

Contractors' signs hung on wire fencing and sheets of plywood promoting Empire Electric, London Painting, Coconut Grove Glass & Mirror. When finished the Winterhaven would look out, like its many glossy neighbors, past palm trees and the dune line to the wide, perfect, entirely artificial beach and to the freighters lining up on the blue horizon beyond it for the Port of Miami.

Ordinarily when you took this short walk, on the corner of the alley behind the Deuce you'd pass the camp of the large homeless woman with the walker. She lived by the One Way signpost there, sticking handwritten messages to it on take-out paper plates saying "Do Not Park on Yellow Curb," or documenting in scrawled and obsessive detail whatever drug deal she'd lately seen going down.

Ordinarily, on this short walk or on any other stroll around South Beach, you'd be brushed by the slipstreams of the young and tattooed swooshing by on their Rollerblades. You'd pass Cubans, Haitians, and Asians chatting outside bakeries and corner stores. You'd see tanned volleyball players and over-muscled gym addicts and among them the tourists, eyeing the daily parade of vanity and color with pleasure and suspicion.

Ordinarily, when you took this short walk at nine on a mid-October morning, the temperature and humidity would be broiling. Ordinarily, the sky would blaze so dazzling that every building gleamed, heat stunned, and without sunglasses you had to creep in shadows or go half blind.

Nine o'clock on the morning of Friday, 15 October 1999, however, wasn't ordinary at all. Moving north through the far end of the Florida Keys, 130 miles southwest of Miami, Hurricane Irene had driven all light and color from the sky, and emptied the streets of all human concourse.

Far ahead of Irene's center, one of the storm's rainbands was sweeping in from the east, through the upper side of the storm's circulation—the fourth, and the worst so far. The sky, what little of it could be made out through flying curtains of rain, was a mass of low, gray-black cloud so heavy that morning seemed unable to dawn. The wind was nowhere yet near hurricane force, but already the rain was driving in virtually horizontal; it seemed to shoot through the street so fast that it shone and sparkled, and as it struck it stung like hard pellets, each fat drop hitting flesh like a solid object.

In the turbulent gloom only the homeless woman was still out, inadequately tented in a cocoon of clear plastic—only her, and me. I crossed Ocean Drive toward the beach; as I left the shelter of the buildings, so the wind gained power in the open space. Walking began to involve leaning forward against it; palm trees bucked and swayed, fronds rattling and hissing as the wind fretted through them.

Vision blurred in the gray-white haze of rain. I advanced through the dune line, and decided instantly to turn back. Though the rain was bearable, the sand driven on this unceasing rush of air was a stinging, flaying assault against my skin. It felt as if all the exposed pieces of my body were being rapidly ground with a fine grade of sandpaper. I looked briefly across a dim murk of foaming breakers, and hastily retreated.

The contractors' signboards rocked and thudded against the fence rails around the Winterhaven, loud and monotonous. Twigs and leaves raced about the sidewalks. Already the curbside of the road outside my apartment was calf-deep in water, the bottom of the camber filling as the storm drains overloaded. Inside I dried off, then lay back to catch the Tropical Update on the Weather Channel. The wind was loud enough to smother the noise of the air conditioner; rain was being driven through the window frame, pooling on the sill, spilling to spread across the floor. Indeterminate objects clattered down the alley behind the building, metal and plastic racing and rolling, pinging into walls and iron fences.

The forecast said Irene would move more or less due north, up the west coast of the Florida peninsula toward Naples and Fort Myers. In that case, the eye wouldn't likely pass nearer than a hundred miles to Miami; with hurricane force winds not extending more than fifteen miles from the center of the storm, the city shouldn't experience much worse than what this rainband was sending in now. There had been a tropical storm warning in effect since the evening before, meaning we could expect wind speeds between thirty-nine and seventy-three miles an hour within twenty-four hours; this rainband was surely in the bottom of that range. It would pass soon enough, and then the worst Irene had for us would come through toward late afternoon.

There was, however, an edge of caution in the delivery of this forecast. Irene's central circulation had been "wobbling and re-forming all over the place," as one of the Weather Channel's engagingly peculiar cast of presenters put it—and there was a hint of an easterly nudge in the track as well, a tendency to lean over toward urban, populous Dade and Broward counties.

Still, this was nothing to get unduly exercised about. Irene was a Category 1, "minimal," and she was barely that. The airport was staying open, as were government and county offices, parks, and libraries. People should be alert for tornadoes—there was already one sighted, spinning down to the sea off Blue Water Key—and they should certainly expect a good deal of flooding. Jerry Jarrell said carefully but sternly, trying to warn the anticipated target area on the west coast without inducing unnecessary alarm, "There'll be damage. There'll be trees down, and mobile homes destroyed."

From the general tone of the local coverage, however, it seemed the worst that Miami's citizens had in store was a long, wet, and ugly commute. Somewhat bizarrely, swimmers were advised only to swim at guarded beaches. Who might wish to go swimming in the present conditions was hard to imagine (in South Florida, of course, you never can tell what people might take it in mind to do), but this advice pretty much summed up an overall sense that Irene need not be taken too gravely in Dade County.

Toward noon I ran through the rain to my car, edged it out of the standing water at the roadside, then set off on the short drive past downtown to the Rickenbacker Causeway and Virginia Key; I'd assumed that HRD's maps discussion would be taking place as normal. As it turned out, I'd assumed wrong.

It was a month to the day after the P-3s had flown in Floyd as that storm approached landfall. Gert had recurved in midocean, passing east of Bermuda to fade out in the North Atlantic, and Tropical Depression 11 had brought calamitous rains to Mexico. Typhoon York had hit Hong Kong, flipping an airliner on its back as it tried to land in ninety-mile-per-hour winds, but miraculously killing only two of those onboard; Typhoon Bart had killed twenty-six in southwest Japan, Typhoon Dan had ground across Luzon, and immediately after Floyd, a little fizzle of a thing called Tropical Storm Harvey had blown up in the central Gulf of Mexico.

For a while, NHC worried that Harvey might go into Tampa. Fronted by a wide, shallow area of continental shelf, that low-lying city and its surrounding metro zone are particularly vulnerable to even a moderate storm surge—which, when it comes (as it surely must) will funnel up into the bay, bringing widespread salt flooding—but this particular storm confounded the forecasters.

They said Harvey would go northeast, and he didn't; he went southeast instead, across the lower tip of the peninsula. He was a moisture pump, giving the Everglades a thorough soaking, and briefly flooding parts of Naples, but he left little impression otherwise, bar one truly exquisite sunset, streaking the whole sky with bright lilac and lemon yellow.

We were past the peak of the season; after several increasingly fraught weeks, it seemed things were finally calming down. At HRD, after Florida's brush with Floyd, the sense of relief in the building was physically tangible. On Friday, September 17, after the last advisory on the remnant storm was issued in the morning—sending it on its way through Maine toward the Bay of Fundy—the thankful sense of a Category 4 catastrophe so narrowly averted spawned a cascade of Andrew stories over lunch.

The extent of the disaster in North Carolina wasn't clear yet, and meanwhile, with Miami spared, it was as if the specter of doom could be brought out, confronted, and gratefully laughed at. Releasing all their tension, the HRD staff asked one another, do you remember this happening, and that? Mike Black recalled helping a neighbor who'd gone through Andrew hiding in her closet as the front door blew out and the storm roared in down the hallway. He went up the front steps the next day, looked in, and he said, "That's interesting wallpaper."

She told him, "That's not wallpaper. That's leaves pasted flat all over the wall."

One of the support staff had been pregnant, and the mix of terror and low pressure had started provoking contractions. In the howling night she'd lain on her bed, but Andrew was taking pieces of the roof off, and water started coming in through the ceiling. Her husband told her it was OK; they were only losing tiles; she lay there feeling the house shake and thump, hearing and feeling the wind, the deep, groaning reverberation as each gust came in, and she wondered how much more than tiles they might yet lose.

All the while she looked again and again at her watch, and prayed for it to end; retelling the tale now she shook her head, the fear still vivid. She remembered how, about seven in the morning when the worst was past, she went to the front door and couldn't open it because a tree had fallen against it. She went out another way and looked at her front yard and was bemused to find that all her plants had vanished. She found a street sign lying there; when she read it, she realized it had blown to her house from twenty blocks away. Then, surreally, the phone rang.

Unlike the power lines, a lot of the phone lines were buried; people were finding that they could still call one another. Mike Black had seen the latest radar coverage; now he was ringing up friends and colleagues and neighbors, making sure they were all right, letting them know it was over. He told her, "It's nearly done. There's just one more rainband."

She looked around at what was left of her home. She said, "It's OK, Mike. It doesn't matter anymore now. Another rainband? Hey, send in the next hurricane, why not? It can't do any worse."

Those who'd taken less damage tried to help their friends and relatives and found themselves walking or driving into places that looked like war zones. There were no landmarks left, no trees, no street signs; where once there had been homes lay only scattered piles of debris. They'd go past the houses they were looking for without being able to recognize them; one guy walked past the house he was born in, and he didn't know it anymore.

You knew when the worst gusts were coming, said Hugh Willoughby, when you heard the car alarms going off. The wind would rip toward you, setting off a string of alarms coming nearer and nearer. . . .

Soon afterward, Frank Marks went up in a light plane with a tornado expert to do a damage survey. Out on the Great Plains, this man was used to slim tracks of wreckage; now they went around in circles over Biscayne Bay looking at Andrew's aftermath, and after a while Marks asked him, "Are we doing what we're doing already? Or do you want to tell us when we're going to start doing it?"

The swath of ruin left by Andrew was twenty-five miles wide. The tornado expert turned away from the window and told Frank simply, "I don't know where to start."

Now, after Floyd, they swapped their stories on Virginia Key and thanked God that at least this time it hadn't happened to South Florida again.

Harvey came and went. The first day of autumn came on September 23, and with it the first cold front, dropping dawn temperatures at Crestview in the panhandle to a most un-Floridian 43° Fahrenheit. The atmospheric sluice gates in the mid-Atlantic—the patterns of hot sea and low shear in the early part of the season that let Cape Verde hurricanes develop, and barrel through toward the islands and the United States—were starting to close.

If anything happened now it would emerge from the still-steaming waters of the Caribbean or the Gulf. HRD watched thunderstorms flare and fade, but their options to fly any potential new system were thin. They had fifty-two hours of plane time left, enough for five missions, but they only had one P-3 and one flight crew—the other plane was leaving for Austria—and they had no money. Considering one bundle of convection waxing red and orange on the infrared just south and east of Jamaica, Frank Marks shrugged and told them, "I'm sorry, guys. But we're not doing genesis."

They couldn't afford to fly a genesis experiment, but they did still hope to get more work done on their main priority, the air-sea interaction study—not least because the expiry dates on the batteries in a lot of the instruments they'd use were either past already or imminent. If necessary, they'd borrow hours out of next year's already much-diminished plane budget to do it; as ever, they were back to counting time and pennies while they waited on the weather.

At four in the afternoon of Monday, September 27, while HRD kept their eyes on the Caribbean, there was a fire inside the Cray C90 supercomputer in Federal Office Building 4 in Suitland, Maryland. This was the central nervous system of NOAA's forecasting operation; this was the computer that ran nearly all the global models on which hurricane prediction depends.

Two of the power supply units inside the C90 were damaged; the dry chemicals used by the fire department to put out the blaze contaminated other components of the computer as well. Three days later Silicon Graphics Incorporated, the computer contractor, determined that "the computer has been significantly damaged. Silicon Graphics does not believe that the computer can be repaired. The Cray C90 is inoperative."

Using other computers and backup procedures, roping in aid from the military and other agencies, a patched, jerry-built system was knocked into place to try to keep the National Weather Service turning out their forecast products. Inevitably, this system could not be as effective. Models that normally ran four times a day were down to two runs daily, and their resolution was coarser; the forecasters weren't blinded, but there was certainly some degree of myopia. As one researcher put it glumly, "Here we are in the mighty U.S. of A.—and we're relying for our hurricane forecasts on computers in Bracknell and Tokyo and Ottawa."

While engineers wrestled with the lamed hardware in the early days of October, TD11 stumbled into Mexico past Veracruz, drowning hundreds, and TD12 formed in midocean, a thousand miles east of the Lesser Antilles. Both were ill-formed and hard to read; at NHC's maps discussion on October 6, the forecasters and their support staff debated intently whether these were really solid cyclonic systems at all. Satellite imagery was inconclusive; there was much uncertainty as to whether the models were properly initialized and whether they were developing either proto-system in plausible directions.

Especially in the Gulf and the Caribbean, late season storms are harder to call anyway, even if your principal forecast tool hasn't burst into flames. They're closer to land, and they bloom in a bitty, fragmented atmospheric environment; scraps and wedges of low pressure, of circling air and rising thunderstorm fall across the sea off the different American landmasses, colliding and interacting with each tropical wave that comes through in a blurred and jumbled profusion.

Day after day, patchy eruptions of rain and lightning stumbled and faltered over the sweltering sea; the map was blotched with orange messes of ill-organized disturbance. Another broad, shapeless area of low pressure formed off Colombia, in the same place where Mitch was born; it nudged unsteadily northwest toward the Mosquito Coast, then turned a hint more to the north. By Tuesday, October 12, NHC was sufficiently concerned about it to send a plane out to see if it was Tropical Depression 13 yet; the plane found the makings of a low-level swirl, with wind speeds nearing twenty-five miles an hour on the eastern side of the circulation. Jamaica, Cuba, and the Cayman Islands could expect heavy rain soon; South Florida likewise, maybe twenty-four hours later.

The system held together overnight, becoming slowly better organized; by Wednesday morning the winds were exceeding forty miles an hour, and the first advisory on Tropical Storm Irene was duly issued at eleven o'clock. It was hard to tell from satellite pictures, but it looked to be centered about 160 miles west-southwest of Grand Cayman, traveling a shade west of north at maybe eight miles an hour.

The Caymans put up a tropical storm warning. Farther north, the Cuban government announced a hurricane watch for their westernmost province of Pinar del Rio, for the Isle of Youth to the south of it, and for the city and environs of Havana. On the Tropical Update, John Hope advised all residents of the Gulf Coast states, and certainly all Floridians, "to start taking inventory . . . watch this very carefully now."

At HRD's maps discussion that Wednesday, Sam Houston handed the latest fan of model tracks out. It looked as if Irene would cross the western tip of Cuba inside forty-eight hours, but after that the guidance splayed out; BAM Shallow offered a northwest path, while the other models swung all around the top of the compass to where BAM Deep took Irene on a northeast track into the Everglades. In itself, that degree of variance isn't necessarily unusual—even if key parts of the mainframe aren't charred and fused—but there were additional problems here anyway.

Thanks to the infinite common sense of international politics, the air force reconnaissance planes couldn't go into Cuban airspace. They had to go the long way around to get inside this storm; there wouldn't be a plane there now until two in the afternoon, and in the meantime the model runs were starting from a central fix determined off the satellite pictures—an imprecise data point at the best of times, and all the more so with a large, sloppy, cloud-covered sprawl of a thing like Irene.

Nonetheless, said Houston, if the storm moved on the official forecast track, pretty much due north, "we'll be into the first rain in a few hours. The bands are forming over Cuba already. And right now, it's in a very favorable environment for development—it's got warm water, and really low shear."

A trough of low pressure was digging down off the central United States; what path Irene followed would hinge a lot on how fast and deep that barrier pushed south. The storm might get squeezed, and start braking as it neared Cuba; even if it crossed the island, it could be held offshore from the Gulf Coast for four or five days yet. If that happened, it might spin up stronger—and it could get pressed more east into southern Florida, instead of making north toward the panhandle.

"Officially," said Houston, "NHC keeps it well west of Naples as a minimal hurricane in seventy-two hours. My feeling is the trough'll push it more toward landfall around Naples by then, about Saturday lunchtime, or maybe up by Tampa later on that day. But until the recon's in, we really don't have a good initial motion. The air force will go in today and tomorrow, then we're tasked to fly on Friday morning. But whatever we do, we're looking at increasing rain in Miami by the weekend—and if it goes into Naples, we may well get tropical storm force winds here. It's going to be messy. This could be a very wet, flooding-type scenario. . . ."

It looked like an untidy situation all around. Irene might offer a chance to do the air-sea study, but to do that to any purpose, you had first to know the state of your candidate patch of deep, warm ocean before a storm moved over it. Early in the season, Pete Black had mapped two Gulf warm eddies out west of the Florida peninsula, the kind of features that almost certainly helped Opal and Camille become so intense, so fast—but now Irene looked likely to travel too far east of the water he'd sampled.

The new storm would more likely cross the Loop Current in the Florida Strait, a stretch of water cramped by both politics and geography. On top of that, the current's fast—so if it's moving through the strait at three miles an hour, the body of water you surveyed in any given area might well have left that area by the time the storm then arrived on top of it.

They talked their way around the awkwardness of all this until finally Marks said, "Hey, guys. I didn't put Cuba there. Cuba's been there a lot longer than me, and we always knew it might be a factor in this. But Irene doesn't look likely to become too much of a system anyway. It'll get punched out crossing the mountains down there, it'll hit shear, then it'll hit southwest Florida—it's got no time to develop, has it?"

Pete Black wasn't so sure. Cleo in 1964 was a Category 1 leaving Cuba, it spent four or five hours crossing the Straits, and even in that short time it cooked up pretty fast—but Irene was shrouded in all manner of uncertainties besides that one. With hints of a clear eye starting to form in new images at two o'clock that afternoon, it began to look as if the initial satellite fix had been way too far south. The storm was already looking both nearer and stronger, and it was very likely moving faster than anyone had first thought. If recon now confirmed this, there could be a hurricane watch posted for Key West inside twenty-four hours.

Sure enough, once the air force plane got inside Irene, the fix on the storm's center had suddenly to be jogged an entire degree north. From the satellite pictures, they'd misread Irene's location by sixty miles—a margin of error that rendered any model run based on it pretty much worthless.

A hurricane watch was duly issued for the lower and middle Keys in the five P.M. advisory that Wednesday afternoon. Wind speeds in Irene had increased by then to fifty miles an hour; authorities in the Keys asked non-residents to start a voluntary evacuation, with the likelihood that this would soon become a mandatory order.

The first rainband came through Miami Beach that evening. The wind wasn't fierce, but it was enough to blow a fair slant into the torrents of shining water as they fell outside the Deuce on 14th Street. As the street ran inches deep with rain, a tiny, withered old homeless woman, little more than a skimpy bag of rags and bones, scuttled into the bar's doorway to shelter from the downpour.

After forty-five minutes or so, when the worst was done, Colin, the English barman, went and asked her to move on. It was still raining, and I raised my eyebrows at that. Colin shrugged and said, "Hey. It's a cruel world out there."

Irene was a Category 1 hurricane the following morning. The maximum winds were now reckoned at eighty-five miles an hour, confined to a tight core only fifteen miles across—but the circulation overall was much, much larger than that. An enormous spread of rain and thunderstorms now covered the western two-thirds of Cuba, drenching an area of that island 400 miles long; farther north, two more torrential rainbands spiraled through Miami that Thursday, one early in the morning, the next toward the end of the day during the rush-hour commute.

The storm had paused a while by the Isle of Youth, 125 miles south of Havana, then set off on a northeast track in the afternoon at nine miles an hour. South Florida was warned to expect at least ten inches of rain—the I-95 corridor from Miami up through Fort Lauderdale was taking three to six inches from the rainbands already—and the hurricane watch in the lower end of the Keys was upgraded to a warning. The forecast now anticipated a landfall on the west Florida coast, probably up around Tampa; still the problems with degraded models and inaccessible Cuban airspace left HRD's people uncertain if that was right.

Working on the wind field analysis, Sam Houston remained more inclined to a landfall farther south, around Naples or Fort Myers—but in truth, anyplace from Tampa down to Everglades City made him anxious.

Southwest Florida had seen rampant growth in the past two decades; now he feared that even a Category 1 landfall in that area would expose all the same shoddy building practices that had contributed so much to the devastation seen in Andrew.

After Andrew, Dade and Broward counties had brought in the South Florida Building Code, a notably more stringent set of rules governing construction in a hurricane-prone area. Unfortunately, no other local governments around Florida had followed suit.

Houston said, "I'd hope that Andrew would have alerted people, at least to get them to inspect things better, but it's a concern among everyone here that we've got all this coastal development going on and that people aren't necessarily living in the best-constructed houses. On the west coast you've got whole retirement communities over there, a lot of mobile homes, and these are people on fixed incomes—so even if it's only a Cat 1, if it starts stripping off their siding, to those people that's a major event."

It was an event getting steadily closer; Irene went past Havana and out into the Straits of Florida late that Thursday afternoon. Still no one felt too confident about where she planned on ending up; to all intents and purposes it could be anyplace from Miami to Tallahassee, and hurricane watches were now posted halfway up the state on both sides of the peninsula.

After the fire in the Cray computer, said Houston, "I'm seeing what I think is a degradation in the numerical models. In the ten years I've worked here I've seen those models improve greatly, dramatically—but right now, I've got doubts about how good this forecast is. And if this had happened during Floyd . . ."

He fell silent; that last idea didn't bear contemplation. Meanwhile, Miami was now under a tropical storm warning and a hurricane watch. As the eye crossed the north coast of Cuba, a big flare of deep-red convection bloomed on the infrared; far from weakening as it passed over land, the central pressure had actually fallen by eleven millibars instead. Havana reported gusts at seventy-eight miles an hour. Max Mayfield said, "We're a little bit concerned. Any time we've got a hurricane moving over those warm waters, we're *very* concerned."

Jerry Jarrell predicted a strong Category 1, maybe a weak Category 2 by the time Irene had crossed the Straits. The official forecast track was nudging east as well, confirming Houston's hunch that landfall down by Naples looked more likely than a strike on Tampa farther north up the coast.

It was Thursday evening; as the rain teemed down, the first reports of shallow flooding around the city were coming in already. In the morning, the fourth rainband came through, as the center of the storm moved into the Keys. Around noon I ran through the continuing downpour to my car, and set off for the lab on Virginia Key.

The sky was a low, thick, bulbous murk; the rain sluiced down from it, and broken palm fronds skeltered through sheets of water across the road. At the stoplights before the toll gates onto Rickenbacker Causeway, the wind was strong enough that the car rocked and shuddered unevenly in its grasp; overhead, the traffic lights swung wildly on their crossbars. Clouds of silver-gray rain raced through the streets; the causeway was curtained in spray, sheened in water, its surface laced with scampering, scurrying ripples. The thin stretch of beach beside the road was gone; chopping and tossing, the sea pushed up close around the feet of the palms to the verge of the tarmac.

It was, surely, going to be one of the season's more interesting maps discussions—but when I got there the building was closed. In the soaking gloom the great hulk of the lab stood locked and lightless, looking blankly down on the bucking, rocking trees around the parking lot.

Rob Rogers drove up; he'd dropped his wife off downtown, where he said the tunnel effect created by the high-rises had made the wind seem especially fierce. With a hint of anxiety he said, "You could feel how a car could just get picked up and flipped."

Of the HRD staff, only Sam Houston and a student named Mark Croxford were inside the building. The others were either flying in the storm, looking to their homes and families, or helping out at NHC—where the forecasters were clinging barely to the right side of chaos. Though their post-Andrew bunker had in theory been built to withstand a Category 5, here we were in only the shallow end of tropical storm force winds a hundred miles from the center of a minimal Category 1—yet around eleven o'clock their electricity had gone just as they were trying to get the latest advisories out, there'd been trouble with the backup generators flaking out, the computers had been sporadically crashing, it took two or three hours to get everything back up, and in among all that their forecast was beginning to look decidedly ropey.

Croxford and Houston scrambled back and forth from the computer room to the fax machine to the monitor screens on the floor above. The power was going on and off here too; high on the wall the Weather Channel flickered and buzzed, unheeded in the thickening dimness. Around the high atrium the wind hissed and groaned, gusts thumping and pounding against glass and concrete in the roof. The building boomed and echoed with the noise of it; sheets of rain streamed down tall, smoked windows, leaving the causeway and Miami beyond it blurred past recognition.

Houston was using dropsonde data from the P-3 to sketch out the wind field; he was producing graphic analysis of how far the hurricane force winds extended around the core, and how far winds of tropical storm force reached out beyond that. It was vital information for the emergency management people, because just knowing where the eye is only gets you to first base. You need also to know where the winds start getting bad ahead of it, and how long that gives you before life starts becoming disorderly—which moment, it appeared, was closing fast upon us.

The wind field whose scope and strength Sam Houston was measuring was howling right outside the walls. In the darkened building, he calmly fed his latest graphics through the fax machine to NHC; the computer connections weren't reliable enough to send them electronically anymore. Then he went to look at the radar. Irene was a big, sloppy vortex of livid green rainfall lumbering up the Keys—and she very plainly wasn't going to southwest Florida. On each stuttering loop as the images rolled, from the track of the empty, scrappy eye within the ragged green sprawl, the hurricane's movement was very clearly northeast.

"That's not going to Naples," said Houston quietly. "That thing's coming here."

An oceanographer appeared from one of the floors below. Quickly Houston told him, "I'd get out of here. It's going to go right over us. I think we're going to get slammed. And don't use the elevator—the power's going to go any minute."

He started getting ready to drive across town to NHC, shaking his head all the while. "This forecast's a bust," he muttered, "and they're sitting in the dark over there. It is so incredible what a wimpy little thing like this is doing. And look, there's an eyewall forming too; we're going to get blasted right here."

He'd seen big trees down on Key Biscayne already, trees that had stood through Andrew; though not a remotely comparable event, Irene now looked set to be the worst impact on Dade County since that disaster.

"We should be under a hurricane warning," said Croxford.

Houston shook his head. "It's too late. We're getting toward fifty miles an hour sustained; we're going to have that on the Key here inside an hour."

Of all the models, only one—just one out of a dozen—had foreseen Irene making toward Dade and Broward counties. That model was CLIPER, the oldest and simplest of them all.

It was one o'clock; Houston reckoned the eye was over Marathon and would be upon us by late afternoon. Calling ahead to NHC before he left, he learned that they now thought it would go through Hollywood, midway between Miami and Fort Lauderdale, in which case Miami would get the east-front quadrant of the storm, the very worst part of it. In four or five hours . . .

It was enough time to cross town to NHC, and then get home to Miami Beach before the eye came through. The drive was horrendous. Here and there, plywood boards and bits of fencing hurtled through the traffic from construction sites; at one point I saw a shopping trolley go skidding between the cars across the road. All the while water flew in sheets across the highway, vast puddles lay axle-deep, and near the forecast center the ironically named suburb of Sweetwater was already turning into a shallow lake; cars crawled and stalled in water up to their radiators.

Irene was arriving over the beginnings of a premature rush hour; as people realized what was happening, anyone who could get away from work now struggled to make their way home through the flooding rain. There were times when it felt about as close to driving underwater as you could get, when you couldn't see farther than the car's hood in front of you—and two people would indeed drown in their cars, unable to distinguish between canals and flooded roads, and driving into the former by mistake.

I got to NHC about two o'clock; the center of the storm was coming onshore through the Everglades, heading northeast toward Dade and Broward counties. Gusts of seventy-seven miles per hour were reported in Homestead, just south of Miami. Knowing the media criticism that would surely soon be coming his way, Jerry Jarrell picked his words carefully as he told reporters in the conference room, "We're over hurricane force in gusts, and that's what's reasonable for a tropical storm warning—and I'd say that's not the last of that we'll see. Everything's crawling north, so the stronger gusts will work their way up further."

He tried to explain how hard it is to call a storm like this one. He said, "This has been a tough center to define. Radar usually gets a good fix on these things, but sometimes the radar doesn't see everything that's going on. We've been seeing a reorganization of the eye going left to right, left to right, and that's why we rely on the reconnaissance aircraft to get in there and say, 'This is the fix. This is where the center actually is.'"

Mike Black and Peter Dodge were flying the landfall as he spoke. Black would subsequently report that Irene was the bumpiest, meanest ride of the season, more turbulently ill-organized than Bret or Dennis or Floyd had ever been.

With little more that he could do at NHC, Black's namesake Pete, meanwhile, had set off into the storm to see how high the sea was coming against the causeway leading out to Virginia Key. Forty-five years after he'd run into his parents' garden during Carol, his boyish zest before the forces of nature remained undimmed—sufficiently so that after a while when he hadn't come back, Frank Marks and Hugh Willoughby began to get concerned and thought they'd better go after him. Five blocks from Black's house, Willoughby's truck stalled and died in the rising water; they had to wade the rest of the way knee-deep in flood.

Five people would die that way, walking into water that concealed fallen live power lines—including two eleven-year-old twins and their friend, and the twins' mother who ran in after them to try to save them as they died. This, remember, was a *minimal* hurricane—yet it was indirectly responsible for the deaths of seven Americans, and it wrought $800 million in damage to flooded homes, crops, and businesses.

On the road back to South Beach in midafternoon, it wasn't hard to see why. The downpour was horizontal, constant, and immense, a gray wall of water streaming through the driven air. On the causeway, the water racing across the road was inches deep, with a glinting, foaming surface as if whole rivers were now falling from the sky—which, quantitatively speaking, they were. Flags and ads on the lampposts beat frantically in the wind, torn and shredded; the palm trees rocked and shook, their fronds flying loose all over the drowning road. The sea in Government Cut tossed and bucked, churned to a dirty, pale green color, and it was everywhere smothered in deep sheets of misty spray so dense it looked like a blanket of fog.

I got home about three-thirty; the power was out, and so was the phone. Already big branches were down, and in some places whole trees; everywhere was strewn with broken vegetation, with felled street signs clattering here and there among the sodden whirl of leaves. Many streets were flooded knee-deep—and the worst was yet to come.

The eye passed through western Broward between five and six o'clock; for about an hour, Miami took the worst Irene had to offer in the northeast quadrant of the storm. On Miami Beach, the sustained winds were at the top of the tropical storm force scale, bordering on Category 1, with hurricane gusts certainly topping eighty miles an hour. At first they came out of the east, off the ocean; as the center passed through they turned to roar up from the south along Collins and Washington, blowing out a window in the apartment across the landing from mine, bringing down a huge tree in the school playground across the road.

Normally, surely you would have heard the smashing of the glass, or the giant, wrenching snap and thud of that tree falling to earth—but there was only the noise of the wind, a deep, physically sensible groan, beating and thumping against the walls and against the leaking, shuddering windows.

Daytime turned black. For a while I lay in the darkness, listening; several times I went down to the front hallway and watched unidentifiable scraps of rubbish and plant life flying down the road through steeply slanted masses of rain. Water was coming in off the street, spreading across the floor; eventually I realized that it was now so deep outside that if I didn't move my car soon, then come the morning I'd very probably not be moving it at all.

In the drenched and moaning gloom I waded past substantial chunks of tree limb rocking and jerking in the road, and found that the passenger side of the car had water three inches deep in the front and back already. I nudged it out to shallower water in the middle of the road, the wind tugging and shoving at it, the windshield wipers trying feebly to cope—then I drove around in Irene for a while. Some streets I decided against—too many trees—and others were flooded worse than mine.

I was thinking two things. First I was thinking, why is it you can never find a place to park on South Beach?

And second I was thinking, What if Irene had been Mitch?

One day, without any doubt, it will be—born in the same place, duping the forecasters, and just deciding on Cuba and Florida instead of Honduras. Because when storms are born in the southwest Caribbean, the historical record says plainly that Cuba and Florida are the places they most often like to go.

"The edge of a major storm," said Hugh Willoughby the next day, "is very much like what we've just been through. There's considerable disruption, but it's manageable—but in the heart of a major storm, you'll go from that manageable level of disruption to absolutely murderous conditions in just a couple of hours."

The forecasters would subsequently take a pounding in the media for "getting Irene wrong"—but of course it wasn't as simple as that.

Miami had been put under a tropical storm warning. Probably a hurricane warning would have made more sense, but when all the models wanted to take the storm into the southwest coast, you could only really say that with twenty-twenty hindsight. Moreover, it wasn't a school day; if it had been, they'd probably have gone to a hurricane warning anyway, to avert the dangers inherent in having the city's children trying to get home from school during whatever conditions might actually obtain.

Those conditions grew worse than expected because the track forecast was indeed wrong—but though the fire in the main computer certainly didn't help, James Franklin for one wasn't prepared to use that as a get-out clause. The fire didn't disable every model, after all; UKMET in Bracknell and NOGAPS in Monterey got Irene wrong just like the other ones did. Instead, said Franklin, "we had a model run twice a day instead of four times a day. So, OK, the guidance was wrong twice a day—but if we hadn't had the fire, it would probably just have been wrong four times a day."

The bottom line, as any forecaster will tell you, is that there will *always* be occasions when the forecast is wrong. In this particular case, "wrong" is actually a harsh word to use anyway; if you want to be absolutely literal you can certainly use that word, but it would be more precise to describe the forecast on Irene as being merely at the bad end of average.

That's because the southern end of Florida is only a hundred miles across, and that distance is the average margin of error in any twenty-four-hour forecast. Statistically, therefore, whether Irene went through Dade in the east or Naples in the west, NHC can argue that with Irene they remained (just about) within the accepted error band that inevitably exists in the present state of the art.

If you want that art to get better and that error band to shrink, the only way to achieve it is you spend more money on research. You do that to improve the track forecasts, in the hope that the path of awkward storms like Irene can be better predicted in the future. You do it to improve the intensity forecasts, so the next Opal doesn't suddenly explode up to Category 4 just offshore and catch thousands of late evacuees on the highway. And, most difficult of all, you do it to improve the rainfall forecast.

Andrew came ashore as a borderline Category 4/5, blew down huge areas of south Dade, and yet was only directly responsible for fifteen deaths. Floyd came ashore as a Category 2, but it killed nearly four times as many people. In Miami, Irene was only barely a Category 1, but it was still a major rainmaker, it killed seven people, and it produced a large order of unhappiness and dislocation.

Parts of Miami stayed underwater for days. South Florida doesn't drain fast; it's flat as a board, the ground's a thin sponge of swamp overlaid on a rock-hard pancake of fossilized silt, and any excess water just sits on it. Add to this the fact that the water management authorities can only run off an inch from the canals every twenty-four hours—partly because of the physical limitations of the floodgates, partly because they have to maintain the salinity balance of Biscayne Bay—and an event like Irene is going to wash in through front doors citywide every time.

It's a mystifying truth, however, that in this and in so many other ways, people are still routinely surprised by what a hurricane can do. The first crucial point to be grasped is that even a minor storm can generate a major disaster. Indeed, two of the most damaging hurricanes in United States history were both only Category 1 storms; Diane in 1955 and Agnes in 1972 had calamitous impacts, almost entirely brought about by freshwater flooding from the rain that fell inland.

Unfortunately, therefore, it must be noted that all the media talk after Floyd that that storm's inundation was "a 500-year event" is simply nonsense. Setting aside the fact that it's a meaningless statement in the first place (because we don't have data going back 500 years), it doesn't take much study of the record to realize that flooding events like Floyd happen a great deal more often than twice per millennium.

They actually happen more than twice per century—but though this lesson is important, there's a second lesson in the record that's more frightening altogether. Minor storms are problem enough—but what if we start seeing more major ones?

The tropical update reads as follows: in the next few decades, there are going to be a lot more major hurricanes in the Atlantic basin. An event like Irene will be merely commonplace; Mitch and Floyd will have many siblings.

The thinking behind this forecast holds, in essence, that hurricanes in the Atlantic basin follow a multidecadal pattern; that there's a natural cycle in which periods of intense activity lasting from twenty to forty years are interspersed with similarly long periods that see far fewer major storms.

The historical record definitely supports this idea. During the last twenty-five years of the nineteenth century there were a lot of major storms, culminating in the calamity at Galveston in 1900. Then things fell much quieter in the early years of the twentieth century, until Miami was destroyed in 1926.

For forty-three years after that, major hurricanes became almost routine. There was the Lake Okeechobee disaster in 1928, and 1933 saw more Atlantic tropical cyclones than any other year on record—twenty-one, over twice the average. Two years later, the Labor Day storm went through the Keys, and the forties were simply horrendous. Florida was battered by eleven full-grown hurricanes in ten years, with a major direct hit on Dade County in 1945; superimpose the tracks of that decade's landfalls on the peninsula, and it looks as if the state's had a nest of vipers thrown across it.

Three more hurricanes hit Florida in 1950; Hurricane King was the second major landfall in Dade County in five years. In the fifties North Carolina took multiple hits before the sixties were rung in by Donna; in three days of

September 1960, Donna killed fifty people in ten states. In 1965, Betsy then hit both South Florida and New Orleans, causing the biggest damage bill yet seen—$1.2 billion in contemporary dollars in Louisiana alone, with fifty-eight dead in that state and seventy-five Americans in total.

Hurricane Inez two years later had winds at one point touching 175 miles per hour; from Guadeloupe to Hispaniola, through Cuba and the Keys and on into Mexico, over a thousand people died. In 1969 Camille, the century's second Category 5 American landfall, went ashore in Mississippi—then the active period ended.

The difference is striking. Averaged out over the long term, a major hurricane hits the Atlantic seaboard of the United States once every three years. In the twenty-five years from 1970 to 1994, however, only two major hurricanes did that—those two being Hugo and Andrew.

Obviously, there are caveats. Not every year in an active period sees massive destruction; similarly, even for an inactive phase 1992 was a particularly quiet year, with only one major storm and only six named storms in total. Unfortunately, that one major storm was Andrew—so if you lived in south Dade, 1992 wasn't a quiet year at all.

Nonetheless, the larger pattern is plain. From 1926 to 1969, there was an average of three major hurricanes per year; from 1970 to 1994, there were half as many. So why does this happen?

During the periods when a larger number of intense hurricanes occur, the surface of the Atlantic is measurably warmer, and an overall regime of lower wind shear across the ocean is measurably more conducive to letting hurricanes build. It looks likely that this in turn is caused by more or less regular, large-scale changes in the flow of the world's ocean currents; that every few decades nature throws a switch in the sea, the Atlantic heats up, and more big storms brew.

What should concern us now, therefore, is that after a quarter-century of relative peace, it's beginning to look very much as if nature threw the switch again in 1995.

During the 1995 hurricane season Drew Delaney was living on St. Thomas in the U.S. Virgin Islands, a young barman leading the paradise life; work was fun, and the diving was great. True, it did seem a busy year for storms—in late August and early September, Hurricanes Iris and Luis both brushed the Virgins—but Delaney was enjoying himself too much to worry about some unlikely calamity. When Marilyn emerged in the mid-Atlantic on September 12, he and his friends just figured she'd brush past them too.

Marilyn was a Category 1 when she went over Martinique and Guadeloupe; once west of those islands, she started strengthening. On St. Thomas, Delaney's crowd thought they'd have a hurricane party; there was a huge bar in an old sugar mill they could go to, with good music and a giant video screen. The building had stood up to all the storms it had seen in the past, so why not now?

Marilyn didn't brush St. Thomas; the northeast eyewall went right over the island, with winds gusting to 130 miles an hour. In the noise of the bar, with the drinking and the music and *Pulp Fiction* on the big screen, Delaney didn't realize at first how bad it was getting outside; he only realized it when the roof started coming off. He looked up and saw the exploding beams flying upward taking the screen with them, and the screen was still working; astonished, Delaney watched Bruce Willis blow away into the howling black darkness.

Five people died on St. Thomas that night; 80 percent of the island's homes and businesses were destroyed, 10,000 were made homeless, and Marilyn's damage bill there and elsewhere was $1.5 billion. Delaney says it changed his life forever. His was one of the homes blown to pieces; he had close friends among the dead. "Sad to say," he says now, "it's all too possible to take for granted what you've got—until you lose it."

Midway through the alphabet, Marilyn was the thirteenth named storm of 1995, and the seventh hurricane, but the season was far from done with. Within days Noel and Opal followed; it was the first time since tropical cyclones were named that the Atlantic had produced an O storm, and still it didn't end. Four more storms made a total of nineteen; there had not been a year so busy since 1933. Five of them were major hurricanes—Felix, Luis, Marilyn, Opal, and Roxanne—and five of them made American landfalls.

It's no coincidence that, from 1994 to 1995, the average surface temperature of the ocean in the Atlantic cyclone basin had jumped by one-half a degree centigrade. It doesn't sound like much, but in a body of water that large, it constitutes a massive increase in the amount of energy available to fuel hurricanes.

On its own, one such bad year would be a statistical blip—but the sea stayed warmer, and 1996 was bad too. There were thirteen named storms, no less than six of which grew to Category 3 or worse, causing havoc from Costa Rica to North Carolina.

Statistically, even two bad years might still be a blip—and a major El Niño event in 1997 did then produce a much quieter season. Once El Niño faded, however, 1998 produced catastrophe. There were fourteen storms, ten of them were hurricanes, and three of them were Category 3 or worse. Bonnie hit North Carolina, causing widespread damage there and in Virginia; Earl hit the Florida panhandle; flooding from Frances in Texas and Louisiana cost half a billion dollars—and that was only the beginning.

Hurricane Georges made seven landfalls, in Antigua, St. Kitts and Nevis, Puerto Rico, Hispaniola, Cuba, Key West, and Biloxi; 600 people died, mostly in floods and mud slides in Haiti and the Dominican Republic, while the damage bill was close to $6 billion. And then there was Mitch.

Driving through Miami in the middle of Irene a year later, the idea that the switch in the ocean has been thrown, and that a new active period is upon us, seemed all the more plausible. Already, in the four years before 1999, there had been thirty-three hurricanes; no previous four-year period in reliably recorded history has ever been that busy. Now, the season not yet finished had produced Bret, Cindy, Gert, and Floyd; when Lenny then blew up in November to grind across the Dutch island of St. Maarten, that would make five Category 4 hurricanes in one year, and that's never happened before either.

The sea has stayed warmer, the shear regime has gotten weaker, and the hurricanes have grown both stronger and more numerous. Moreover, says Chris Landsea at HRD, "once the Atlantic gets into that mode, it appears to stay in it for a while. So I'd say we'll see it like this for another twenty or thirty years now."

I t gets worse.

Insurers calculate the return period for a disaster like Andrew over a long timescale; they come out with an average likelihood that an event of that magnitude will recur every thirty or so years. Unfortunately, Landsea doesn't think that figure is realistic, because the climate simply isn't that stable. In a quiet period, certainly, you may well live a good long time without seeing a major hurricane. On the other hand, in a busy period like the one we appear to be entering now, Miami can expect a severe impact *every ten years.*

Moreover, South Florida is now massively more vulnerable, because massively more people live there, engaged in massively more complex and interwoven economic activity. In a sense, this applies to the entire hurricane-prone coast of the United States; during the twenty-five years of the last quiet period, an awful lot of people have decided it would be nice to live on the beach. From Texas to Long Island, the rate of increase in the coastal population continues today at over 4 percent a year—so all those people now find themselves in a place of residence where the danger has markedly increased.

For South Florida, nonetheless, the threat is especially acute. The eleventh most populous state of the union in 1980, Florida today ranks fourth; Dade and Broward counties alone have a population of nearly 4 million, and 600 more people move into the state every day. In consequence, all along the coastline, swamp and mangrove have been and continue to be rapaciously transformed into condo and suburb. Where once the hurricane was nature's reset button, brutally flushing out the unpeopled bays and glades, there now stands a burgeoning world of malls and marinas, retirement communities and amusement parks. Unfortunately, it rather seems as if countless land-use decisions involved in that process will now turn out to have been fantastically reckless.

That's because, if Landsea and his colleagues are right—and it certainly looks that way—then in the next two or three decades there are going to be twice as many storms of at least Category 3 stature bearing down on all that teeming development.

"What it means," says Hugh Willoughby, "is that the occasional $5 billion damage toll is going to be a lot less occasional. There are several places along the coast—Miami, New Orleans, Galveston/Houston—where multiples of tens of billions of dollars are possible."

One doomsday scenario has a Category 3 coming into New York, pouring the ocean into the subway system, and leaving La Guardia Airport under twelve feet of seawater; it's possible, but unlikely. There is, however, one climatological track—one course that storms have taken in the past—whose human and economic impact today would be little short of apocalyptic.

It involves a storm like Floyd at the peak of its power going down Governor's Cut onto 8th Street in downtown Miami, continuing past the airport through west Dade, and crossing out from there into the Gulf of Mexico. Once back over warm water the storm reintensifies, and then it hits New Orleans. It tips Lake Pontchartrain into the city from behind it, and it blows the ocean up the river in front of it.

The cumulative damage in such an event could easily exceed $100 billion—but a bad strike on Miami alone, as noted earlier, could well be an $80 billion hit in itself. This would certainly jolt the Caribbean and at least parts of Latin America toward recession. Virtually all the region's major banks have their headquarters in Miami; trade spills through the port and the airport. Let a storm trash all that, and the effects would ripple outward from New York to Buenos Aires, from London to L.A.

It may not bear contemplation, but this is the prospect that good and credible science lays before us—good science done by brave men on a puny budget—and it's what the people of Honduras already understand far too well.

In the ruins of Barrio Pedro Diaz, in the wrecked wasteland of dust and hovels by the Choluteca, Paola Sanchez and her brother Santo may know little of sea surface temperatures, of vertical wind shear or the Coriolis effect—but they know what hell looks like. Like their colonial forebear Cabeza de Vaca on the Cuban shore nearly five centuries before them, they know what happens when the devil's music starts to play. And now, as Paola said, they could only watch in fear to see what the river did the next time it rained—because they know that when the hurricane comes, it's not a thing that's over in a day or a week.

Wealthy and politically well-connected, Arturo Corrales in Tegucigalpa might be thought to inhabit a different world—but his concern for the future of his wrecked country was exactly the same. In the head office of his family's engineering and surveying business, authoritatively surrounded by maps, blueprints, computers, and satellite images, he described how the riverbeds of Honduras now lay choked with sand and mud and sediment; how their courses were markedly more shallow, so that even a normal rain risked bringing more floods.

He told me bluntly, "It will happen again."

Five months after the storm he said, "As an engineer I'm telling you, Mitch has not gone yet. He's still here. He came to stay."

316
ABNT20 KNHC 010321
TWOAT
TROPICAL WEATHER OUTLOOK
NATIONAL WEATHER SERVICE MIAMI FL
1030 PM EST TUE NOV 30 1999

FOR THE NORTH ATLANTIC . . . CARIBBEAN SEA AND THE GULF OF MEXICO . . .

A NON-TROPICAL GALE CENTER . . . LOCATED ABOUT 1350 MILES EAST-SOUTHEAST
OF BERMUDA . . . HAS NOT BECOME ANY BETTER ORGANIZED. FURTHER
INFORMATION ON THIS SYSTEM CAN BE FOUND IN ATLANTIC HIGH SEAS
FORECASTS ISSUED BY THE TROPICAL PREDICTION CENTER UNDER WMO HEADER
FZNT01 KWBC AND UNDER AFOS HEADER NFDHSFAT1.

ELSEWHERE . . . THERE ARE NO WEATHER SYSTEMS THAT POSE A THREAT OF
TROPICAL STORM DEVELOPMENT. TODAY IS THE LAST DAY OF THE 1999 ATLANTIC
HURRICANE SEASON . . . AND THIS OUTLOOK WILL BE THE LAST ONE ISSUED FOR
THE 1999 SEASON. ISSUANCE OF THIS PRODUCT WILL RESUME ON JUNE 1 2000.

HAVE A NICE WINTER . . .

FRANKLIN

Appendix 1

15 MOST DEADLY ATLANTIC HURRICANES

Location	Year	Deaths
"The Great Hurricane," Martinique/Barbados	1780	22,000
Galveston, Texas	1900	9,000
FIFI, Honduras	1974	9,000
MITCH, Central America	1999	9,000
FLORA, Haiti/Cuba	1963	8,000
Pointe-a-Pitre Bay, Guadeloupe	1776	6,000
Newfoundland Banks	1775	4,000
Puerto Rico/Carolinas	1899	3,500
Guadeloupe/Puerto Rico/Lake Okeechobee, Florida	1928	3,400
Cuba/Caymans/Jamaica	1932	3,000
Central Atlantic	1782	3,000
Martinique	1813	3,000
El Salvador/Honduras	1934	3,000
Western Cuba	1791	3,000
Barbados	1831	2,500

Source: Rappaport and Fernandez-Partegas. I've added Mitch to their list. All death totals are approximate, some very much so.

15 MOST COSTLY
U.S. HURRICANES

Hurricane	Year	Category	Damage
ANDREW, Florida/Louisiana	1992	4	$30,475,000,000
HUGO, South Carolina	1989	4	$ 8,491,561,181
AGNES, Northeast U.S.	1972	1	$ 7,500,000,000
BETSY, Florida/Louisiana	1965	3	$ 7,425,340,909
CAMILLE, Mississippi/Alabama	1969	5	$ 6,096,287,313
DIANE, Northeast U.S.	1955	1	$ 4,830,580,808
FREDERIC, Alabama/Mississippi	1979	3	$ 4,328,968,903
New England	1938	3	$ 4,140,000,000
FRAN, North Carolina	1996	3	$ 3,200,000,000
OPAL, Florida/Alabama	1995	3	$ 3,069,395,018
ALICIA, Texas	1983	3	$ 2,983,138,781
CAROL, Northeast U.S.	1954	3	$ 2,732,731,959
CARLA, Texas	1961	4	$ 2,223,696,682
JUAN, Louisiana	1985	1	$ 2,108,801,956
DONNA, Florida/ Eastern U.S.	1960	4	$ 2,099,292,453

Source: Hebert, Jarrell, and Mayfield. Damage totals are given in 1996 dollars. The final bill for Floyd remains to be posted, but figures so far range from $3 to $6 billion in current dollars. It should be noted that Pielke and Landsea produce a different table, rating each storm *if it were to happen today*; by that measure, the Miami hurricane of 1926 would be by far the worst. Their paper on these normalized damages is listed in the selected resources.

Appendix 3

UPDATE AND FORECAST

There is absolutely no reason for a hurricane to make landfall. NOAA
must be done away with! The military must take control of our weather.
The reason NOAA allows our friends to die and their property
to be distroyed [sic] is simply avarice—there are
too many six-figure jobs involved.
—Earl in Alabama

Where do I get one of these six-figure jobs?
—Chris Landsea in Miami

Bill Gray's long-term forecast for the 1999 hurricane season turned out to be a good one. Four hundred miles east of the Windwards, Tropical Storm Jose was christened on the afternoon of Monday, October 18, three days after Irene came through Miami. Jose became a Category 2 hurricane, causing severe flooding and at least two deaths in Antigua and St. Maarten.

At the end of October, Tropical Storm Katrina made landfall in Nicaragua; two weeks later, Lenny was born 175 miles southeast of Jamaica. Lenny peaked as a Category 4 hurricane just south of St. Croix on November 17; weakening somewhat as it lurched across St. Maarten, it still caused around a dozen more fatalities. As further evidence that we're into a new active regime, there had been no Category 4 storm in November since Greta in 1956, and no year with five such storms at any time since records began.

In December 1998, Gray had forecast fourteen named storms, nine of them hurricanes, four of them majors. What the Atlantic actually produced was twelve storms, eight hurricanes, and five majors—so Gray and his team were pretty close. Given that at least two tropical depressions might well have become named storms in other circumstances—one was too short-lived before it fell into Mexico, while another in midocean didn't get paid much attention because Floyd and Gert were up and running on either side of it—the forecast couldn't have been much closer.

Gray's work has practical worth in fields from emergency management to the insurance business; sporadically, the latter industry has helped to fund his research. The American taxpayer standing in the path of the storm may, however, be interested to learn that Gray has not been funded by NOAA for several years, and that he often finds it hard to continue his work from one year to the next.

Maybe that's because NOAA's money is thinly spread across a vast range of responsibilities; maybe it's because Gray can be impolitic when he questions the resources deployed on numerical computer modeling. He's far from the only scientist who questions the worth of the large-scale climate models now seeking to produce long-range global forecasts, but as we've seen, even the models specifically applied to a hurricane's behavior over the next hundred hours can still on occasion perform pretty poorly.

They can get a storm like Floyd right on the button—then along comes a slow, meandering brute like Lenny and the models get utterly baffled. On Friday, November 19, as Lenny's eye drifted erratically between St. Maarten and Anguilla, with the model guidance continuing both widely divergent and mostly wrong, in NHC's forecast products Lixion Avila's Discussion No. 25 had him pretty much throwing up his hands in exasperated surrender.

He wrote, "Models have not changed their tune and for several days have been indicating a faster northeast track that has not materialized yet. Enough has already been said about model output . . . time will tell."

The phrase "time will tell" is surely the forecaster's equivalent of a helpless shrug, and twenty-four hours later, the situation was no better. In Discussion No. 29 Avila wrote, "I have no choice but to forecast a turn toward the northeast as indicated by track models. However . . . there is little confidence in this forecast."

Six hours later Discussion No. 30 announced, "The diffuse center of capricious Lenny appears to be moving toward the east-southeast about 5 knots . . . against all models . . . in this particular case . . . models are practically useless . . . and the situation is similar to Mitch."

To record the occasional failure of the models should not be taken as any implication that they've been a poor investment. On the contrary, the average track error for hurricane forecasts has been halved since 1970, and the models have been the principal engine driving that improvement. Their failures merely show that they are, in Hugh Willoughby's apt phrase, "Not a bad idea, but a work in progress."

The difficulties presented by storms like Mitch, Irene, and Lenny, therefore, simply illustrate how much more research is needed for that work to go on progressing—yet those engaged in the field battle forward in a penny-pinched environment, scrambling for funds in barely veiled frustration.

On Virginia Key, HRD finished the 1999 hurricane season $400,000 in the red. At the time of writing, Willoughby expects a funding increase of about $500,000 for budget year 2000—a 20 percent increase in his baseline allocation. That's enough to come out roughly even at the end of the 2000 season, though only if, as planned, HRD does very little flying in whatever storms the new season may produce. Willoughby describes the projected new budget as "survival money, but not enough to innovate. There's no spare money to hire new people, or to do anything else but keep on keeping on."

It might be pointed out that if all that $500,000 raise for HRD does indeed come through (and it looks as if it will), it still represents only 0.01 percent of the average annual damage bill for hurricanes in the United States. Cheap at the price? I can only leave it to those 40 million Americans now living on hurricane-prone shorelines to consider whether this is a sufficient disbursement of their tax dollars in pursuit of their better protection.

Had the new money not materialized, Willoughby would have thought seriously about writing his letter of resignation—and his frustration is widely shared. As Floyd loomed over the Bahamas and Bill Clinton returned early from New Zealand, NHC director Jerry Jarrell, his deputy Max Mayfield, and senior hurricane specialist Miles Lawrence flew to Washington to brief the president on the hurricane's likely path and impact. Jarrell said he'd wanted to ask Clinton for more money—as much for research at HRD and elsewhere as for his own team—but somehow, in the course of the presidential conversation, "There was not an opportunity afforded me to do that."

NOAA was supposed to be contributing one quarter of an $8 million budget to a multiagency program called the United States Weather Research Project. So far, they hadn't come up with their share of the money, and the other bodies involved (NASA, the National Science Foundation, and the Department of Defense) were getting antsy.

Jarrell sighed and said, "We spend four times that much on Clinton's security, so this is not a lot of money to bid for—but we're asking for peanuts and we're not even getting peanut shells. It's insane. We're looking at a huge disaster—like 1926, like Andrew, like Floyd could have been—and in my estimation, we're not doing anything to prevent it."

I imagine Jarrell meant "anything like enough" to prevent it. In total, the sum spent annually on airplanes, satellites, NHC, HRD, other NOAA agencies, and the wider academic range of hurricane research is something a little short of $100 million. By a complex calculation (taking into account a 340 percent increase in the coastal population from Texas through Virginia since 1950) it can be shown that the result of this investment is an average annual saving in U.S. property losses of around $1 billion and, altogether more important, of over 200 American lives.

So you can either settle for that, or you can try to do better. Given the credible threat of an increase in major hurricane activity, I know which way I'd go.

In the immediate future, meanwhile, Bill Gray's long-term forecast for hurricane season 2000 predicts a slightly quieter year than 1999, but still busier than the average. As of April 2000 his team foresaw eleven named storms, seven of them hurricanes, with three of those growing to Category 3 or worse. They also warn of an above-average probability of a major U.S. landfall, with a 39 percent chance of it happening on the Atlantic seaboard and a 34 percent chance on the Gulf Coast. More generally, they put the chance overall of a major landfall somewhere between Brownsville and Maine at 60 percent.

So if you've not bought storm shutters yet, now might be a good time to start thinking about it.

—May 2000

FORECAST 2001

Once again, the long-term forecast produced by Bill Gray and his team for 2000 turned out pretty well. There were more named storms overall than they'd predicted—fourteen, against a forecast of eleven—but only eight of them became hurricanes (against a forecast of seven) and their call that the season would produce three major storms was exactly right. Given the level of uncertainty involved, this is further confirmation that Gray and his colleagues are doing a good job.

Although 2000 was yet another very active season, it was also in the main a merciful one. Hurricane Debby briefly scared a lot of people in South Florida, before weakening and stumbling into the Dominican Republic, but in the end only two systems made U.S. landfall. These were Tropical Storms Gordon and Helene, which both went onshore in the Florida Panhandle in rapid succession.

Gordon caused twenty-four deaths, mostly in flooding in Guatemala, and one American died when Helene spawned a tornado in South Carolina. Soon afterward, torrential rainfall produced by the disturbance responsible for Tropical Storm Leslie killed another three people in South Florida; the associated damage bill was estimated at $700 million.

Of the major storms, Alberto and Isaac stayed far out at sea. The season's most destructive event was, therefore, Hurricane Keith, which pounded

Belize and the Yucatan Peninsula with winds of 125 miles an hour or worse for several days. Nineteen people lost their lives, and the damage bill in Belize alone was $200 million—a major impact on a small and fragile economy but, sadly, an impact that went largely unremarked.

So what does 2001 hold in store? First issued in December 2000, Gray's long-term forecast is for less activity than we've seen in the past record-breaking six years. The call is for nine named storms, five of them hurricanes, two of them bad ones—in other words, an average year.

Americans should not, however, take false reassurance from this prediction of a smaller number of storms in 2001 than there have been in previous years. What matters is not how many storms there are, but where they go— in particular, where the bad ones go—and Gray suggests an increasing likelihood that a major hurricane will make landfall in the United States.

For 2001 there is, he says, a 63 percent chance of such an event—this against a long-term average of 52 percent. His reasoning is that during the twentieth century overall, roughly one-third of all major hurricanes hit the United States, but in the past six years, of twenty-three such storms, only three have come ashore along the U.S. coastline.

Put another way, a disastrous U.S. landfall is, in statistical terms, pretty much due. Gray says, "Climatology will eventually right itself, and we must expect a substantial increase in landfalling major hurricanes on the U.S. East Coast and in peninsular Florida in the coming few decades. Due to the great increase in coastal population and property values in the southeast in recent years, we should expect to see hurricane damage at levels never before experienced."

So it may happen in 2001, or it may not. But sooner rather than later, it definitely will happen.

—March 2001

GLOSSARY

AOC. Aircraft Operations Center for NOAA, based at MacDill Air Force Base in Tampa.

AOML. Atlantic Oceanographic and Meteorological Laboratories, run by NOAA on Virginia Key in Miami.

ATC. Air Traffic Control.

AXBT. Airborne Expendable Bathythermograph, an instrument taking the temperature of the sea through depths down to 1,500 feet. Called BTs for short.

BAM. Beta and Advection Model, a computer model for forecasting hurricanes that considers the wind flow steering the storm overall, then adds a northwest push to it of about three miles per hour. It does this because, over the surface of the rotating spherical earth, that's the direction in which the hurricane's internal dynamics would naturally incline it to travel if there were no other weather about.

CLIPER. Climate and Persistence, a statistical computer model for forecasting hurricanes; the most rudimentary of the suite of models used by NHC.

Coriolis effect. The atmospheric impulse imparting spin to a hurricane as the planet rotates beneath the wind moving across it.

dropsonde. An instrument deployed into hurricanes to measure wind speed and direction, moisture content, temperature, and barometric pressure.

FIU. Florida International University.

GFDL. Geophysical Fluid Dynamics Laboratory, a NOAA laboratory on the campus of Princeton University; also the computer model named after this lab. One of the most reliable and sophisticated forecast tools presently at work at NHC.

GPS. Global Positioning System, the satellite network used by dropsondes to give precise location fixes on storm data.

HRD. Hurricane Research Division, part of AOML.

JAX ATC. Jacksonville Air Traffic Control.

maximum sustained wind. Different countries use different measures to determine this index of a storm's potency. In the United States, the wind has to blow for sixty seconds at a given speed before that speed is deemed to be "sustained."

NHC. National Hurricane Center, the hurricane-specific forecasting agency run by the U.S. National Weather Service on the campus of FIU in Miami.

NOAA (pronounced "Noah"). National Oceanic and Atmospheric Administration, part of the U.S. Department of Commerce.

NOGAPS. Navy Operational Global Atmospheric Prediction System, the U.S. Navy's computer forecast model run at Monterey, California.

NWS. National Weather Service, part of NOAA.

rawindsonde. A balloon packed with instruments for observing meteorological conditions, routinely launched around most of the world (in some places more often and more efficiently than others).

shear. The degree of difference in the speed and direction of winds at different altitudes. If it's all blowing the same way from the earth's surface to the top of the troposphere, you have "low vertical shear" and more hurricanes; if it isn't, you have high shear and fewer storms.

SOPTRAVI. The Honduran Ministry of Public Works, Transport, and Housing.

tropical wave. A parcel of disturbed weather originating over Africa, and most commonly the seed for Atlantic hurricanes.

tropical depression. A weather system with a closed circulation where the wind rotates around a center of low pressure. Often built in the Atlantic out of a tropical wave, the TD is precursor to a tropical storm. TDs are numbered but not named.

tropical storm. A system in which the maximum sustained wind exceeds 39 mph, at which point the storm gets a name.

tropical cyclone. The technically correct term for the weather system known around the world as a hurricane, cyclone, or typhoon. On the Saffir-Simpson scale used in the United States, a tropical storm becomes a hurricane when the maximum sustained wind exceeds 74 mph.

troposphere. The lower layer of the earth's atmosphere, to about 50,000 feet, in which the temperature decreases with altitude.

UKMET. The United Kingdom Meteorological Office's computer forecast model; the only non-American model in use at NHC.

SELECTED
RESOURCES

INTERNET

The National Hurricane Center's Web site carries a wealth of current and historical information as well as up-to-the minute forecast advisories and discussions during the season:
http://www.nhc.noaa.gov

The Hurricane Research Division is at:
http://www.aoml.noaa.gov/hrd/

Chris Landsea posts a fantastically useful crash course in tropical meteorology on the HRD site, titled Frequently Asked Questions (FAQ):
http://www.aoml.noaa.gov/hrd/tcfaq/tcfaqHED.html

For information on the 1999 Hurricane Field Program:
http://www.aoml.noaa.gov/hrd/HFP99/index.html

For advice on storm shutters:
http://www.aoml.noaa.gov/hrd/shutters

For Bill Gray's seasonal forecasts:
http://tropical.atmos.colostate.edu/forecasts/index.html

BOOKS

Barnes, Jay. *Florida's Hurricane History*. University of North Carolina Press, 1998.

————. *North Carolina's Hurricane History*. University of North Carolina Press, 1998.

Doehring, Duedall, and Williams. *Florida Hurricanes and Tropical Storms*. University Press of Florida, 1997.

Fisher, David E. *The Scariest Place on Earth*. New York: Random House, 1994.

Hess, W. N. (ed.). *Weather and Climate Modification*. New York: John Wiley & Sons, 1974.

Jennings, Gary. *The Killer Storms*. Philadelphia: Lippincott, 1970.

Larson, Erik. *Isaac's Storm*. New York: Crown, 1999.

Lester, Paul. *The True Story of the Galveston Flood*. Philadelphia: American Book and Bible House, 1900.

de Maria, Mark. "A History of Hurricane Forecasting for the Atlantic Basin 1920–1995," chap. 9 in *Historical Essays on Meteorology 1919–1995*, ed. J. R. Fleming, American Meteorological Society.

Millas, José Carlos. *Hurricanes of the Caribbean and Adjacent Regions 1492–1800*. Miami: Academy of the Arts and Sciences, 1968.

Ousley, Clarence (ed.). *Galveston in 1900: The Authorized and Official Record of the Proud City of the South-west before and after the Hurricane of September 8th, and a Logical Forecast of Its Future*. Atlanta: William C. Chase, 1900.

Parks, Arva. *Miami: The Magic City*. Tulsa: Continental Heritage Press, 1981.

Pielke, Roger E. *The Hurricane*. London: Routledge, 1990.

Simpson, R. H., and H. Riehl. *The Hurricane and Its Impact*. Oxford: Blackwell, 1981.

Tannehill, Ivan Ray. *Hurricanes: Their Nature and History.* Princeton University Press, 1943.

Will, Lawrence E. *Okeechobee Hurricane: Killer Storm in the Everglades.* St. Petersburg: Great Outdoors Publishing Co., 1971.

PAPERS

Aberson. 1998. "Five-Day Tropical Cyclone Track Forecasts in the North Atlantic Basin," *Weather and Forecasting* 13, pp. 1005–15.

Bosart et al. "Environmental Influences on the Rapid Intensification of Hurricane Opal over the Gulf of Mexico," unpublished.

Broeker, W.S. 1991. "The Great Ocean Conveyor," *Oceanography* 4, pp. 79–89.

Drury and Olson. 1998. "Disasters and Political Unrest: An Empirical Investigation," *Journal of Contingencies and Crisis Management* 6, pp. 153–161.

Emanuel. 1999. "The Power of a Hurricane: An Example of Reckless Driving on the Information Superhighway," *Weather* 54, pp. 107–8.

———. "Thermodynamic Control of Hurricane Intensity," *Nature* 401, pp. 665–69.

FEMA, Federal Insurance Administration. "Building Performance: Hurricane Andrew in Florida. Observations, Recommendations, and Technical Guidance."

Goldenberg and Shapiro. 1996. "Physical Mechanisms for the Association of El Niño and West African Rainfall with Atlantic Major Hurricane Activity," *Journal of Climate* 9, pp. 1169–87.

Goldenberg, Landsea, and Shapiro. "Are We Seeing the Beginning of a Long-Term Upturn in Atlantic Basin Major Hurricane Activity?," paper delivered at U.S. Office of Naval Research Tropical Cyclone Symposium in Melbourne, Australia, 9–13 December 1996.

Hebert and McAdie. "Tropical Cyclone Intensity Climatology of the North Atlantic Ocean, Caribbean Sea, and Gulf of Mexico," NOAA Technical Memorandum NWS TPC-2.

Hebert, Jarrell, and Mayfield. "The Deadliest, Costliest, and Most Intense U.S. Hurricanes of This Century." NOAA Technical Memorandum NWS TPC-1.

Henderson-Sellers et al. 1998. "Tropical Cyclones and Global Climate Change: A Post-IPCC Assessment," *Bulletin of the American Meteorological Society* 79, pp. 19–38.

Krishnamurti and Oosterhof. 1989. "Prediction of the Life Cycle of a Supertyphoon with a High-Resolution Global Model," *Bulletin of the American Meteorological Society* 70, pp. 1218–30.

Krishnamurti, Oosterhof, and Sukawat. 1994. "Numerical Prediction of a Bangladesh Tropical Cyclone," *Terrestrial, Atmospheric and Oceanic Sciences* 5, pp. 245–75.

Krishnamurti et al. 1999. "Improved Skills for Weather and Seasonal Climate Forecasts from Multi-Model Super Ensemble," Florida State University Report No. 99-5.

Landsea, Gray, Mielke, and Berry. 1994. "Seasonal Forecasting of Atlantic Hurricane Activity," *Weather* 49, pp. 273–84.

Marks and Shay. 1998. "Landfalling Tropical Cyclones: Forecast Problems and Associated Research Opportunities," *Bulletin of the American Meteorological Society* 79, pp. 305–23.

Olson. 1997. "Un-therapeutic Communities: A Cross-National Analysis of Post-Disaster Political Unrest," *International Journal of Mass Emergencies and Disasters* 15, pp. 221–38.

———. "Toward a Politics of Disaster," *International Journal of Mass Emergencies and Disasters,* scheduled for August 2000.

Pielke and Landsea. 1999. "La Niña, El Niño, and Atlantic Hurricane Damages in the United States," *Bulletin of the American Meteorological Society* 80, pp. 2027–33.

———. "Normalized Hurricane Damages in the United States 1925–1995," *Weather and Forecasting* 13, pp. 621–31.

Rappaport and Fernandez-Partegas. "Deadliest Atlantic Tropical Cyclones 1492–1994," NOAA Technical Memorandum NWS NHC-47.

Ross and Wilkinson. 1970. "Citizens' Responses to Warnings of Hurricane Camille," Social Science Research Center, Mississippi State University.

Saffir, H. 1972. "Report on the Nature and Extent of Structural Damage Caused by Hurricane Camille."

Shay, Goni, and Black. "Effects of a Warm Oceanic Feature on Hurricane Opal," unpublished.

Willoughby. 1988. "The Dynamics of the Tropical Cyclone Core," *Australian Meteorological Magazine* 36, pp. 183–91.

———. 1999. "Hurricane Heat Engines," *Nature* 401, pp. 649–50.

Willoughby and Black. 1996. "Hurricane Andrew in Florida: Dynamics of a Disaster," *Bulletin of the American Meteorological Society* 77, pp. 543–49.

Willoughby, Masters, and Landsea. 1989. "A Record Minimum Sea Level Pressure Observed in Hurricane Gilbert," *Monthly Weather Review* 117, pp. 2824–28.

Willoughby et al. 1985. "Project STORMFURY: A Scientific Chronicle 1962–1983," *Bulletin of the American Meteorological Society* 66, pp. 505–14.

ACKNOWLEDGMENTS

I spent four weeks of March and April 1999 in Honduras. In Tegucigalpa I stayed at the Apart Hotel Los Proceres, which I recommend to anyone spending time in that city; particular thanks to Fatima Rivera Vega for looking after me during my stay. My thanks to Ivan Romero Nasser at the Honduran embassy in London for steering me there, and for much other assistance.

Rufus Legg, Deputy Head of Mission at the British embassy in Tegucigalpa, was a generous and informative host. I'm especially grateful to Gustavo D'Angelo and David Throp of the Save the Children Fund, and to the other staff of that agency in the capital and Choluteca. Anyone wishing to help the people of Honduras could contribute to the fine work being done by this organization.

Thanks are due to Rafael Galindo and Miguel Angel Aplicano in Concepción de María, Kathya Pastor, Marc Dawson, and Abraham Alvarado Bolaine of SOPTRAVI, Andrew Pinney of the British Red Cross, Patricia Cervantes of the UN, Todd Amani of USAID, and to Ney Scoggins, Nany de Flores, Augusto Larios, and Doña Vilma Reyes de Castellanos at Tegucigalpa City Hall.

Thanks also to Ofelia Barahona, Sagrario D'Avila, Arturo Corrales, Alejandro Banegas, Victor Leonardo Ruiz at the Koko Loko, Tom Taylor at the Tobacco Road Tavern, John Dupuis of *Honduras Tips*, Howard Rosenzweig at the Casa de Café in Copán, and to Cambridge ecologist Mike Hands. I especially thank those *sindicatistas*—members of a banana workers' trade union—whose names, I regret to say, are probably better left unprinted.

On Guanaja, my thanks and best wishes to David Greatorex rebuilding at the West Peak Inn, to Odette Borden at the Alexander, and to Captain Al Veverica and his friends and family at the Thirst & Last. I'm deeply indebted to Tom and Linda Fouke, Don Pearly, and Chris and Alice Norris for their time and hospitality at the Bayman Bay. I'm happy to report that the resort continues to recover from Mitch and hosted twenty-eight guests for their

Y2K party. Apparently the band complained about wet paint on the new pier facilities—but it's a miracle there's anything there to be painted at all.

Many other people, both on Guanaja and in the rest of Honduras, gave time to tell me their stories; too many to name here. I'll just say that when I asked Paola and Santo Sanchez what they'd want the reader to know they said simply, "Just tell them what happened here. Just tell people what happened to us."

I hope I've managed to do that job for them.

During my first visit to Florida in May 1999 I stayed at the Lily Guest House on Collins Avenue in Miami Beach, and very pleasant it was. During the hurricane season, I had an apartment at the Bayliss on 14th Street; the building is run from the Beachcomber Hotel on Collins, and if you're on South Beach for any length of time it's a great place to stay. My thanks to Scott and Barbara for looking after me there. The Governor's House on Broad Street in Charleston was by far the best place I stayed when on the road; thanks also to Philip and Dawn for a good time in Raleigh.

My lease at the Bayliss was swiftly and painlessly arranged by Melissa MacDonald at Income Real Estate. The best deal on a car for three months was offered by Alamo; they were courteous, efficient, and commendably unfazed when I gave them back trashed vehicles—one damaged by vandals, the other by Irene.

I'm particularly grateful to Maurizio and his staff at Kafka's Cyber Kafe on Washington Avenue for my endless use of their computers at exceedingly reasonable rates, and for the equally endless supply of good coffee and sandwiches. Kafka's is also a splendid secondhand bookstore, and well worth a visit.

For good company, my thanks to Casual Robert the Pastry Chef from Cleveland, not the least for taking me mountain biking in Florida. This may sound a contradiction in terms when the second highest elevation in the state is Disney's Magic Mountain, but after you've juddered over enough mangrove roots you realize that (this being America) anything is possible. Greetings also to Melissa, Christal, Kate, Colin, Pete, Marilyn, Mike, Drew, and the two Ashes at the Deuce. The next Swedish lemonade's on me.

. . .

Thanks are due to my editor, Rowland White, for inspirational encouragement and much sharp guidance; I'm grateful to Deborah Brody in New York for her parallel contribution. As ever, thanks to my agent, Rachel Calder, and all at Tessa Sayle for standing by me. More important than anyone, my thanks to Rebecca, Joe, and Megan for their patience and support when I was away from home for so long.

In Miami and elsewhere, many academics, meteorologists, emergency management officials, and other public servants gave me considerable quantities of their time with unfailing patience and generosity. One consequence of this was an inordinate quantity of taped interviews; particular thanks to Rosie Hepworth for transcribing a large proportion of that material.

My first lesson in tropical meteorology was given by Julian Heming of the U.K. Met Office in Bracknell; my thanks for that, and for many valuable introductions. Thanks also to Manuel Lonfat for giving me a bed during the evacuation of Miami Beach—a practical lesson if ever there was one.

I'm grateful to Professor T. N. Krishnamurti at Florida State in Tallahassee for organizing an informative session with him and his students, and to Ryan Boyles at North Carolina State for his insights into the weather in general and Floyd in particular. At FIU in Miami, Professors Richard Stuart Olson and Jose Mitrani of the International Hurricane Center were invaluably helpful, the former on the economic, social, and political impacts of natural disasters, the latter on structural engineering and construction management.

Over the last couple of years, there's been a political push to emasculate South Florida's building code for the benefit of the construction industry; Mitrani's a vigorous campaigner against this outrageous project, and I wish him well in his efforts. On this issue and related matters, my thanks also to Herb Saffir, to Charles Danger, director of the Metro-Dade building department, and to Wendy Jennings of that office.

Space did not permit me to cover this subject in the detail it deserves; I was similarly unable to cover the work of Professor Kerry Emanuel at MIT in Cambridge, Massachusetts. Emanuel has devised a new prototype model for forecasting changes in hurricane intensity; as an approach to this critical problem it's both ingenious and highly promising. Emanuel is a lucid and inspiring teacher, and answered my many questions with urbane good grace.

Chuck Lanza at Miami-Dade's Office of Emergency Management gave a brisk and canny résumé of the many threats posed to his city by severe weather. I'm also grateful to engineers Erle Peterson and Frank Reddish of that office for their time and enlightenment, and to Monroe County's Director of Emergency Management Billy Wagner for a lot more of the same.

The staff of the National Hurricane Center put up with my presence on more than a few occasions when they'd surely have preferred to be left to their work. I'm thankful for their patience and consideration, and for the illuminating hours they spent explaining their work. This book owes a great deal to Jerry Jarrell, Max Mayfield, and Frank Lepore, to forecasters Lixion Avila, James Franklin, and Jack Beven, to meteorologists Christopher Burr, Fiona Horsfall, and Colin McAdie, and to librarian Bob Britter. I should note that Jerry Jarrell retired early in 2000; he was considered by many in the profession to be the best director NHC ever had.

The staff and students at the Hurricane Research Division tolerated an even greater degree of intrusion with endless good cheer; they maintained that good cheer in often stressed and trying circumstances, and were good company all around. I am indebted to these people, and their colleagues at AOC, for the opportunities they gave me not only to try to understand hurricanes but to see them up close.

My thanks to Sim Aberson, Bob Black, Mike Black, Pete Black, Joe Cione, Mark Croxford, Peter Dodge, Matt Eastin, John Gamache, Stan Goldenberg, Sam Houston, Daniel Jacob, John Kaplan, Chris Landsea, Rob Rogers, Sandra Taylor, Eric Uhlhorn, and Erica Van Coverden at HRD; to Greg Bast, Stan Czyzyk, Barry Damiano, Phil Kenul, Terry Lynch, Jim McFadden, Gerry McKim, Sean McMillan, Richard McNamara, Ron Phillipsborn, Dave Rathbun, Jim Roles, and Dave Tennesen at AOC.

Above all, my thanks to Hugh Willoughby and Frank Marks. They taught me a great deal, and not just about meteorology. If there are mistakes in this book, they're mine; if the book's any good, it's due to them. May they fly safe and learn much.